Charles Lanman

**Leading men of Japan**

Charles Lanman

**Leading men of Japan**

ISBN/EAN: 9783742823106

Manufactured in Europe, USA, Canada, Australia, Japa

Cover: Foto ©ninafisch / pixelio.de

Manufactured and distributed by brebook publishing software (www.brebook.com)

Charles Lanman

**Leading men of Japan**

Emperor of Japan.

WITH AN HISTORICAL SUMMARY OF THE

EMPIRE

BY
CHARLES LANMAN
AUTHOR OF "THE JAPANESE IN AMERICA," ETC., ETC.

BOSTON
D. LOTHROP AND COMPANY
32 FRANKLIN STREET

# PREFACE.

THIS volume is the direct outgrowth of my work entitled *The Japanese in America*, which was published ten years ago, and widely circulated in the United States and England. It is divided into two parts, the first of which contains brief biographical sketches of the leading men who in recent times have been honorably identified with the marvellous career of the Island Empire of the Pacific. A goodly number of names have necessarily been omitted, for the reason that I could not obtain the needed data to do them justice; and, I regret, for the same reason, that several of the notices in the volume are far more brief than they deserve to be. I may say, however, that so far as I have been able to go, my statements will be found entirely authentic—the great bulk of my information, including the translations, having been obtained from Japanese scholars and various well informed friends residing in Japan. With the exception of the first two sketches—of the Emperor and his father—I have arranged them in alphabetical order, intending thereby to avoid even the appearance of favoritism. This is the first time that sketches of so many men from the Orient have been brought together in a single volume for the edification of the Western world, and I cannot but hope that these records will do something towards making the people of America and Europe better acquainted than ever before with the gifted, elevated, and progressive character of the Japanese people and Government.

In the second part of this work I have introduced a bird's-eye view of the History of Japan, which I contributed to Johnson's Universal Cyclopædia, together with several chapters bearing on the outlying possessions of the Empire, or directly connected with its history.

C. L.

WASHINGTON, Jan., 1882.

# CONTENTS.

### PART I.

| | |
|---|---|
| THE EMPEROR OF JAPAN | 7 |
| KOMEI TENNO | 19 |
| ARISUGAWA TARUHITO | 24 |
| ENOMOTO TAKEAKI | 27 |
| ENOUYE YOSHIKADSU | 31 |
| FUJITA HIO | 33 |
| FUKUCHI GENICHIRO | 37 |
| FUKUZAWA YOUKICHI | 43 |
| GENPAKU SUJITA | 64 |
| GOTO-SHO-JIRO | 66 |
| HEIHACHIRO | 67 |
| HIGASHI FUSHIMI | 78 |
| HIROYUKI KATO | 81 |
| IJICHI MASAHARU | 83 |
| INOUYE KAORU | 85 |
| ITO HIROBUMI | 101 |
| ITAGAKI TAISUKE | 103 |
| IWAKURA TOMOMI | 104 |
| KABAYAMA SUKENORI | 108 |
| KAWAJI TOSHIYOSHI | 110 |
| KATSU AWA | 112 |
| KAWAMOORA SMIYASHI | 114 |
| KIDO TAKAYOSSI | 115 |
| KONO BENKAI | 121 |
| KURIMOTO-JO-WUN | 122 |
| KURODA KIYOTAKA | 127 |
| NEESHIMA JO | 130 |
| MIURA GORO | 132 |
| MORI ARINORI | 135 |
| MOSHITSU OTSUKI | 138 |

| | |
|---|---:|
| MUMETA GENJIRO | 140 |
| NAGANORI ASANO | 145 |
| NARUSHIMA KIUHOKU | 146 |
| OKI TAKATO | 161 |
| OKUBO TOSHIMICHI | 163 |
| OKUMA SHIGENOBU | 177 |
| OTORI KEISUKE | 181 |
| OYAMA IWA-O | 183 |
| OYANO IWAO | 185 |
| RAI MIKISABURO | 187 |
| SAIGO TAKAMORI | 190 |
| SAMESHIMA NAONOBU | 206 |
| SAIGO TSUGUMICHI | 208 |
| SANJO SANETOMI | 210 |
| SANO TSUNETAMI | 213 |
| SATO SHUNKAI | 215 |
| SHIBURAWA EICHI | 216 |
| SHIMADZU HISAMITSU | 221 |
| SOYESHIMA TANEOMI | 223 |
| TANAKA FUJIMARO | 225 |
| TANI KANJO | 227 |
| TERASHIMA MUNENORI | 230 |
| TOYAMA MASAKAZU | 232 |
| TSUDA SEN | 234 |
| YAMADA AKIYOSHI | 240 |
| YANAGIWARA SAKIMITSU | 245 |
| YOSHIDA KIYONARI | 246 |
| YOSHIDA TORAJIRO | 251 |
| BIOGRAPHICAL ADDENDA | 256 |

## PART II.

| | |
|---|---:|
| THE EMPIRE OF JAPAN | 261 |
| THE ISLANDS OF OKINAWA | 302 |
| THE OGASAWARA ISLANDS | 317 |
| COREA | 326 |
| ORIGIN OF THE AMERICAN EXPEDITION TO JAPAN | 391 |
| ADDITIONAL NOTES | 409 |
| FOREIGN BIBLIOGRAPHY OF THE EMPIRE | 411 |

# LEADING MEN OF JAPAN.

## THE EMPEROR OF JAPAN.

THE Emperor of Japan was born in the Christian year 1852, or, according to the Japanese calendar, in 2512; a date showing that the Imperial dynasty had its origin in the seventh century before the Christian era. His name is Mûts-hito, the son and rightful heir of Osa-hito (or Komei Tenno, the name given after death), who died in 1867, after a reign of twenty years. Soon after that event the abdication of the Tycoon, known formerly by the name of Hitoty-bash, took place at Osaka; and as that was the pivot upon which the Japanese revolution was balanced, it is proper that we consider here the circumstances of this abdication.

The question of opening a port in the "inland seas" to foreign trade had been pending at that time for more than three years. In 1865, or perhaps 1866, the Government of the Tycoon was forced by the strenuous urging of the foreign representatives in Japan to consent that the port of Kobe should be opened on and after January 1, 1868. Immediately after this fact had been proclaimed a strong opposition was manifested by the leading Daimios, because it neither had been properly discussed by the authorities, nor received the sanction of the Emperor. This opposition arose not so much from any objection to the opening of a new port, as from the consideration that the Tycoon's government had virtually been forced by the foreign powers to yield to them a right which required the royal sanction, and because it was a question in which the whole people were greatly concerned. By the more thoughtful statesmen of Japan, this premature concession was considered an act of cowardice; therefore hurtful to the national honor. Memorials were written and circulated throughout the Empire against the measure as well as against the previous blunders of the Tycoon's government, in regard to foreign intercourse. Other demonstrations were also of frequent occurrence, and thus the fire was kindled which was to consume the foundations of the Tycoonate.

In the latter part of 1867 the Tycoon and the leading Daimios were summoned to the seat of the Imperial government, for the purpose of discussing the question of opening the port of Kobe, and they accordingly assembled in Kioto. The diplomatic agents of all the treaty powers, with their respective fleets, assembled in the Bay of Osaka, to watch the proceedings of the assembly. As the Tycoon had formerly made a hasty concession, he now advocated the immediate opening of the port of Kobe; but the other Daimios (for he was in reality one of them) still opposed the measure. Seeing clearly that the political tide was turned against the Tycoonate, Hitotybash found it necessary to resign his hereditary office; his abdication, which was soon presented to the Mikado, was at once accepted; and then, without further delay, the question of opening the port of Kobe was agreed to by the assembled Daimios and sanctioned by the Mikado. Thus an end was put to this question as well as to the hereditary Tycoonate. The reader may think it strange and illogical that the very question which caused the overthrow of the Tycoonate, a political institution which had lasted three hundred years, should have been settled thus without difficulty. Nevertheless, such was the fact. But the end of the old institution would have soon come, irrespective of this question; for even those who belonged by hereditary right to the Tycoon's government, and faithfully supported it, and who had sufficient foresight, had long before advocated the abdication, because they had discovered that the old system was decaying from the effects of corruption, and that the demoralization was too general to allow of the continued existence of the long-established hereditary system. Thus, at the age of fifteen years, the Mikado, or Emperor of Japan, began his rightful reign.

At that time the residence of the Mikado was at Kioto, thirty miles from Osaka, while that of the Tycoon had been at Yedo. In 1868, those of the Daimios who were dissatisfied with the course pursued by the Tycoon began to manifest their hostility, and soon made known that they would not obey the orders of the Emperor. It then became necessary to put down this rebellious spirit by force of arms. Anarchy prevailed in various parts of the country, but especially in Yedo, where demonstrations were made against the Tycoon's household; a naval engagement took place in the Bay of Yedo; a serious fire occurred in Kanagawa; and then in the district between Osaka and the Mikado's capital, several battles were fought which resulted in the total defeat of the rebels and their disastrous flight. Their forces amounted to about thirty thousand apparently well-disciplined troops, while the Imperial army was very much smaller; but the tide had turned, and the Imperial government was triumphant; and, while the Tycoon fled for safety to his palace in Yedo, the Mikado, with his Regency or the Great Daimios, who were his chief advisers, was living in comparative peace in Kioto.

Since the year 1868 many remarkable events have occurred in Japan, and the reign of the young monarch promises to be unprecedented in its influence on the welfare of the Empire. During the troubles which followed the abdication of the Tycoon, the Mikado resided temporarily at Osaka, and it was in that city that his coronation took place on his reaching the requisite age of sixteen years. Almost the first step which he took after that event was to grant an audience to the representatives of the foreign powers, a concession that never had been made before by the Imperial dynasty. It filled the Japanese people with astonishment, and made them almost doubt the reality of the Imperial personage; nor was it much less astonishing to the Europeans to realize their situation in being permitted to see what millions of Japanese had never dreamed of seeing — the person of the Imperial ruler of the nation. It was not long, however, before all doubts were removed by the enactment of official measures calculated to impress the most skeptical conservatives that a new era of progress and civilization had dawned. A second step of the Emperor was to establish upon a firm temporal foundation the Imperial government, which had for so long a period been considered merely spiritual in its character. This was a consummation for which the patriots throughout the Empire had been pining for scores of years.

Before the close of the year 1868 the Mikado resolved to remove his residence to Yedo, and this event was commemorated by a royal decree, a part of which we may translate as follows: "Being now established in my reign, and in the government over all my people of Japan, I have taken into consideration that Yedo is well adapted for the seat of government, inasmuch as it is the most central, the greatest and the most populous city in the Empire. I therefore decree that Yedo shall be the seat of my government, and this city shall henceforth be called Tokio, or the Eastern Capital. This I do because I consider my whole Empire as but one body, and therefore I am anxious to show no partiality to either of the eastern or western provinces. Let all my subjects be informed that this is my decree."

The disappointed followers of the Tycoon, having been unsuccessful in their movement against the forces of the Mikado near Osaka towards the close of 1868, retreated to the island of Yesso, intending to make a final effort there to retain power. As related in our sketch of General Saigo, they were the possessors of a naval fleet, commanded by Admiral Enomoto, who had under him a number of French officers. They made an attack on Hakodate, captured the place, and remained undisturbed there during the winter. In the meantime, while the Mikado and his great Councillors of State were not unmindful of these operations, certain important negotiations or transactions were taking place in Yedo. The representatives of all the foreign powers whose fleets were then at anchor off the port of Yokohama, having signified to the youthful Mikado that they were anxious to present their credentials to him, a favorable answer was returned, and the reception took place on the fifth of January, 1869. It was a grand affair, and was glowingly described by the local press. Soon after that event, the Mikado made a visit to Kioto, married a wife, and returned to Tokio, where he had determined to remain permanently, and where also the great Daimios of the realm had congregated in obedience to the Imperial order.

In the beginning of the summer reinforcements by sea and land were despatched by the Imperial government to Hakodate, for the purpose of entirely quelling the rebels, who there made a final effort at resistance. The insurgents under Enomoto were not only in a wretched plight in regard to food and clothing, but they were disheartened, so that the hostilities were of short duration, and the Imperial forces soon beheld their flag waving over the subdued port and fortifications of Hakodate. After the surrender, the leading rebels were imprisoned, but the rank and file were treated with great kindness. Not only were they all subsequently pardoned, but many of them have since been appointed to offices of trust and honor. Enomoto, their leader, was appointed Envoy Extraordinary to Russia. Indeed, the disposition of the Emperor to treat his erring subjects with the kindest consideration was something unprecedented in Japan. He even invited Hitoty-bash, the ex-Tycoon, to take part in the government; but the offer was not accepted.

Animated by noble instincts, the Emperor of Japan has ever since made no discrimination in appointing the responsible officers of his government, whether they were formerly supporters of the Tycoon or not; but he has always been anxious to find men of ability and lofty principle to assist him in public affairs, and he has usually been successful in his efforts.

He has set aside the prejudicial distinctions which formerly existed in regard to appointing certain officers from certain classes; and though there still exists a marked line of distinction between the members of the royal family and the rest of the inhabitants — the nobility, the middle class, and the common people — yet what may be called aristocratic vanity is no longer tolerated, either by the Emperor or his subjects. A farmer or a mechanic may now become the head of any bureau or department, according to the personal worth of the man. Such things were altogether unknown in Japan in former times. Members of the middle class, or samurai — not to mention the nobility — were not permitted to marry legitimately the daughters of farmers and mechanics. But all such restrictions have been abolished by law, and now a farmer may marry the daughter of a nobleman or a samurai, and the daughter of a mechanic may become the lawful wife of a nobleman.

Among the events which thus far have distinguished the reign of the Mikado, perhaps none is so important as that which was brought about by the foremost Daimios, Satsuma, Chosiu, Hizen and Tosa, in voluntarily yielding up their feudal rights into the hands of the Emperor. This, which occurred on the fifth of March, 1869, was followed by similar concessions by nearly all the other Daimios of the Empire, and the abolition of feudalism was fully consummated before the close of that year. In rendering this truly wonderful sacrifice, these noblemen solemnly declared that their single object was to raise the national standing by perpetuating the centralization of power in the Imperial government, and thereby enabling the Empire to take its place side by side with the other civilized nations of the world. These sentiments were welcomed with enthusiasm, and the great deed of the fifth of March was imitated by the other Daimios so rapidly, that in a very few months the Empire was nominally unified.

How wonderfully have the desires of the Japanese patriots been hastened to a complete fulfilment! In proof of the earnestness which has ever animated the Mikado himself, we have but to glance at some of the results of his enlightened policy. He has sent ambassadors abroad for the purpose of informing themselves in regard to affairs of state; regular legations have been established in Germany, England, France, Italy, Russia, Austria, China, and the United States, and consulates in many of the ports of the world; railways have been built and steamship lines established; lighthouses have been built all along the coasts of the Empire; telegraphic lines have been constructed on land and sea; a regular army and a navy have been organized on the models of the western nations; institutions of learning and for benevolent purposes have been founded and liberally endowed; and able young men have been sent to foreign countries by hundreds, to be educated, to assist in the progress of the Empire towards a perfect civilization. Old laws have been revised, new laws have been instituted, and ancient usages that were barbarous have been abolished. Indeed, the laws of the Empire are to-day far more lenient than is generally supposed; the principles of the administration of justice are almost as perfect as those of the United States, and the habit of executing them is universal. The wicked are inevitably punished according to law, and the just and good are rewarded by the state in many ways. Even the old restrictions in regard to religious observances, which were very zealously enforced by the Tycoon's government, have been greatly modified, and while we do not know that any proclamation for universal freedom in matters of conscience has been issued, it is clear that the spirit of the time decidedly tends in that direction. The question is a question of time only. In all these movements it seems plain that the young Mikado is the head and front, as he is the supreme ruler of the Empire.

One of the most remarkable events which has signalized the reign of the Mikado, is the Imperial proclamation or decree which was promulgated by him on the fourteenth of April, 1875. It had for its object the creation of a deliberative body, whose resolutions, founded upon such knowledge of the wishes of the people as may be obtained without direct representation, will be submitted to the Council of State, and, if approved, will then be referred to another organized body to be moulded into the forms of law. Of this document we have two translations before us, and upon the whole we think the following one will give the best idea of the original :

"On ascending the Imperial throne we assembled the nobles and high officers of our realm, and took oath before the gods (or heaven) to maintain the five principles, to govern in harmony with public opinion, and to protect the rights of our people.

"Assisted by the sacred memory of the glorious line of our ancestors, and by the union of our subjects, we have attained a slight measure of peace and tranquility. So short a time, however, has elapsed since the late restoration, that many essential reforms still remain to be effected in the administration of the affairs of the Empire.

"It is our desire not to restrict ourselves to the maintenance of the five principles which we swore to preserve, but to go still further, and enlarge the circle of domestic reforms.

"With this view we now establish the Genroin to enact laws for the Empire, and the Daishin-in to consolidate the judicial authority of the courts. By also assembling representatives from various provinces of the Empire, the public mind will best be known and the public interests be best consulted, and in this manner the wisest system of administration will be determined. We hope by these means to secure the happiness of our subjects and ourself. And, while they must necessarily abandon many of their former customs, yet must they not on the other hand yield too impulsively to a rash desire for reform.

"We desire to make you acquainted with our wishes, and to obtain your hearty coöperation in giving effect to them."

The other translation interprets the Emperor as saying: "We likewise call together the local officers, causing them to state the opinions of the people," etc.; and in this connection a Japanese newspaper makes the remark that the freedom of the press has in that country preceded the conferring of any political power on the people, and that this inversion of the usual order of events is something quite remarkable.

Of all the events connected with the reign of the present Emperor, the most important occurred on the twelfth of October, 1881, when he issued a Decree or Rescript, for the establishment of a Constitutional Government. As a Japanese scholar wrote:

"This may seem to be nothing to outside nations, but if you take into consideration the rapid growth and influence of public opinion and the steady progress of political ideas among the people, it is the most important event in the history of the nation."

### IMPERIAL DECREE.

We, sitting on the throne which has been occupied by our Dynasty for over 2500 years, and now exercising in our own name and right the authority and power transmitted to us by our ancestors, have long had it in view gradually to establish a constitutional form of government, to the end that our successors on the throne may be provided with a rule for their guidance.

It was with this object in view that in the eighth year of Meiji we established the Senate, and in the eleventh year of Meiji authorized the formation of local assemblies, thus laying the foundation for the gradual reforms which we contemplated. These, our acts, must convince you, our subjects, of our determination in this respect from the beginning.

Systems of government differ in different countries, but sudden and unusual changes cannot be made without great inconvenience.

Our ancestors in heaven watch our acts, and we recognize our responsibility to them for the faithful discharge of our high duties, in accordance with the principles and the perpetual increase of the glory they have bequeathed to us.

We therefore hereby declare that we shall, in the twenty-third year of Meiji, establish a parliament in order to carry into full effect the determination we have announced; and we charge our faithful subjects bearing our commissions to make, in the meantime, all necessary preparations to that end.

With regard to the limitations upon the Imperial prerogative and the constitution of the parliament, we shall decide hereafter and shall make proclamation in due time.

We perceive that the tendency of our people is to advance too rapidly, and without that thought and consideration which alone can make progress enduring, and we warn our subjects, high and low, to be mindful of our will, and that those who may advocate sudden and violent changes, thus disturbing the peace of our realm, will fall under our displeasure. We expressly proclaim this to our subjects. By command of His Imperial Majesty,

SANJO SANETOMI,
First Minister of State.

In his personal appearance the Emperor of Japan is rather tall, compared with his countrymen generally; and he has a healthy physical constitution. He has had several children. Unlike many of the princes and royal personages of Europe, he is not addicted to self-indulgence, but takes delight in cultivating his mind; sparing no pains nor personal inconvenience to acquire knowledge. Although still young he frequently presides at the meetings of his Privy Councillors, composed of the first, second and third Ministers of State, together with the Sangi, or Councillors, whose numbers are not limited, but now comprise about ten honored names. He often visits his executive departments, and attends at all the public services where the Imperial presence is desirable. While prosecuting his literary as well as scientific pursuits, he subjects himself to the strictest rules, having certain hours for special studies, to which he rigidly conforms. In his character he is said to be sagacious, determined, progressive and aspiring; and from the beginning of his reign he has carefully surrounded himself with the wisest statesmen in his Empire, and these have naturally assisted in his own development; so that it is almost certain that history will testify that the crown of Japan has been worn in the present century by one who was worthy of the great honor. From all the glimpses that we have been able to obtain of this youthful Emperor of the far Orient, we are led to believe that in his unselfish patriotism, and in his zealous aspirations, almost free from prejudices, to adopt from other nations all that he deems beneficial for the promotion of the national welfare, he bears a striking resemblance to Peter the Great, of Russia. With such a vigorous ruler and such a progressive people as his subjects are proving themselves to be, the Empire of Japan may well count upon a future of prosperity and happiness.

## KOMEI TENNO.

AS we have given an account of the present Emperor of Japan, it cannot but prove interesting to Western readers to learn something of his father, known as Kômei Tennô, who came to the throne in 1846, and died in 1867.

He was the fourth son of Kôjin Tennô, his mother being Shini-taiken-mon-in, who was the daughter of a Kuge named Ogimach-Sancmitsu. Kôjin Tennô died in the second month of the third year of Kôka (1864), and in the third month of the same year Kômei Tennô succeeded his father, and ascended the throne of Japan, being at this time sixteen years of age. Though so young, he was clever and endowed with sound judgment.

In the fifth month of the same year, an American vessel-of-war arrived off Uraga, and demanded that trade should be opened between the two countries. In reply to this demand Tokugawa Iyeyoshi, the then Shôgun, replied through one of his councillors, Okubo Tadatoyo, that Japan had from time immemorial abstained from all intercourse with foreign nations. The vessel therefore left in the sixth month.

In the ninth month of the following year the ceremony of the enthronement of Kômei Tennô was performed at Shi-shin-den (Hall of Ceremony). In the fourth month of the second year of Kanyei (1849) an English man-of-war arrived at Uraga, and in the fifth year of the same a Russian war vessel came to Shimoda. In the sixth month of the following year the American Envoy Perry arrived off Uraga with four vessels of war, bringing books and other presents to the Shôgun, and requesting that a treaty for purposes of trade might be drawn up between the two countries. Up to this time the only foreign vessels which had visited Japan had been the Korean and Dutch ships which came to Nagasaki. This arrival of American men-of-war was therefore altogether strange. The Dutch presented to the Government a memorial praying that the authorities would listen to the demands of the foreign powers; or that otherwise they might endeavor to open the country by force. Orders were therefore given to the different Daimios to construct fortifications at Omori and at Shinagawa.

At the castle in Yedo consultations were held as to the best steps to be taken. The decision was made known to the Imperial Court at Kiyôto by a member of the Shôgun's council named Wakizaka. The Emperor was much disturbed by these events, followed as they were by the appearance of a Russian Commander with four men-of-war at Nagasaki, likewise demanding that the country should be thrown open to trade.

At this time, as peace had prevailed in the country for some three hundred years, the power of Tokugawa exceeded that of even Taira-no-Kiyomori or Ashikaga Toshimitsu. The samurai were entirely given over to luxury, thinking of nothing but dancing, singing and the like, and in no way occupying themselves with military studies. Thus their spirit had almost become extinct. When the state of affairs was made known throughout the country there was great excitement. Messengers were flying in every direction;

foreign vessels were threatening the shores, and thus the Bakufu authorities decided in order to gain time for preparation and to evade the present difficulties, to grant the demands. In the meantime they requested the Imperial Court to make preparations for war. In reply to the Gorojiu (Shôgun's Council) Hotta, the Prime Minister of the Mikado, replied that as the question was one of supreme importance it was the will of the Emperor that the Gosanké (the three families of Mito, Owari and Kii related to Tokugawa) and the whole of the Daimios, should consult together and make known to His Majesty the result of their councils, when he would decide what steps to take. While this was in progress, however, the Regent Ii Kamon-no-Kami concluded treaties with the foreign powers and opened certain ports for the purposes of trade.

The ex-Daimio of Mito, having received from the Mikado secret orders, raised the cry of Sonnô-joi! (Honor to the Emperor and expulsion of foreigners.) For this he was put in confinement by Ii Kamon-no-Kami. But the cry was taken up and became a popular one, and such men as Hashimoto Sanai, Rai Mikisaburo (the son of the great historian), and other prominent scholars, were made the victims of the wrath of the Bakufu and lost their lives.

In the first year of Bunkiu (1861) the sister of Kômei Tennô, Katsu-no-Miya, was married to Tokugawa Iyemochi. This was done in order to heal the differences which existed between the Imperial Court and the Bakufu. But the whole country was indignant at the course taken by the Bakufu in not following out the wishes of the Emperor with regard to expelling barbarians. Hence various evils arose. The Satsuma samurai having killed an Englishman at Namamuga, the English attacked Kagoshima with a fleet of seven men-of-war. In the third year of Bunkiu, Chiunangon Sanjô Saneyoshi and seven other Kuge fled to Chôshiu. By the order of the Imperial Court they were deprived of their rank, and the Chôshiu samurai were forbidden to enter Kagoshima.

In the sixth month of the first year of Gangi, a Chôshiu samurai named Fukubara, came to Fushimi and petitioned that the Daimio of Chôshiu and his son might be permitted to reside at Kiyôto, and that their title and rank might be restored to Sanjô and his companions. At the same time a Chôshiu samurai named Maki, stationed himself near Kiyôto, with a force of four hundred men. The inhabitants of the capital were thrown into a great state of alarm. H. I. H. Prince Arisugawa and seventy others petitioned that the Lord of Chôshiu and the eight Kuge should be pardoned, but Nashushima Noriyasu, the Daimio of Aidzu, demanded that they should be chastised. On hearing of this the Chôshiu men became infuriated and attacked the city of Kiyôto in the ninth month. The troops of Hitotsubashi guarded the Nakatachiuri gate while those of Yasushima were guarding the Hamaguri gate. Kabata, the commander of the latter, fell into an ambuscade of the Chôshiu men, and was killed, his troops being entirely routed. The Chôshiu men were advancing victoriously when they were attacked and utterly routed by the Satsuma and Kawana troops. Both the Chôshiu commanders Fukubara and Kurushimi were killed, and the rest either committed suicide or fled and hid themselves. By order of Nuriyasu, the greater part of the city of Kiyôto was destroyed by fire.

In the meantime there was great alarm at the court. Some wanted to remove the Emperor to

Kamo, but Noriyasu decided that he should remain. Prince Arisugawa and seventy Kuge being placed in confinement. In the same year a combined attack was made by the Dutch, American and other vessels upon Shimonoseki, and the affair was finally settled.

The troops of Tokugawa surrounded the provinces of Nagato, Chôshiu and Inô, but they could not make headway against the Chôshiu men, who obtained possession of Kokura in Bungo.

In the eighth month of the second year of Keiô (1866) the Shôgun, Tokugawa Iyemochi, died at Osaka. In the same month the Emperor died of small-pox at the age of thirty-six, and the whole country was plunged into mourning.

Thus although the great event of the Restoration, which placed the present Emperor in possession of full powers, took place in the following year, all those which brought it to pass occurred in the reign of Kômei Tennô, and thus his life was an eventful one and subject to constant anxiety.

## ARISUGAWA TARUHITO.

HE was born on the nineteenth of February, 1835, and is the present representative of the family founded by Prince Toshihito, the seventh son of the Emperor Go-Yozei Tenno, who reigned from 1587 to 1611. He was carefully educated at the Court in Kiyoto, where his youth and early manhood were passed, and attracted considerable attention from his elders, the young Prince giving ample evidence of possessing talents far exceeding those of the ordinary run of mankind, whether noble, bourgeois or peasant.

On the fifth of February, 1868, the Emperor took the final step towards the restoration of his imperial authority. By a decree issued on that day, Tokugawa Naifu and his followers were stripped of their honors and dignities, and a large army sent to overrun their territories. Recognizing the ability of the Prince, the Emperor placed him in supreme command of the "Army of Chastisement," handing him at the same time a brocade banner and sword of justice, as the insignia of his important functions.

Marching against the adherents of the deposed Shôgun, now a contumacious rebel, the army under Prince Arisugawa — who was assisted by Saigo Takamori (Kichinosuke) — defeated the enemy in various engagements and marched by several roads to the assault of Yedo, capturing on the way the strong fortress of Oshi-no-Gioda. Arrived before

Yedo, complete and unreserved surrender saved the city from the horrors of fire and plunder, Prince Arisugawa mercifully consenting to accept the submission of Tokugawa, just as the stormers were assembled and the torches lighted which would have laid Yedo in a smouldering mass of blood-stained ruins. The hot-bed of sedition being now under control, strong detachments were sent out in various directions to destroy the scattered band of disaffected ronins and followers of the Aoi, who still maintained a desultory resistance throughout the eastern provinces. The operations directed by Prince Arisugawa were attended with complete success, and on the entry of the Emperor to Yedo — thenceforward known as Tokio — on the twenty-sixth of November, 1869, His Imperial Highness had the satisfaction of returning into the hands of His Majesty the brocade banner and sword of justice in token of the complete pacification of the north and east. Rewards and honors were attendant upon the valuable services of the Prince, and he was shortly afterwards entrusted with the task of quelling the disturbances at Fukuoka, a duty which was quickly accomplished with slight bloodshed, and unaccompanied with the fearful scenes of slaughter which usually accompanied a victory in the times to which we refer.

In the eighth year of Meiji (1875) Prince Arisugawa was appointed to the Senate, shortly afterwards taking his seat as President of that august body upon the retirement of Mr. Goto Shokiro.

Two years subsequently — in 1877 — the renowned Saigo Takamori raised the standard of rebellion in Satsuma, and commenced the sanguinary struggle which deluged with blood the southern provinces of Japan. The supreme command of the Imperial forces was conferred upon Prince Arisugawa, who landed in Kiushiu with his army. After many battles fought at first with varying success, the great rebellion was crushed and feudalism in Japan drowned in blood on the fatal field of Shirayama, where the gallant Saigo, the chivalrous Kirino, and many other dauntless leaders, fell upon their swords, and thus spurned the mercy their conqueror would gladly have accorded them.

On his return to the capital, His Imperial Highness was appointed Field-Marshal in the Imperial service, at the same time retaining his position as President of the Senate, and received the order of the Chrysanthemum, the highest decoration in the gift of the Emperor.

Upon the change in the Government at the commencement of the present year, the subject of our too brief sketch was appointed Sa-Daijin, or Junior Prime Minister, an exalted office he still holds.

His Imperial Highness was entrusted with the administration of the Government during the recent absence of the Emperor in the provinces; nothing, however, occurring which called for any exertion of his well-proved tact and ability.

Prince Arisugawa is recognized as among the foremost workers in the party who desire to join with closer ties the destinies of their country to those of Western nations, and, as no small proof of the sincerity and earnestness of his purpose, we find serving as a midshipman on board of Her Majesty's ship *Iron Duke*, the son and heir of His Imperial Highness, Field-Marshal Prince Arisugawa Taruhito.

# ENOMOTO TAKEAKI.

IN after years when the hand of time has swept away existing prejudices and misconceptions, ample justice will be done by the conscientious historian to the chivalrous and devoted subject of this sketch, who in a remote portion of the Empire remained constant to the fealty he owed his feudal superior; and, disdaining like so many others to sever a tie consecrated alike by honor and gratitude, maintained a desperate struggle against the whole might of the Empire until the very hopelessness of the attempt rendered further resistance a crime. Then, and not till then, did Admiral Enomoto surrender his untarnished sword to the victors : defeated, but not dishonored, he wrested admiration from his foes, and how well and faithfully he served his former master afforded a bright augury, since amply fulfilled, of the loyalty afterwards so often proved.

Sprung from the best blood of the Tokugawa, Enomoto was despatched to Holland with two companions in the year 1863, to study the art of maritime war. Of his career in the land of canals and dykes, but still teeming with memories of great naval heroes whose glorious example must have excited a spirit of emulation in the young sailor, we have unfortunately no record, and we next hear of him in the autumn of 1867, when he returned to Japan on board the *Kaiyo Maru*, a man-of-war built by the Dutch for the Shôgunate.

Enomoto received the appointment of Assistant-Administrator of the Navy, an important position he occupied when those troublous times fell upon the country, during which he inscribed with his sword a stirring record on the page of history.

When the downfall was apparent of the feudal system, which under the rule of the Tokugawa had preserved Japan from the horrors of internecine strife for nearly three centuries, the last Shôgun was urged to commit *hara-kiri*, an insane proposal strongly and successfully opposed by Enomoto and others. Refusing, however, to despair of ultimate victory while a single hope remained, the admiral got his squadron — consisting of seven men-of-war — under way, and while the vanguard of the Imperialists entered the capital, he sailed from Shinagawa at night in the midst of a terrific storm of wind and rain. Negotiations which subsequently took place resulted in the surrender to the Imperial authorities of a portion of the war vessels, the remainder — still under Enomoto's command — being bestowed upon the Tokugawa. Dissatisfied, however, with the conduct of affairs, Enomoto again sailed from Shinagawa, taking with him eight men-of-war and transports, a letter he left behind criticising the action of the government officials explaining sufficiently the reasons which prompted a step he must have since often and deeply regretted.

Enomoto then gathered together such scattered fragments of the Shôgun's forces as could make their way to the seashore, as almost every means of egress was beset by overwhelming numbers of their adversaries. With these reinforcements a descent on Hakodate was determined upon, and, after some hard fighting, the town and district was captured. Here a conference was held with the foreign consuls, and, although we do not affirm that such a course was recommended or joined in by the representatives of the foreign powers, still as a matter of history these last remnants of the once powerful Tokugawa established a republic in Hakodate, Enomoto being elected President, Matsudaira Toro (now Consul at Vladivostock) Vice-President, and the other necessary officials duly appointed. Enomoto then sent a petition to the Imperial Government, through the kindly offices of the captain of a British man-of-war, and prayed that the island of Yesso should be granted to the Tokugawa clan, who would faithfully hold the "Northern Gate" of the Empire against all comers. This petition was refused and a powerful expedition fitted out to crush the last embers of disaffection then remaining in Japan.

The blow at last fell. After long continued resistance and the exhibition of a dauntless courage never surpassed in the brightest days of chivalry in old Japan, the day at length came when the generous offers of the Imperial commander had to be accepted, and Enomoto with his remaining comrades were transferred to the capital under arrest.

The Imperial clemency was shortly afterwards extended to the subject of this memoir, and he again entered the service of his country. Quick promotion soon followed.

In 1874 he received a commission as Vice-Admiral in the Navy, and was afterwards appointed Envoy Extraordinary and Minister Plenipotentiary to the Court of St. Petersburg. During his stay in the capital of Russia, the admiral studied the language of the country and also French. His proficiency in the latter is considerably above the average, and he has translated from it into Japanese a work called *The State of Corea.*

On returning from St. Petersburg the admiral received further official promotion, and was appointed Naval Minister of the Empire.

Of commanding personal appearance, affable in manner, and possessing in an unusual degree the rare combination of admirable qualities requisite to produce an able administrator and successful leader, Admiral Enomoto is justly regarded as one of the most prominent men in the Empire. In 1881, he was attached to the Imperial Household, and is superintending the building of the new palace for the Emperor.

## ENOUYE YOSHIKADSU.

THIS rarely-gifted but ill-fated scholar was allied to a family of samurai, and was born near the castle of Fukuoka, Japan, July 6th, 1852. His father was poor and his early education was neglected, but his natural abilities having been reported to General . K. Kuroda, that dignitary sent the young man to Nagasaki to be educated ; in 1868, by the same patronage he was sent to America, and, under the guidance of Gilbert Attwood (one of the best American friends of the Japanese students) obtained a knowledge of the English language at Boston and its vicinity. He then turned his attention to law, entered the Harvard law school and made rapid progress; participated in various debates, and received from Harvard the degree of LL. B.; and several essays which were printed in the work entitled *The Japanese in America*, were greatly praised by the press in America and England. In 1874 he returned to Japan, and was appointed to a position in the Navy Department; but as he had lost the mastery of his native language, his services in that capacity were not satisfactory, and he resigned. He then established a private school for teaching the English branches of learning, but the Government wanted his services in the Imperial University, where he made himself of great use as a Professor of Law and English Literature ; he also delivered lectures regularly outside of his routine duties on subjects connected with law; and although he married and was pleasantly settled in life, the fact (added to depression caused by bad health) that he had lost his Japanese tongue, preyed upon his mind, until by his own act his days were ended in January, 1879. In the following year an account of his life and character were written by Mr. Kentaro Kaneko, and with his collected writings was published in Tokio, a copy of which was presented to the present writer by Mr. Enouye's pupils. That he was a young man of high character and very great abilities, was the universal verdict of his countrymen, and his untimely death was a public calamity.

## FUJITA HIO.

FUJITA HIO was a native of Mito, son of Fujita Itsusei, and his family was descended from Onono Takamura. At a certain time an ancestor of his house became a retainer of the Daimio of Mito. In his early days he was fond of military exercises, and he learned the arts of war from his father. After that he went to Yedo and acquired the sword-exercise from Okada, and the spear practise from Ito, always neglecting to pay the slightest attention to literature. In the seventh year of Bunsei an American ship which was sailing about stranded on the coast of Hidachi. The crew landed at Otsu-mura, attacked and robbed the people, and threw the village into confusion. As soon as this news was reported, Hio's father was very much excited, and said to his son: "As you know, during the past few years, foreign barbarians have visited our coast very often, and sometimes they have made use of cannon, and so caused great disturbance among the people. But, alas! all our countrymen are contented with a momentary peace, and they take no heed of the danger of the future. I am deeply sorry for them, that they have no courage or spirit of patriotism. Now I advise you, my son, to go to Otsu-mura immediately, and to watch what the foreigners are doing; and when an opportunity occurs, slay them all, and afterwards report personally to the Government what you would have done, and bravely accept the judgment of the authorities. This will not be a service of the highest importance for the country, but we should be quite satisfied to manifest our *yamato tamashi* (conservative feeling) even in so small a way." Hio, having listened to his father's advice, quite sympathized in the scheme, and a stern resolve to carry it out was exhibited in his face. While he was making preparation for departure upon this errand, a report was brought from Otsu-mura to the effect that the Americans had retired, and that no foreigner remained on shore. He was disappointed and felt great regret at this circumstance, as it interfered with the execution of his father's order. At that time he was only nineteen years old.

Not long after this it came to his reflection that the famous scholar Hokuwan had been noted for his want of military knowledge, and that Zuiriku, who was skilful in arts of war, was equally unfamiliar with literature. For this reason each was laughed at for his special ignorance by the ancients. Therefore Futija resolved to give attention to literary studies, and went to Yedo again and became intimate with Kameta and Ota, who were distinguished members of society. With them he learned the history of the Japanese political system. At this time Keizaburo, the second son of the Mito Daimio, wondering greatly at the assiduity of Fujita, wrote a motto consisting of two large characters, "*Fu soku*," or "Without rest," and gave it to him. Fujita hung this inscription on the wall of his study, where he could always look at it. While he was in Yedo his father died, whereupon he returned home, and after that was appointed Hensiu of a school named the Sho-ko-kuwan of Mito. In the course of his labors, he brought about the discussion of certain social principles in a manner that excited much admiration and favor among his followers and the public, who were delighted with his arguments, so that his fame suddenly increased very rapidly. Just then Seisiu, the Daimio of Mite, was very sick, and the question of appointing his successor was agitated throughout the province. The opinions of the people were not unanimous. Fujita thought Keizaburo, the second son before mentioned, would be the most suitable heir to the name and rank, and he went to Yedo secretly and had an interview with Matsudaira, Daimio of Moriyama, to endeavor to put his views in force. On all occasions he earnestly urged the selection of Keizaburo. His arguments were so eloquent and reasonable that the Bakufu government sanctioned the nomination which he advocated, and the new heir was honored by receiving the name of Nariaki from the Shôgun. Obtaining the joyful intelligence of his success, Fujita returned home, and began to employ himself in the service of the local government of Mito. His uniform kindness and his high character led his society to be much sought after by the most eminent men of the time. He was also distinguished for his ability in composing poetry — a faculty which he frequently exercised. In the first year of Kokuwa the Bakufu government ordered the lord of Mito to retire from his office and be confined in his private house, and Fujita was also imprisoned at the same time at a village called Komme.

Fujita was imprisoned three years. After his liberation he published some volumes entitled *Hidachi Obi*, and *Kuwaiten Shishi*. The chief purpose of these books was to demonstrate that his master, Nariaki, respected the Imperial government with all his heart, while he was at the same time endeavoring to assist the Tokugawa rulers. He also advocated the plan of colonizing Hokkai Do (Yezo) upon a system which, if carried out, would doubtless have greatly improved the condition of that island. All the intelligent and virtuous men quite sympathized with the statements and the arguments put forward in these works, and many scholars assembled day by day at Fujita's house for the purpose of enlarging their knowledge of literature under his guidance. In the sixth year of Kayei an American ship of war appeared in a bay in the neighborhood of Yedo, and a desire to communicate with the Government was expressed. At that time the Bakufu authorities suddenly released Nariaki of Mito from confinement, and requested him to submit a plan for the defence of the sea coast. Fujita went to Yedo with his lord and was employed in projects for strengthening the fortifications along the shore. But the Tokugawa officers being afraid of the foreigners, they agreed to negotiate a treaty without first obtaining the permission of the Emperor at Kioto. Fujita was exasperated by the cowardly conduct of the officials then in power, and wrote some verses in which his resolute temper was plainly indicated. All the patriotic feeling of society was aroused by the spirit which Fujita manifested, and he was honored by a special recognition of his services from the Emperor. While he was making this visit to Yedo a severe earthquake occurred, on the second of the tenth month of the first year of Ansei. Fujita hurried to the private room of Nariaki his master, and took him out into the garden for safety; but unfortunately the house was shattered to pieces as they were leaving it, and a large beam fell upon Fujita and caused his death. He was fifty years old.

## FUKUCHI GENICHIRO.

THIS prominent member of the "Fourth Estate" of Japan was born at Nagasaki in 1840. While yet a young man he acquired a knowledge of the Chinese and Dutch languages, and forthwith became a kind of professional interpreter. About the year 1858, he removed to Yedo, where he devoted himself to the study of English, French and German, and became an interpreter in the Foreign Department of the Tycoon's Government. In 1862, when an embassy was sent to the United States and Europe, Mr. Fukuchi was made a member and rendered important assistance by the use of his various acquirements. During the excitement attending the Restoration, he published the first newspaper ever issued in Japan, and, not hesitating to express his opinions with the utmost freedom, he offended the Imperial Government, was thrown into prison for his temerity, but soon released on the condition that he would not continue to issue his journal.

A few months afterwards he was invited to a position in the Treasury Department, and when it was decided to send a commission to the United States to investigate the banking and commercial systems of the country, he was made one of the members, with Messrs. Ito and Yoshikawa; and on his return he published a valuable book on the subjects which the commission had investigated.

When the Iwakura Embassy was organized in 1871, Mr. Fukuchi was asked to take the position of First Secretary, which he accepted, and accompanied the Ministers in their tour of observation around the world. On his return to Japan in 1873, he resumed the profession of a journalist in Tokio, and became the editor-in-chief of the *Nichi-Nichi-Shimbun*, which has ever since been one of the leading newspapers in the Empire.

In 1875 he became an officer of the Dai-jo-kwan, and acted as Secretary of the Assembly of Local Governors until its dissolution. He subsequently held an honorable position connected with the city government of Tokio. During the late rebellion in Satsuma, he joined the Imperial forces, and sent regular letters to his journal from the field of conflict. On his return to Tokio his friend Mr. Kido, then a private counsellor of the Emperor, had him presented at the palace, where he gave a minute account of his observations in Satsuma, which audience was followed by a dinner and the presentation of many valuable presents by the Emperor.

In 1878 he was again called to assist the Assembly of Local Governors; and in 1879, when the regular local parliament was opened, he was chosen a representative for the city of Tokio, and was made speaker or chairman of that important assembly or parliament. When General Grant was in Japan, Mr. Fukuchi was chairman of the special committee designated to assist in the various demonstrations organized to honor the noted American.

In casting about for a brief quotation which would give the foreign reader an idea of Mr. Fukuchi's style of writing, we have selected the following, which, though written when his duties as the regular editor of the *Nichi-Nichi-Shimbun* had ceased, is undoubtedly from his pen; and it is especially interesting because of the fact that he had himself formerly been punished for disobeying the press laws. Alluding to the editors of the *Japan Gazette* and the *Mainichi Shimbun*, he proceeds as follows :

"They are contemporaneous newspaper writers. They are the controversialists living in one country. One of them is, however, limited by law in asserting his opinion, and is occasionally brought before the courts as a criminal, while on the contrary, the other uses his pen free from any peril of the law. A great difference exists between the positions occupied by these newspaper writers with regard to the limit and extent of their privileges, or the restrictions imposed upon them in our country. Toyama Unzo, the editor of the *Mainichi Shimbun*, has been summoned before the Yokohama Saibansho for having re-published in his paper a paragraph which appeared in the *Japan Gazette*, and was sentenced to one year's imprisonment.

"The paragraph in the *Japan Gazette* is not altogether correct, and it is clear that that paragraph was written by the editor as a pure invention. But according to the sentence pronounced by the Yokohama Saibansho upon Toyama, the latter is declared guilty for reproducing the said paragraph in the *Japan Gazette*, for the purpose of causing trouble by announcing changes in the Government and disquieting the country. Referring to the action with regard to Toyama, the *Japan Gazette* has expressed an opinion criticising it as " strained and severe," but we can say nothing about this judgment. Considering which of the two editors mentioned above has committed the greater crime, we find that the editor of the *Japan*

*Gazette* published the offensive paragraph first, and the *Mainichi Shimbun* translated and republished it; and on this account, the former cannot be considered less criminal than the latter. Taking the sentence passed upon Toyama into consideration, it is evident that the editor of the *Japan Gazette* ought not to escape imprisonment for one year—the same term as Toyama suffers for the offence he committed. Both the *Japan Gazette* and the *Mainichi Shimbun* are pursuing the same business in Yokohama, and they have published the same matter in their respective papers. For so doing, the editor of the *Mainichi Shimbun* was condemned to one year's imprisonment, but the editor of the *Japan Gazette* is permitted to escape without receiving even censure. May we say that this is his good fortune, or say that it is the misfortune of the *Mainichi Shimbun?* We do not know which.

"The editor of the *Mainichi Shimbun* is a Japanese subject and governed by the Japanese law, while the editor of the *Japan Gazette* being a subject of England is under no obligation to our law. In Japan, newspaper regulations are in force, under which the native newspaper writers may criminate themselves; but there are no such regulations in England, and no English subjects who conduct newspapers receive even warnings. The editor of the *Mainichi Shimbun* is therefore condemned to one year's imprisonment for having published the same paragraph as the *Japan Gazette*, while the latter is free even from censure. Great is the difference of fortune of men of the same occupation! shall we sympathize with the unfortunate editor of the *Mainichi Shimbun?* Or congratulate the good fortune of the editor of the *Japan Gazette?* No, we do neither; but we regret that owing to the existence of the extra-territoriality clause, the editor who published a *paragraph in his paper for the purpose of causing trouble, by announcing changes in the Japanese Government and disquieting the country*, has fortunately escaped the punishment which his crime deserves.

"In order to punish newspaper-writers for their improper conduct, the press regulations were established; but they were not intended to prevent free discussion; they were also intended to prevent offensive expression of opinions, which might influence general feeling and violate the peace of the country. Thus the editor of the *Mainichi Shimbun* was condemned to one year's imprisonment for having reproduced a paragraph in the *Japan Gazette*, calculated to disturb the government and people; consequently the original writer of that paragraph, the editor of the *Japan Gazette*, is equally a criminal, guilty of the same offence. Owing to the strong protection he enjoys under extra-territoriality, we cannot punish him directly by our law, but we cannot pass over his offence without discussion. Our Government ought to bring an action against him before the British Court in Yokohama, urging his proper punishment; if it be rejected there, the case should be appealed to the Supreme Court at Shanghai. Although there are no press regulations in England, the law of libel is now in force, and those who write for the purpose of creating trouble, by announcing changes in the Government, thereby disquieting the country, are turbulent persons and public enemies, who are prosecuted in any country of the world. If the English judge possesses right and just discrimination, like that used by the judge of the Yokohama Court, he will consider the opinions expressed by the *Japan Gazette* dangerous and turbulent, and he will punish the editor accordingly. The *Japan Gazette* and *Mainichi Shimbun* differ in their language, one being English and the other Japanese; but with regard to their crime for having published offensive matter, they are equal. For this reason, we believe that the Government cannot condemn one without proceeding against the other. But up to this date, neither the native or foreign press has advised an action against the editor of the *Japan Gazette* to be brought by the Japanese Government. Persons may ask the following questions, to which, we fear, we are unequal to give satisfactory answers. How is it that a paragraph in the *Japan Gazette* of a dangerous and seditious character cannot create a disturbance? What is the reason that the influence upon the people caused by this paragraph differs because of the Japanese and English language? How can we say that the Japanese read no English newspapers? How can we say that there is no danger to apprehend from spreading such unfounded reports in foreign countries by publishing them in the *Japan Gazette*?

"For the reasons referred to, we believe that the Government of Japan will bring an action against the editor of the *Japan Gazette*, before the British Court, and also that, notwithstanding the existence of the extra-territoriality clause, the Government will not permit his crime to escape investigation. We have no doubt, therefore, that the fortunes of the two editors guilty of a similar offence will be made equal."

It seems to us that the most able journalists of London or New York would hardly acquit themselves with more ability and propriety under the same circumstances.

## FUKUZAWA YOUKICHI.

HE was born in Nakatsu, Buzen, or what is now called Oida Ken, about the year 1834. He applied himself to the study of Chinese at an early age, and subsequently went to Osaka, where he acquired a knowledge of the Dutch language. In 1858 he went to Tokio, where he continued his studies with great zeal. In 1860, under the patronage of a naval officer, he went to America, where he remained several months. On his return he brought to his country the first Webster's Unabridged Dictionary that was ever imported. In 1862 he again went abroad, this time to Europe, where he purchased a number of foreign books. In 1866 he graduated from the student into the author, by the publication of a volume entitled *Sei Yo Jijo; or, Western Habits*, a collection of translations, as is well known, from foreign literature. This was the first work of the kind that had appeared in Japan, and it instantly gained a wide popularity. After the appearance of the *Western Habits*, Mr. Fukuzawa again visited the United States, and on his return he was appointed one of the instructors in the old Kai Sei Jo, a position which he held till the breaking out of the war of the Restoration. He had already established his private school, the Keiogijiku, and begun to win recognition as a teacher. The political agitations consequent on the civil war drew attention to his *Sei Yo Jijo*, and increased its author's reputation. Printed in an easy character, and treating of interesting subjects in an attractive style, the masses were not deterred from reading and appreciating it by the criticisms which some purists made on its form and methods. The "Mita fashion" became *the* fashion, in spite of the opposition of science.

In the seventh year of Meiji he published his celebrated *Gakumon no Susume; or, Progress of Education*, in which he advanced the opinion that Death is a democrat; and that the samurai who died fighting for his country, and the servant who was slain while caught stealing from his master, were alike dead and useless. This attack on the dignity of the military class aroused fierce opposition, and filled the newspapers with angry discussions. The debate excited universal attention, and resulted, we cannot doubt, in a general advance in public sentiment on the subject of natural rights. In the following year, the now famous schoolmaster opened a lecture hall in connection with his academy, and delivered, for its inauguration, an eloquent public address, by which act he imported the lyceum into his country. And as he gave a new sphere to the form, so he was no less instrumental in developing a scholarly association of a more retired character, the Mei Roku Sha, or Society of the Sixth Year of Meiji. This organization, established by Mr. Mori on his return from America, chose Mr. Fukuzawa as its first president, an honor which he resigned in favor of the young founder. He has, however, retained a leading connection with this body, which includes such representative men as the Mitsukuris, Nishimura, Kato and Nishi.

Though it is rather as a public instructor and a critic of government in the abstract than as an active politician that Mr. Fukuzawa has wielded influence, still in the debate on the establishment of a House of Commons, according to the plans proposed by Itagaki and Goto, his influence was earnestly exerted on the more conservative side, his opinion being that the time was not rife for such an experiment, while he advocated the formation of local assemblies as a preliminary step. His moderate views in this discussion, however, have not brought him into the confidence of a strong party in the Government, who look upon him as too extreme a radical. But his services to the cause of popular education and the evident sincerity of his patriotism make him universally esteemed.

He is married, and when congratulated by a friend on the birth of a son, he simply replied, "Yes, I am fortunate, but after all, the child is nothing but a poor Asiatic." His love of learning was developed at an early age, and the moment he became impressed with the low condition of moral and intellectual culture in Japan, he was fired with a strong desire to do all in his power to elevate his countrymen, and has filled his self-appropriated mission with a success that is quite unprecedented in the annals of the East. It is now about eighteen years since he entered upon the life of a schoolmaster in Yedo; his school has been what we in America would call a boarding school. In it are represented all the provinces of Japan, and while his present number of pupils is from three to four hundred, the children whom he has educated can be counted by the thousand. Notwithstanding his constant and arduous labors as a teacher, he has found time to translate from English into Japanese a considerable number of valuable books, which have been published and had a wide circulation. He has always been averse to holding public office, and all that he has done has been done as a private citizen. With regard to the letter which follows, we have this explanation to make : The author had been upon a visit to his native place, and while enjoying the scenes of his boyhood, and talking with the friends of early days, he resolved to send to the latter a communication in regard to their condition and future welfare. His motives and the manner in which he carried out his purpose were fully appreciated by his old friends. They had the letter printed in Yedo, in pamphlet form, and proceeded to give it the widest circulation. For writing such a paper fifteen years ago he would probably have lost his life ; but now he is universally applauded, not only for his courage, but for his wisdom and sincerity, and to all human appearances he promises to become one of the greatest benefactors of his race. The letter in question is sufficiently interesting on account of its merits alone, but what gives it importance is the fact that it comes from a native of Japan, and was written in the year 1872.

The letter is as follows :

"Man, in common with the brutes, is gifted with the senses of feeling, sight, hearing, smell, and taste, but is the only one of created beings who has a spirit or mind. It is this which makes him a human being, gives him power to conduct himself according to nature, and by which he is enabled to obtain knowledge, and learns how to provide for the wants and comforts of life, and treat his fellowmen with consideration. But more than this, it is a peculiar characteristic of human beings that they have the ability to secure liberty of mind and of actions. In this particular, from the most ancient times, the Chinese and Japanese have been ignorant. Liberty or freedom is not self-will — it is the power with which we do all we choose, without obstruction from others. It is right that the father and child, the master and retainer, and the husband and wife should all have this liberty — none of them to be interfered with in their proper desires. Men were not created with the blight of evil in them, and they are not led astray by nature. When they do things that are wrong against their fellow-beings, they offend both nature and heaven. Small offences deserve to be despised, but large ones ought always to be punished, and this without any regard to the position of the offender — whether a nobleman or a peasant, an old or a young man.

"The liberty of which I have spoken is of such great importance, that everything should be done to secure its blessings in the family and the nation without any respect to persons. When every individual, every family, and every province, shall obtain this liberty, then, and not till then, can we expect to witness the true independence of the nation; then the military, the farming, the mechanical and the mercantile classes will not live in hostility to each other; then peace will reign throughout the land, and all men will be respected according to their conduct or real character.

"All the human family came from one pair — a man and a woman — who were created by heaven; then came the conditions of parents and children, of brothers and sisters, which are to continue through all time. Heaven made no difference between man and woman in regard to freedom, but intended them to be equal. In looking at the history of China and Japan from the earliest times, we find that men often had several wives, whom they treated like slaves or criminals, and the husbands were not ashamed of their conduct. Was not this wicked on the part of the men, and most pitiful for the women? When men thus treat their wives, the example has an evil effect upon the children, and they do not treat their mothers with respect, nor listen to their instructions. When this is the case the mother is only a nominal mother, and the children are no better off than orphans, and their condition most unhappy. And when we know that the fathers are seldom at home, but away attending to business, who is there to instruct the children?

"The famous Confucius in his *analects* says that there should be one husband and one wife; and while the modern Chinese and Japanese believe this to be right, they do not always act upon his advice. Most certainly there should only be one pair, and between the husband and wife there should always be true friendship and courtesy. When they treat each other as strangers or without due regard, it is impossible that domestic life should be happy. When men have a plurality of wives, the children, as a whole, have one father and several mothers; and the laws of Confucius as well as of nature are disobeyed. If it is right for one man to have several wives, then why not allow one woman to have several husbands? I would ask any candid man how he would like to be treated by a woman as many husbands now treat their wives? But in another of his works Confucius tells us that in his time, it was common for men to exchange their wives, according to caprice, and he expressed his great sorrow on account of the bad customs of his time. He was a great philosopher, but I do not find that he condemned the particular custom alluded to, and hence I cannot but think that he was an insincere man, or has contradicted himself in his writings. He is sometimes a difficult writer to understand, and cannot always be well understood without the help of Chinese scholars.

"Let me now speak of the children. It is their duty to be good and obedient to their parents. The Government is always ready to help those who treat their parents kindly, but the children must never do this from interested or sinister motives. As is well known, the custom prevails that because the mother carries her child for three years in her arms, so the child should mourn for three years after the death of its mother as well as its father. But this is all wrong; it is against nature, and looks too much like a business transaction. It is well known, also, that children are always punished for disobedience to parents, but parents are not punished when they treat their children with unkindness. This is not right, and there is no reason for this inequality or distinction. It is wrong for parents to look upon their children as they do upon their furniture — which they may have made themselves or can buy with money — for those children are each a gift from heaven, and should be highly valued for that reason alone. Until they reach the age of ten years, they should be instructed by their parents in all useful things — with parental love should be directed in the good way. When old enough to attend school they should be sent to those appropriate to their station, and they should strive to become useful members of society. All these things should be done by parents, as a return to heaven for blessing them with children. (Here the line of argument is leveled at some of the ancient customs of Japan. For example, it was formerly the case, that parents might even destroy their children without being punished under the law; but if children killed their parents, then the offenders were severely punished; and instances are recorded where children have been torn to pieces by wild beasts for having taken the lives of their parents.)

"When children have reached the age of twenty years, then they are called men or women: are free to act for themselves; must obtain their own support; are no more subject to the orders of their parents, and are at liberty to do as they please in all things. But they must not forget in their subsequent lives to be kind to their parents, and always to help them when necessary. It is written in the books of enlightened nations, that when children have reached the age of maturity, the parents may advise, but never command them; and this is a golden custom which should last into eternity.

"The way to bring up children is not only to teach them how to read and write, but they should be made familiar with the right way in everything under the influence of good example. If parents are wicked, mean or vulgar, the children are apt to be like them; example is far more telling than words, both for good and evil. If parents are bad, how can they expect their children to be good? This is far worse for the children than if they were left orphans. Some parents love and treat their children well as far as they know, but from ignorance often force them to do things that are not for the best. Such parents are criminals and opposed to the wisdom of heaven. Without meaning to do so, they degrade their children to the level of the brutes. To love in a proper way should be their ruling idea. There are no parents in the world who do not feel an interest in the behalf of their children, and yet, to be degraded in mind, is worse than to be without health. The love of which

I speak, which only looks after the body, is what I would call maternal, or merely animal love. As human faces differ in appearance, so is it with human hearts; but the aims of the truest love should be exalted.

"One of the peculiar facts connected with civilization is, that as it advances, bad people become more abundant; then it is that men have trouble in taking care of their property and persons; then comes the idea that the people must have representatives, whose business will be to form a substantial government, make laws, punish the wicked, and help those who need help in every way. If the people, in the aggregate, were always good, then there would not be any necessity of organized government. The head of a government is its ruler, and the people who keep him are officers. Such a government is indispensable for the prosperity of a people and for national defence. There are many kinds of business, as you know, but the business of governing the people is the most difficult and important. The dutiful and attentive, in every sphere of life, ought always to be rewarded according to the justice of heaven. The people who live under a good government should not be envious of the officers who receive large salaries, for generally speaking, such men earn by hard work all they receive. They should be respected. On the other hand, the rulers and officials must not forget the duties they owe to the people; their work should not be out of proportion to their pay; the same justice should prevail between the officials and the people, which prevails between the master and servant.

"All this is merely a summary of my ideas of human society, and on a few pages of paper it is quite impossible to enter more fully into so important a subject. To become well informed upon it, it is necessary to read books; not only those of Japan, but those of China, India and all the western nations. In these days there are many Japanese scholars who are well informed in the literature of foreign nations; but it is said that they quarrel among themselves. Such conduct is foolish and wicked, and does great harm. Scholars have something more to do than merely to read and write, which accomplishments are not difficult to acquire, and so it is most unwise for them to spend their time in literary and scientific squabbles. If our scholars continue to do this, they will remain just as ignorant of foreign nations as are the Chinese. Long arguments will do well enough after we have become informed in regard to other nations. We should apply our mental powers to acquiring all we can through the English, French and German languages as well as the Chinese. If one man is partial to one language, that is no reason that he should insult those who prefer another language. But after all, the first thing for us to study is the present condition of our country; learn what is good and what is bad, so that we may act accordingly. It were better for us to stop quarrelling about the goodness of different literatures, and devote more attention to the interests of our nation. Since our country was first opened to foreign commerce, many unworthy foreigners have been found in the open ports who endeavor to impoverish and keep ignorant our people, and all for their own selfish advantage. The trouble is, that foreign nations are judged by our scholars by their bad specimens; and for that reason our people are too often unwilling to receive the good inventions from abroad. The unworthy men alluded to fear and try to put down the literature of western nations, for fear that its influences will stop their enterprises. When we are able to read the books of the different nations of the world, and become acquainted with its real condition and with international law, then we shall be able to preserve our virtues and protect our liberties; and thus solidify and make our nation permanent, until the time comes when we shall be called the Great Empire of Japan. In my opinion there ought to be no delay in our becoming well acquainted with the literature of foreign nations, and especially with that of the western nations.

"To my old friends in my native place do I send these words. I hope you will be spared to act upon the advice I have given you. From this day forth I hope your eyes will be opened to see that my words are true; that you will earn your support by systematic industry, refrain from interfering with the liberties of your fellow citizens, be strong in intellect, and put away all low and unworthy thoughts and pursuits, for in that way alone can you secure the welfare of your families and of the nation. Who would not think, as I do, of his native place, and wish for the best happiness of old friends? May what I have said not be forgotten by you in future years!

"Y. FUKUZAWA."

The following extract from a lecture by Mr. Fukuzawa, will give the reader another phase of his remarkable mind:

"Our principal aim at present ought to be the increase of our national power. Let us accumulate wealth. Let us strengthen our military forces. Let us encourage education and the publication of useful books. All these are the means to make us strong at home and respected abroad, and when we have become conscious of our national strength, then it will be time to manifest that consciousness in our relations with the foreigner. Since our country was opened, the ignorance of our people in all that concern foreign countries has been a constant stumbling-block ; but on the other hand, foreigners are just as ignorant of our country as we are of theirs. However, during the last twenty years our countrymen have been working hard to make themselves acquainted with foreign commerce, literature, military systems and law.

"Our principal men have, with the object of promoting our own progress, constantly studied the civilization of the western countries, and, after mature consideration, have introduced into this country what met their approbation, and this work they are still pursuing. It may, therefore, safely be asserted that the Japanese are better acquainted with foreign countries than foreigners are with Japan. If we, for instance, compare the number of Japanese who are able to read and speak foreign languages, with the number who can read and speak Japanese, then we shall find that the former is many times larger than the latter. Englishmen and Americans who enjoy the advantage that their language is very widely spread over the world and spoken everywhere, do not trouble themselves to learn foreign languages, and very naturally so. But if they do not know the language of a country it is impossible for them to know the manners and customs of that country. But this ignorance of our affairs is no slight drawback in our intercourse with foreigners. During the last twenty years only a few resident foreigners have associated with our countrymen, read our books, and studied our national customs and manners, with the exception, that is, of a few individuals. The rest who are generally considered to know something of Japan have only a crotchety idea of Japan and its people.

"The Christian missionaries look upon our people as savages without religion, and are intent upon converting them without considering what are the morals of our educated classes. The professors of jurisprudence, without acquainting themselves with our manners and national customs, demand that the law of the land be noised at once. Whether it be religion, jurisprudence, literature, or military system, the foreigner knows only what is used in his own country, and seeing only that side of the matter he tries to graft it upon this country of which he knows nothing, and if he fails in his attempt then he is apt to throw the blame on the people of this country whom he calls both ignorant and savage. How shallow! And if this occurs with those who are old residents in our country, then we can easily imagine what the foreigners living at home in their own country think of us. Not only are they ignorant of our morals, art and industry, but many of them do not even know in what part of Asia Japan is situated, and whether she is an independent country or not. Looking at the map they may think Japan a part of the Chinese Empire to which it is next neighbor. Our learned men are in the habit of blaming our countrymen for their ignorance of foreign countries, and profess to be much grieved at it. I, on the contrary, feel aggrieved at the foreigner's ignorance of Japan.

"It is a common trait of human nature to despise what one does not know, and this was the reason why the Japanese, until quite recently, looked down upon foreigners as barbarians. But the foreigners are just as the Japanese were formerly. They do not know what to them is a foreign country, namely, Japan.

They are still more ignorant of our affairs, and therefore they look down upon us with still greater scorn. And now those living at home and having no contact with Japan: how do you think that they estimate our country? But when the general opinion is tainted by such ignorance and finds expression in public acts and measures, our foreign intercourse becomes sadly hampered.

"It is, therefore, of the utmost importance, at present, that we show foreigners what our country and our people really are. I do not mean that we should boast and brag before foreigners, telling them that Japan is the most powerful and richest country upon the surface of the globe. Civilization consists of many and various elements. There may be something in our civilization that excels every other thing in the world, and in other respects we may be inferior to other people. Leaving aside the question of who is in the van and who is in the rear, I want that we shall show ourselves to the world as we really are. As for the manner how to accomplish this, it is not to wait until the time shall have come when foreigners shall have learned to speak the Japanese language and read Japanese books; it is for our countrymen to write and publish books in foreign languages, and to publish newspapers in foreign languages. This, however, cannot be done yet; and if we search for other means, then the most powerful is to exhibit to foreigners what our countrymen are able to do. As the adage says: 'One learns more from one look at a thing than from a hundred tales about it.' Therefore it is a most appropriate means to take part in foreign exhibitions, and such expeditions as those of the Seiki Kuwan and the Tsukuba Kuwan, which were fitted out by the navy department in January, 1878, have also a remarkable effect.

"It is only in the last twenty years that our countrymen have learned the art of navigating the high seas, and now we have with our hands built ships, fitted them out, and navigated them to places which the Japanese had never seen before, and where the people had never before seen Japanese. It is, therefore, not surprising that we have excited their wonder, and I do not hesitate to say that the voyages of these two men-of-war have greatly increased the respect for Japan. Although it is within the last twenty years that we have learned the art of navigation, it is neither within the last twenty years, nor within the last two hundred years that we trained our intellect so as to enable us to learn such an art. That is a characteristic of Japanese civilization that dates back hundreds and thousands of years, and for which we ought to thank our ancestors. We have never been backward or wanting in civilization. What we wanted was only to change the outward manifestation according to the time.

"Not only in navigation but in every other branch, however trifling, let us imitate such elements of European civilization as are useful, and leave alone what is useless. In so doing we shall fortify our national condition. On the great theatre of the world we will show before the eyes of all what we can do, and enter into competition with other nations in art and science. Thus shall we make our country independent and powerful, and that is my ardent desire."

We also submit the following suggestive passages from a lecture recently delivered by this well-known scholar on the subject of the intricacies of intercourse between Japan and the nations of the West:

"Our foreign relations have of late been much and warmly discussed in public. Some want to permit the foreigners to reside in the interior, while others want to introduce foreign capital, and for that purpose associate foreigners with natives in industrial enterprises. The discussion of the advantages and disadvantages of these different schemes has grown hot among the newspapers, and we will leave the same to them; as for ourselves, we will just throw a glance over our foreign relations. The public writers always occupy themselves with reason only, and leave human passions entirely out of sight. If the affairs of this world could be governed by reason alone, then there would be small trouble indeed, and everybody could go to sleep in peace; but are the affairs of the world so governed? Can we depend upon laws and treaties? Is this world really a place where reason reigns supreme? We will not answer these questions. Looked at from the point of reason our foreign relations are based upon the treaties of friendship and peace, concluded between our country and foreign countries, and according to the treaties, our foreign relations give no cause for fear or noisy discussion. Let us see, for instance, what the treaty between Japan and Great Britain says:

Her Majesty the Queen of the United Kingdom of Great Britain and Ireland, and His Majesty the Tycoon of Japan, being desirous to place the relations between the two countries on a permanent and friendly footing, and to facilitate commercial intercourse between their respective subjects, and having for that purpose resolved to enter into a treaty of peace, amity, and commerce, etc.

Art. I. There shall be perpetual peace and friendship between Her Majesty the Queen of the United Kingdom of Great Britain and Ireland, her heirs and successors, and His Majesty the Tycoon of Japan, and between their respective dominions and subjects.

"The above treaty is founded on reason, and is

a very excellent one, and calculated to promote peace and friendship between the subjects of the two countries. As a document it is perfect, but if we come to examine its fruits, then things wear a different look, and we are quite disappointed. By quoting some of the most remarkable events that have occurred we shall now prove to you that treaties are not to be relied on at all. When in the year 1862 Prince Shimadzu of Satsuma was travelling along the Tokaido, an Englishman named Richardson broke in upon the Prince's procession, whereupon the Prince's vanguard killed the Englishman on the spot. For several centuries it has been both custom and law in Japan that it is lawful to kill whosoever breaks in upon a Daimio's procession; the said Englishman, being ignorant of the laws and customs of Japan, in a manner killed himself by riding on horseback into the Prince Shimadzu's procession. There was therefore no cause for complaint. Nevertheless the British Government took up the matter, and in March the following year it despatched some men-of-war by way of threat against our Government, and wrote a very harsh letter, in which it demanded a fine of one hundred thousand pounds, and the execution of the persons who committed the deed; and from the Prince of Satsuma twenty-five thousand pounds as compensation to the family of the man who had been killed. The Government were very much exercised about this matter, and in May the same year it paid the fine. About the same time the Shimonoseki affair took place. This event happened in the following manner: At that time the desire of expelling the foreigners was very intense and very general. Foremost among that party was Mori, the Prince of Choshiu; and he issued an order that any foreign ship, whether man-of war or merchant vessel, that passed Shimonoseki should be fired upon. The Bakufu Government became in consequence extremely anxious, and earnestly besought the foreigners not to navigate the Inland Sea for some time, stating frankly as their reason that, as the people were greatly excited, it was impossible to foresee whether foreign vessels would not be fired upon, which would be in contravention of the recently concluded treaties and entirely contrary to the intentions of the Bakufu government. But the foreigners never heeded the warning, and they went on purpose through Shimonoseki Straits, and thus provoked the fire from Prince Mori's guns. Then the foreigners sent some men-of-war and stormed and demolished the forts there, and the four powers, Great Britain, France, Holland, and the United States, claimed payment of two million dollars as the Shimonoseki indemnity. It is beyond doubt that the amount of this indemnity was fixed quite at random and not fairly estimated. The foreigners were at that time by no means ignorant of our domestic troubles; on the contrary they knew them perfectly well, and took advantage of them to make harsh demands upon us, and extract an indemnity from us, just as if a person should take advantage of a fire having broken out in another man's house, or of a man lying sick in bed, to make extortionate demands upon him. Is this the peace and amity heralded by the treaty? When the Bakufu were beset with difficulties, and the whole country was in a turmoil, then the foreigners, contrary to treaty stipulations, sold arms and ammunition to the Daimios who were in rebellion against the Bakufu, which was then the lawful government of Japan, and thus they helped indirectly to destroy the latter. Is this also peace and amity?

"Since the fall of the Bakufu up to the present time many similar instances have happened. Foreigners are permitted to travel within treaty limits, and to shoot at certain places within treaty limits, and in consequence Japanese women often find themselves insulted by foreigners, and the farmers must see their rice and vegetable fields damaged by foreigners. Our policemen are greatly troubled by such acts, which they, with all their diligence, are unable to repress. Again, the Christian religion was from ancient times strictly forbidden in our country, and notices to that purpose were posted everywhere; but since the Restoration these notices have been removed, the Government considering it surperfluous to keep on posting such notices, which are already firmly impressed upon the minds of the people. We shall not here enter upon a discussion of the merits of that religion, but there can be no doubt that when the notices were removed this was done in spite of the wish of the majority of the people. What was the cause then of removing the notices? Ask your own conscience, gentlemen, and it will tell you without any aid from your humble lecturer. And the lawsuits between natives and foreigners! Almost in all cases the plaintiffs are foreigners: not more than two or three out of every ten natives; because our countrymen do not sue even when they have cause to do so, but rather submit in patience; while the foreigners sue without cause, and without doubt in many cases gain undue advantages. Such is the coal mine affair of Mr. Goto, whom I observe present at this meeting. Mr. Goto is well known to the public. His past life has proved him to be a strong and steadfast character; he was, in fact, one of the founders of the present Government. Even he has been unable to avoid being sued by an English merchant; what may others then expect? Nor do we need any proof that our merchants suffer losses from the foreigners. But the cause of their sufferings is neither in the treaties nor in reason; it arises from human nature. Treaty stipulations and the precepts of reason are easily learned; what is difficult to know is the human heart, and it is therefore a pity to see how eagerly public writers discuss about principles and leave human nature and its practical workings entirely out of sight.

"As we have said already, foreign relations are governed, not by reason, but by passion; and if we want to discuss them, it is human nature and its weaknesses of which we must take account, otherwise our discussion will be vain and vapid. If, then, our public writers consider it possible to admit foreigners freely into the interior and control them by means of the treaties, then there is no necessity for revising our treaties; but we want to see the proof that we have not suffered from the practical working of our present treaties. Unless it can be shown that the treaties have hitherto been carried out according to reason, and borne the fruit they professed to bear, we do not believe that any amount of revision of treaties will make any palpable difference. The present plain treaties have proved barren, and however much they might be improved through revision, it would still be the same. If therefore you, the public, are so anxious to have the existing treaties revised, show me at least what good has come of the existing treaties, and if I see any evidence of it, then I shall gladly submit to your opinion."

In speaking of this noted scholar, the *Japan Weekly Mail* of November 26th, 1881, uses this language :

"One of the greatest names in Japan at present is that of Fukuzawa Youkichi, who for many years back has been the principal of a large school known as the Keio Giguku, in Mita Tokiyo. It is believed, and not without justice, that his efforts have done more towards the growth of Western civilization in Japan, than those of any other man, and it is also held by some whose exaggeration may well be pardoned, that his influence for good or evil might at any moment be turned into an uncontrollable factor." And then the same writer goes on to tell us that Mr. Fukuzawa's last publication is entitled *Complaints of the Time*, and treats quite fully and with great ability the following questions, viz., "National Security and International Competition," "The Power of the Government and National Assemblies," "National Strength," and "Finance and the Development of the People's Energy."

# GENPAKU SUJITA.

AS one of the pioneers whose labors in the early part of the present century led to the present condition of Japan, this man deserves special mention in this volume. He was the physician to the Prince of Obama, and lived at Nagasaki. Having become convinced that the surgical writings of the Japanese were very deficient, and been attracted by a certain book written in the Dutch language, he went to work for the purpose of producing a translation. He did not have even an elementary knowledge of the Dutch language, but this fact did not alarm him. He studied very hard, and it is said often spent a whole day in translating a single phrase. Some of his friends laughed at him and said he was trying to do what was impossible, but he said, "It is possible for a man to do this work; but he must have the help of Heaven."

At the end of four years his remarkable feat was accomplished, and the work on *Analytical Anatomy* was engraved and published in the Japanese language. From this the people of the Empire learned that it was possible to translate Dutch books; also much truth respecting the human frame; and that the energy and perseverance of their countryman, Genpaku, was most remarkable, and a blessing to his country. It should be added, however, that Genpaku was greatly assisted by a number of friends, who were fired with the same ambition as himself, and they formed themselves into a society or league for the accomplishment of their purpose, and the names of those men were Hoshiu Hosun, Nakagawa Iunan, Mine Shiunotai, Toriyama Shoyen, and Kiriyama Shotetsu, the whole of whom are honorably remembered by the scholars of Japan.

## GOTO-SHO-JIRO.

HE was born in the province of Tosa, and was not only well educated, but displayed uncommon abilities even in his youth. He was among the first to take part in the movements which preceded the Restoration, and he became a Sanyo, or member of the Imperial Council, serving with such men as the elder Saigo Kido and Okubo, and to him was assigned the duty of presenting to the Emperor a series of articles bearing upon the adoption of a written constitution. His services in that direction were duly recognized and rewarded, but he resigned in 1868. He also served his country with credit as minister of the Public Works Department; and while a member of the Imperial Cabinet, in 1873, he could not agree to the proposition of making peace with Corea, and resigned his high position and retired to private life. He continued, however, to take a great interest in public affairs, and probably did more than any other man in the Empire to acquaint the people generally with the necessity of a national assembly or parliament. When subsequently the Genro-in or Senate was organized, he was made its Vice President; but in 1873 he again resigned and returned to private life. He next turned his attention to commercial affairs, and was the head of an influential firm; but he soon dissolved that connection, and became interested in the coal mines of Takashima, in the management of which he is understood to have been quite successful.

# HEIHACHIRO.

FOR the following narrative we are indebted to the *Japan Mail* (as we are for many of the facts recorded in this volume), and as the adventures of the hero bordered on the romantic, they cannot but prove interesting to the foreign readers :

"As a boy Heihachirô, a native of Osaka, and born in 1792, was remarkable for cleverness, and for his fondness for literature, fencing, and all the accomplishments which go to make up the education of a samurai. At the age of fourteen or fifteen he set out for Yedo, having received permission from his father, in accordance with his wishes, to complete his education in that city. As he was travelling over Sudzukayama in the province of Isé, a pass nearly as high as that of Hakoné on the Tokaidô, he was stopped by two robbers of great stature, who came up and demanded his money, threatening to kill him unless their demand was complied with. Heihachirô, not being a youth easily frightened by such threats, determined not to yield without a struggle, and clutching one of the robbers, succeeded in hurling him over the precipice. Drawing his sword he then turned on the other, who was also armed, and they fought for some time. Finally they grappled, and Heihachirô managed to disable and bind his antagonist. He then said, 'Your life is in my hands, but I will have mercy and spare you on certain conditions. You are a strong, able man. If I let you go free you must promise me that you will repent and lead a different career. Get your living by honest means, as you are quite capable of doing, and leave your present degraded mode of life.' The fellow promised, and Heihachirô letting him go free, proceeded on his way to Yedo.

"On his arrival there he became a student of the National University, and resided in the house of Hayashi Daikaku-no-Kami, the director of the college. For a period of five years he pursued his studies with untiring diligence, and became the head student of the University and Professor of Literature. He was then compelled to return to Osaka in consequence of the illness of his father, who died very shortly after his return, and Heihachirô succeeded to his position and emoluments. Takaye Yamashiro-no-Kami, the then Governor of Osaka, hearing of the excellent abilities of the new Yoriki, appointed him to the position of judge, which office he discharged with great honor. In those days the judge was both the judge and the law, for legislation being then in its infancy, cases were mostly decided at the will of the judges. The consequence was that such judgments were mostly given as partiality might dictate, or bribes could buy, and the grossest injustice and corruption prevailed.

"But this was not the way in which Heihachirô discharged his duties. All his judgments were delivered in a straightforward manner, and in accordance with strict justice. He never courted the favor of the powerful, nor played into the hands of his friends, neither did he flatter his superiors nor despise those beneath him.

"His chief aim was to promote the welfare of the people, and after his official duties were discharged, he occupied his leisure in teaching a number of pupils fencing and literature.

"As he had now arrived at the age of thirty and had no children, he adopted a pupil of his named Nishida Kakunosuke, who showed signs of great talent. Heihachirô had always been a special favorite with the Governor of Osaka, Takaye, who had long since recognized his abilities, and on many occasions profited by his advice. Unfortunately for him, his patron was recalled to Yedo, and his place was filled by another Governor, a man of totally different character, who refused to listen to any of the representations which Heihachirô made on behalf of the welfare of the people. The latter, therefore, finding all his endeavors set at nought, and the workings of justice interfered with, resigned his post, settled certain property on his adopted son, and retired to his estates, where he devoted his time entirely to the education of his pupils.

"Now in those days a terribly selfish and oppressive spirit prevailed among the official and wealthy mercantile classes, and it had always been Heihachirô's earnest desire to bring about a better state of things and alleviate the condition of the people at large. The crops had for several years past been very bad, and the consequent high price of rice was causing much misery to the farmers and the poorer classes. It was in vain that Heihachirô and his son memorialized Atobe Yamashiro-no-Kami, the new Governor of Osaka, to take some steps to aid the suffering people. Their petitions were rejected and their representations remained unnoticed. Then Heihachirô in anger denounced the selfishness of the authorities, and seeing no other means of affording relief, sold his property and distributed the proceeds among the most needy.

"From the commencement of the year 1836, heavy rain fell unceasingly, and so unusually cold was it that summer clothes could scarcely be worn in the sixth month (August, according to the present reckoning). During the same month there occurred a severe storm which nearly ruined the crops of the fifteen provinces of the Tokaidô and Oshiu, already poor enough on account of the inclement season. The following month there was a still more violent tempest which uprooted trees, wrecked many vessels on the coast, broke down the river embankments, and caused floods which carried away houses and destroyed the remnant of the crops that the former gale had spared. In some regions the people were rendered utterly destitute, and many died on the road-side of starvation. Such terrible sufferings from famine as those endured during this seventh year of Tempô have fortunately rarely been recorded in the history of Japan.

"During the famine the Government authorities acted in the most shameful manner toward the helpless and destitute people. They cared only for their own selfish interests, and did nothing to relieve the starving population. The rich merchants, also, by means of bribes to the officials, taking advantage of the general distress bought up all the rice and other necessaries, and sold them again at outrageous prices, thus making capital out of the general misery, and filling their own pockets at the expense of the starving thousands. Instead of doing any thing for their assistance, they added to their own luxury, and spent their ill-gotten gains in every kind of degraded pleasures.

"To a man like Heihachirô, who had at heart only the well-being of the people, this state of things was unendurable, and in the following year, 1837, he determined to make an attempt to relieve the ever increasing misery, by overthrowing the corrupt officials, and depriving the merchants of their inhuman gains.

"With this intent he got together a body of men to whom he stated his views, and drew out a manifesto to the following effect:

"The Government most gravely mismanages the affairs of the state, and uses no discrimination in its administration. The officials have no respect for the will of the Emperor, and act in utter violation of the laws established by the Tokugawa dynasty. Taxes are for ever being imposed, and those who collect them seem insatiable. However great the sufferings of the people may be, the officials show not the slightest wish to do anything to alleviate them. They and the wealthy merchants indulge in every kind of luxurious pleasure, never showing an atom of sympathy with the distress of the poor. For these reasons it is decided that such officials must be destroyed, and the inhuman merchants be deprived of their wealth, that you, the people, may be relieved from your present misery. Should any uprising take place, select your leaders and come to our assistance, so that you may be transported from the tortures of hell to the happiness of Paradise."

The above was written in the plainest and easiest Japanese style, so that farmers, women and children could read and understand it. At the end the proclamation was inscribed "Punishment from Heaven." It was then enveloped in silk, with the words "Heaven's commands to the farming class," and distributed throughout the provinces of Settsu, Kawachi, Idzumi and Harima, copies being pasted on the pillars of every Buddhist temple and Shintô shrine.

Now the 19th of the second month (April) was appointed as the day on which Hori Iga-no-Kami, the

Governor of East Osaka, and Atobe Yamashiro-no-Kami, the Governor of the western districts, should meet and inspect the various wards of the city. It was also arranged that they should spend some portion of the day in recreation at the residence of a Yoriki, by name Asaoka, which stood exactly opposite the house of Heihachirô. The latter, taking immediate advantage of this opportunity, at once called together his party, made up of Yoriki Dôshin, Rônin, students, and the more wealthy farmers of the neighborhood, the most prominent among whom was Hashimoto Chubei, of Hanniaji-mura, whose daughter was a mistress of Heihachirô, and told them that although their plans of action were scarcely matured, it would never do to let so good an occasion for carrying out their intentions slip by. It was therefore agreed that they should fall on the two Governors when they were feasting in Asaoka's house, and having killed them seize the castle, and after forcing the wealthy merchants to give up their property distribute it among the poor people.

Now by his mistress, Chubei's daughter, Heihachirô had one son named Hanjirô, who was then two years old, and before entering upon his daring project, he secretly had both mother and child conveyed out of Osaka, and sent to some distant province where they could hide in safety.

The appointed day drew near, and orders were conveyed to the neighboring farmers through Chubei, to meet at the house of Heihachirô early on the morning of the 19th instant, as some presents were there awaiting them. On the night of the eighteenth it was the turn of two yoriki named Koidzumi and Seda, both belonging to Heihachirô's party, to keep watch at the Government Office. It was therefore decided that as soon as the two Governors had set out they should fire the Office, and thus cause confusion that would be favorable to the carrying out of Heihachirô's plans.

Unfortunately for their success, one of the conspirators named Hirayama, a Dôshin, distrusting the success of the movement, went to Governor Atobe and disclosed the whole plot. Atobe was thunderstruck by the intelligence, and after consulting with Governor Hori, sent Hirayama early on the morning of the eighteenth to Yedo, to convey the news to the Bakufu, Heihachirô being in the meantime entirely ignorant that he had been betrayed. On the eighteenth the Governors, intending to examine Koidzumi and Seda, ordered them to their presence. They immediately surmised that the plot had been discovered, and attempted to escape. Koidzumi found himself surrounded by a body of samurai, and after bravely fighting for some time, was cut down. Seda, however, succeeded in cutting his way through his assailants, and making good his escape, ran to the house of Heihachirô and informed him that he had been betrayed, and that the whole conspiracy was known. Seeing no other alternative, Heihachirô then decided to commence the fight rather than wait and be attacked.

At eight o'clock on the morning of the nineteenth, rockets and guns were fired to call the forces together. They had fire-arms and several pieces of cannon, and were likewise armed with spears and swords. Heihachirô, after setting fire to his own house, marched out at the head of his men. They fired the city in various parts, and extorting money from the wealthier merchants permitted the poor to take what they pleased. Osaka was very soon almost entirely in flames, the clouds of smoke that rose hanging over the city like a pall. The greatest confusion prevailed; women with their children on their backs, and the aged and helpless carried or led by the younger and stronger, struggling together in their efforts to escape the conflagration.

Heihachirô's forces gradually swelled in numbers, and were divided into two bodies, one commanded by himself in person, and the other by Oye Shôjirô. The authorities, on the other hand, were not idle. Tajama-no-Kami, the commandant of the fortress, with the two Governors doing their best towards defending themselves. Stockades were thrown up round the castle, while the Yoriki and Dôshin were sent out against the rioters. The fight was desperate on both sides, and the sounds of the firing and shouts of the combatants could be heard for miles. In spite, however, of their desperate bravery, the forces of Heihachirô, entirely outnumbered by the Government troops, were in the end utterly routed.

Heihachirô perceiving that there was now no longer any hope of success determined to destroy himself, but just as he was drawing his sword to inflict the fatal cut, he was seized from behind and a voice entreated him to commit no such act. Looking round he saw a priest of tall stature, who addressing him said: "I am the robber who attacked you on Sudzuka-yama many years ago. Acting on your warning I changed my mode of life and entered the priesthood. I have been for a long time in Osaka, and knew that Oshiwo Heihachirô was the boy whom I once attempted to rob; but I was ashamed to show my face, and therefore never made myself known to you. Hearing that you were leading the present attempt, I determined to come to your assistance, but found that it was too late, and that the day was already lost. You once spared my life, and it was owing to your advice that I was led back to an honorable calling. I look upon you as my greatest benefactor, and all I ask is to be able to repay your kindness in the past."

With these words he threw off his clothes and made Heihachirô put them on. Then dressing himself in Heihachirô's garments, and telling him to make good his escape and bidding him farewell, he appeared before the Government troops and called out "I am Oshiwo Heihachirô, and am determined to die on this spot. Come now, therefore, and attack me!" He was soon surrounded, and for a time fought desperately. At last, disabled by many wounds, he jumped into the flames of a burning house, his last wish being to delude his opponents into believing that it was Heihachirô who thus perished. When the body was rescued from the flames, however, although the features were unrecognizable, its remarkable size proved that it could not be Heihachirô, who was a man of small stature, and it was shown to be a trick to induce the authorities to believe that the latter had thus met his death.

The struggle had now come to an end. The rioters were completely routed, but their leader succeeded in making good his escape. The flames of the burning city were not extinguished until the morning of the twenty-first, up to which time eighteen thousand, two hundred and forty seven houses, four hundred large godowns, seven hundred and three smaller godowns and five large bridges had been swept away. Such was the result of this outbreak, which with one exception, the fight at Amakusa, was attended with more serious loss than any disturbance during the whole of the Tokugawa dynasty, and which would probably have been far greater had the plot not been disclosed.

Heihachirô believing that he was more certain of concealment in Osaka, where so great confusion reigned, than if he were to hide in some distant place, went with his son to the house of a cloth merchant named Miyoshiya Gorobei, who lived at Abura-cho, and whose wife was also a daughter of Chubei and sister of his mistress. Here they lay hid in a room that was entered only by Gorobei and his wife, their presence being unsuspected by any other member of the household. The Bakufu were, in the meantime, sending detectives to every part of the country to try and discover Heihachirô's place of concealment, but they could learn nothing of his whereabouts.

Now in Gorobei's employ it happened that there was a maid servant whose famly lived in the neighboring village of Hirano. Her term of service expired in March of this year, and she returned to her home. One day she happened casually to remark that she could not understand why Gorobei had lately been in the habit of using so much rice, for that more was boiled every day than the family could possibly consume, and yet it always disappeared. Now when some gossips in the village heard this, they remembered that the wife of Gorobei was related to Heihachirô's mistress, and they suspected that the merchant might be concealing the leader of the riot. They communicated their suspicions to the authorities, who immediately arrested Gorobei and his wife, and examined them before the court. Then they confessed that from the 23d of February up to the date of their examination, the 27th of March, Heihachirô and his son had been hidden in their house. Detectives were at once sent to the spot, Gorobei's wife being compelled to act as guide. The house was surrounded while a few proceeded to the room where Heihachirô and his son were concealed. Immediately the latter perceived that they were discovered, they set fire to some gunpowder that they had kept by them, and amid the flames and smoke of the burning house, they both committed *seppuku*.

Thus ended the life of a man endowed with singular ability and of marked attainments, at the age of forty-five, his only crime being that he was too anxious for the welfare of the people. As for Gorobei, his property was confiscated, his wife was exiled, and himself died in prison.

A few words about Hanjirô, the child who was sent away into safety with his mother before Heihachirô caused the outbreak which cost him his life. The mother after roaming about the country, finally came to Kagoshima with the child, but still fearing that the Bakufu would discover them, settled in the island of Amakusa. The boy as he grew up showed wonderful talent for all branches of military science. These youthful promises have been amply fulfilled, for the boy Hanjirô has developed into the famous Satsuma samurai and leader KIRINO.

## HIGASHI FUSHIMI.

HIS Imperial Highness, Prince Higashi Fushimi Yoshiaki, is the third son of his Imperial Highness, Prince Fushimi Kuni-iye. He was made Prince Imperial by Emperor Ninko, and became a priest* in 1858, when he adopted the name of Ninnaji-no-Miya. The subject of this memoir is gifted with great energy, a high order of intellect and an equable temperament. He was one of the prime movers in the restoration of the Imperial authority to its original and legitimate preëminence, and at the time of the last war of the Restoration, abandoned the priesthood by Imperial command, and was appointed a member of the Legislative Council of the Empire. Shortly afterwards Prince Higashi was placed in command of the expedition against the rebels in the eastern provinces. At the same time he was presented by the Emperor with an Imperial standard and a sword of honor.

Hearing that the royal forces had been severely handled by their opponents at Yodo and Toba, the Prince-Marshal at once proceeded to the scene of operations, and restored the fortune of the war by inflicting a decisive defeat upon the rebels. He then marched to Osaka, and using it as a base of opera-

---

* Until the Restoration it was customary in Japan for all the sons of the reigning Emperor, with the exception of the heir apparent, to become priests. This was done to avoid the possibility of any disputes arising about the succession to the throne after the death of the occupant.

tions, sent columns to Yamato, the central provinces and Shikoku, reducing these localities to submission.

In March, 1868, Prince Hiyashi was appointed Minister of War, and three months afterwards commander-in-chief at Yechigo. He then invaded Aizu, capturing the Daimio of that district, after which he returned to Tokio in November of the same year, when his important services to the Imperial cause were rewarded by the grant of a pension of one thousand five hundred koku of rice.

His Highness now resigned all his appointments and turned his attention to the study of moral science and art. He applied for and obtained permission to visit Europe, and in the winter of 1870 went to England, where he remained for three years, ardently devoting himself to the study of Western civilization. Shortly after his return to Japan he applied for permission to revisit Europe, with the object of acquiring a further knowledge of military science; but the rising of Eto Shimpei, at Saga, occurring, His Royal Highness was placed in command of the army operating against the rebels. Before his arrival at Saga the outbreak was crushed and he then, in conjunction with the late Okubo Toshimichi, at that time Home Minister, tranquilized the disturbed districts, rewarding the loyal and punishing the disaffected. On his return from this service His Highness was appointed a Lieutenant-General in the Imperial army.

In 1877 the rebellion in the southwest broke out, and Prince Hiyashi was placed in command of the troops armed and disciplined on the Western model. The deeds performed in this rebellion belong to the history of Japan; and His Highness greatly distinguished himself both by his wise counsels and bravery in the field, receiving, on the suppression of this formidable rising, as recognition of his brilliant services, the Order of the Rising Sun of the first-class.

The recent change in the Ministry has again brought His Highness' name prominently before the public, as he has been appointed a general and intrusted with the command of the Imperial Guard, the *corps d'élite* of the Japanese army.

# HIROYUKI KATO.

THIS accomplished scholar was born in Tokio, and is about forty-five years of age. After acquiring a thorough knowledge of his native language and history, as well as those of China, he began the study of the German language, which he soon mastered. In 1872 he was invited to take the secretaryship of the Educational Department; and about that time commenced the publication, in Japanese, of an extensive work, translated from the German, on State and National Law, of which between fifteen and twenty volumes were issued. He also published a number of original volumes connected with the progress of affairs in Japan, all of which were so ably and judiciously written as to command great influence among the people. For his various services as a man of letters, he received two or three titles of honor; and was at one time invited to become a member of the Imperial Household, and had the honor of assisting the Emperor in acquiring a knowledge of the German language. As a natural result of his many acquirements, he was subsequently made president of the University of Tokio, or *Tokio Daigaku*, in 1879, in which capacity he is accomplishing much good for the intellectual welfare of his countrymen. The calendar of that institution for 1880 is now before the writer, and it is certainly a remarkable volume; in all its arrangements equal to any thing of the kind in America and England. It fills five hundred and seventy-five pages, two hundred of which are in English. In contains an historical summary of the institution, from which we learn that the introduction of Western learning into Japan took place about the year 1703, when the University was really founded; that a new and important departure was taken in 1855; and that at the present time, full courses of instruction are given in all the departments of law, science and literature. The total number of officers employed in the institution is sixty-four, of whom fifty-two are Japanese and twelve are foreigners. Among the Japanese professors, who seem to have their full share of hard work, are two—Toyama and Yatabe—who are well known for their superior talents in the United States where they were educated—the first at the University of Michigan, and the second at the Cornell University. With a full corps of such men to help him in his responsible position, President Hiroyuki Kato cannot fail in time to place the University of Tokio on a level with the very best institutions of the kind in any land.

Among the Americans who have heretofore been connected with the Tokio University, we name with pleasure the Rev. D. E. W. Syle, from one of whose lectures on Japan, delivered in the United States, we quote two paragraphs, which are not inappropriate to the foregoing, as follows : —

> It is worthy of notice that Japan has a Minister of Education, a functionary not to be found in either Washington or London.
>
> Altogether, Japan opens a novel and most interesting field to the explorer in all departments. In history, in art, in natural phenomena, in ethnography, and in many other respects, we find in Japan aspects of fact and of detail which are unique and of an exceptional value. No country better repays the traveller, and in none can he be more certain of a courteous welcome. The Japanese have nothing to learn from us on the score of good manners; while we might learn from them more lessons than could be briefly enumerated.

## IJICHI MASAHARU.

HE is a native of the province of Satsuma, and was well-educated in Chinese literature; but as he progressed in life, took a special interest in agricultural affairs. He was among the first to advocate the policy of Restoration, and frequently visited the city of Kioto for the purpose of helping on the cause. He there had charge of the Imperial forces consisting chiefly of Satsuma men, and when a demonstration was made upon the city by the Tokugawa army, he with the help of Yamada, after a severe conflict caused the enemy to retire in dismay. He then went to Yedo, and at a council of war held there, he proposed plans for continuing the conflict, all of which were duly carried out, and finally resulted in the subjugation of all the followers of the Tycoon. For these services he was rewarded with an annual pension of one thousand kokus of rice.

After the war he returned to Satsuma, his native province, and held a leading position; and when the Hans were abolished after the Restoration, and gave place to the more modern Ken or province, he was called to Yedo and became, with Yamagota and Kuroda, member of the Imperial Council; and in 1875 was brought into intimate relationship with the Emperor, as a devoted personal friend. Feeling a desire to return to his native province, he obtained leave to do so, and for a while devoted himself to the pursuits of agriculture. But in 1879 he was again called to Yedo to be near the Emperor, where he has continued until the present time, commanding the highest regard not only of the Emperor, but of all the people, who are acquainted with his faithfulness as a man and an official.

## INOUYE KAORU.

HE was born in the province of Choshiu, received a good native education, and from his earliest years gave promise of future success. At one time, because of his wit and eloquence, he was very popular among the people, and the name by which he was known on reaching the years of maturity, was that of Bunda. When the English, French, Dutch and Americans made their attack on the Japanese fortifications at Shimonoséki, he, in company with his friend Ito Hirobumi, received the proposals made by the foreign envoys. When the Tokugawa forces made an attack on the Choshiu Han he with Omura Masjiro, in command of the Imperial forces, defeated the enemy, and captured the province of Iwaki, and was also successful in other military exploits. And it was during the discontents among the samurai, and because of his loyalty to his sovereign, that an effort was made to assassinate him, and the wounds he then received have remained visible down to the present day. In 1867 he became the highest local official in his native Han to look after the Imperial cause, and devoted himself to foreign affairs, and subsequently became a judge at Nagasaki.

His next official position was that of Vice Minister of the Finance Department in Tokio. In that capacity he did much to promote order in the affairs of the

Government; and it was under his orders that the various provinces during the period of the Restoration gave up their guns before the revolt in Satsuma.

In 1873, when certain affairs connected with the Government did not progress as he thought they should, he resigned from the Treasury.

When the difficulties with Corea arose in 1875, he was requested to visit that country in the capacity of chargé d' affaires, and after having secured an amicable settlement of the troubles, returned to Japan and was honored with a handsome present in money by the Emperor.

He subsequently visited England on business connected with the Treasury Department, and was again successful in his mission. On his return to Japan, he became a member of the Council of State; then placed at the head of the Public Works Department, for which he was honorably decorated, and in 1879 was made Minister for Foreign Affairs, in which position he increased his reputation as a true patriot and a judicious diplomat.

His knowledge of the English language is quite complete, and in all that he does for his country he uniformly displays a thorough knowledge of sound, practical affairs, in his own and foreign countries.

Like all men of his character, during his residence in London, he fortified himself with all the knowledge he could possibly acquire, and hence it is that on all such subjects as the conduct of business in all the departments of Government, and especially in regard to diplomatic and financial affairs, he is a leading authority, and exercises great influence among his countrymen.

With a view of giving the foreign reader an idea of Mr. Inouye's statesmanship, and of his style as a writer, we have obtained the translation of a memorial on the condition of the Empire, which appeared in 1873, and which, besides his own signature, had that of his friend Shibusawa Shigekagu, as follows :

"Although the prosperity or decay of the state undoubtedly depends on natural causes, still they also may be affected by the merits or demerits of the measures adopted by the Government. Not ten years have elapsed since the Reformation, and yet immense progress has already been achieved in various branches. On the one hand the law, which during several centuries had been inoperative, has been revived, while on the other hand the vigorous forms of government and legislation of the five great continents have been searched for whatever was worthy of adoption from them. The feudal system has been changed, and the whole country brought under one rule. Birth is no longer the sole qualification for office, but wisdom and talent are required in its stead. In legislation the law of nations* has been superadded, and in matters of debate the opinion of the majority of the nation† has been exhaustively consulted. As regards education, eight districts have been marked out, to provide instruction for the ignorant populace, while, as regards military organization, six military divisions have been created in order to keep the seditious under restraint. In order to facilitate speedy intercommunication the power of steam has been applied to ships and vehicles, and for the quicker transmission of information the telegraph has been invoked on land and under the sea. Attention has been bestowed on

---

\* This phrase seems rather vague. *Bankoku kōhō* is the usual rendering of "The Law of Nations," but it more correctly represents natural law, or perfect justice.

† The attempt to form a deliberative assembly has recently been finally decided upon.

commerce, and energy directed towards the opening up of undeveloped tracts of land. From the mint, iron-foundries, light-houses, railways, to the streets, roads, house, dress and furniture, every thing shows daily improvements which succeed each other with such rapidity that our advance into the regions of civilization may be compared to the race-horse which leaves every thing behind him. If we continue in this course for a few years without stopping, our civilization will be such that we shall not be ashamed to stand a comparison with any country in Europe or America. Every man who takes an interest in the welfare of the state rejoices and congratulates his fellow.

"But we have nevertheless a cause for grief. No grief is so pure as not to be mingled with joy; no joy so pure as not to be mingled with grief. If then we feel grief we should endeavor to find out its joyful side; if we experience joy, we should reflect on the element of grief which it contains. If we do this the measures we shall adopt will be the right measures, and the state will enjoy a truly enlightened rule.

"The word enlightenment is a single word, but when we consider its application, it must be acknowledged to be employed in two distinct senses. Those who make an enlightened theory of government their chief aim, take it to be outward appearance; while those who consider enlightened capacity in the people to be most important, take it to be a question of actual fact. Those who take it to be outward appearance find the object easy of attainment; those who take it to be a question of actual fact find it difficult to succeed.

"At this moment the populations of every European or American country are diligent in true learning, and they excel in knowledge and intelligence. Every man feels it a disgrace to be unable to live by his own exertions, but our people do the very opposite. The samurai merely understands how to live on the allowance of rice inherited from his progenitors, but not how to acquire a civil or military profession. The peasant merely understands how to practise the ordinary village routine, but cannot improve in the art of agriculture. The tradesman merely understands how to strive for petty profits, but is ignorant of the laws of commerce. All of these are ignorant of the art of living by their own exertions, and although there may be one or two here and there who are distinguished by ability or knowledge, the majority depend on the aid of others, and trust to the chance of fortune, or can do no better than climb on to the conspicuous mound and catch profit in a net.* In the worst cases fraud and deceit are prevalent, and trickery shows itself in a thousand forms. Often beggary and ruin are the consequences. If you drive on such people too fast, and try to make them suddenly enter the region of enlightenment, you are like one who on seeing an egg demands that it become immediately changed into a cock.

"We have thought to ourselves secretly in the midst of the night:—'We have been long at the capital, have once travelled abroad, and have held office for a considerable period. We cannot deny also that we have seen a good deal, so that our knowledge and intelligence must certainly be greater than they originally were. And yet, if we humbly ask wherein are we superior, we find ourselves to be ignorant fellows as before.' This has constantly drawn profound sighs from our bosoms. If our own experience is such,

---

* Vide Mencius Bk. II. Pt. II. Cap. X. § 6 & 7 Legge's Edition.

how much more must it be the case with those who dwell in remote and rural parts. From this it does not require a learned man to see that the enlightenment of to-day does not consider the capacity of the people, but that it is merely a vain race after a theory of administration.

"If the only object in view is a theory of administration, what patriot will not wish for the civilized government of a European or American country. But the samurai who are now in office have never yet trodden the soil of those lands, nor have their eyes beheld their state. All they know is derived from translations of books or from photographs. And yet they are eager and excited in wishing to enter into rivalry with those countries. Still more is it the case with those who have resided abroad for some years. When they return home, some maintain England to be superior to all. Others assert the preëminence of France. Or, it may be, Holland, America, Prussia or Austria. They compare the superiority of each to our own condition, and in commerce, the development of non-productive regions, in legislation, debate, military organization, education, dress and mechanical appliances, in short in every branch the attempt has been made to equip ourselves completely, by including every detail that might be converted to the assistance of our civilization.

"It is, of course, a perfectly natural feeling which has prompted all this, and we cannot condemn it altogether as wrong. But if regard is only had to outward appearance, and no attention be bestowed on the reality, the Government and the people will be widely opposed in feeling. The more beautiful the laws become the greater will be the fatigue of the people. As the activity of the rulers increases the national strength will diminish, and before the work is achieved the country will fall into poverty and weakness. Even the good that may have been effected will not last. And if this is to be the end, how shall we maintain our existence as a nation?

"Thus that which is the joy of all is what we grieve over.

"Although we ought to place our aim high in all matters which affect the Empire, it is necessary that in order to work we should proceed step by step and in regular order, assuring ourselves first of each result attained, and that the theory of administration should not be at variance with the capacities of the people. Assuredly we should not proceed hastily, move heedlessly, or attempt a speedy result in too short a space of time.

"When the military vassals (*i. e.* the Shôgunate) ruled the state, though the system differed in each province, men everywhere held office in virtue of their birth. Those who occupied high rank were all men who had lived in the lap of luxury, and the power was wielded by officials of surbordinate position. The latter were ignorant of the right way to govern, and of law. They relied much on precedent, and as every thing was decided by military force, matters were settled without difficulty, and none of the troubles which arise from confusion were felt. The people, accustomed to long-established abuses, looked upon them as matters of course. No one thought there was any thing to be shocked at in all this, and the country remained quiet for over two centuries.

"But as soon as intercourse with foreign countries commenced the magnitude of the evil became apparent, and order could not be maintained. Since that time men animated by a sense of right and a feeling of humanity have arisen in crowds, and have shed their blood eagerly in order to bring about a reformation. The result has an impulse towards the abolition of old abuses, the reformation of the administration and the purification of the ears and eyes of the Empire. The first object was to widen the range of both sight and hearing. In seeking to widen the range of seeing and hearing, the lesson of shame at resting in the old rut was learnt. When this lesson was learnt it became necessary to sweep away old abuses boldly and resolutely. Upon this the work was proceeded with, but upon no fixed principle, in the hope that by changing every thing from the national polity, the military system, penal laws, religious instruction, arts, civil laws, and trade, down to every kind of accomplishment, all in the space of a moment, we might enter into rivalry with all nations. This was the natural effect of preceding causes, but should not have been left to work itself out spontaneously.

"We will take for an example a physician prescribing for a disease. When the disorder is at its height, he must apply strong remedies, but when it begins gradually to abate, he applies mild restoratives, and awaits the revival of the patient's strength. This is the perfection of the art. The object of the physician is the return of the patient's strength, and he therefore first administers powerful remedies.

"The art of ruling the Empire is exactly the same. When the disorder gradually abates, various measures are initiated, and a general forward movement follows. This is the time to apply mild restoratives. It is necessary therefore that the Government in pursuing its policy should proceed step by step and in regular order, assuring itself first of each result attained before moving further. But hitherto the application of this theory has been unknown. We still imitate the old happy-go-lucky style and busy ourselves with advancing hurriedly in every direction. This is what we cannot feel tranquil about.

"We think we can at the same time point out the causes of this state of things. At the time of the Reformation the Government hastened to select men of talent, and the samurai of the Empire on their side were enthusiastic in their desire to serve it. Every one who had a single accomplishment or speciality came crowding in, and thronged to the foot of the throne. Those who in past time had been diligent and faithful servants could not suddenly be cast off, because they were sometimes destitute of the necessary talent, while those who were famed for their learning could not be dispensed with, even though they had given a little dissatisfaction. Thus outside the official ranks there were men whom it was necessary to appoint to office, and within those ranks there were none who could be dismissed. The want of functionaries to carry on the Government was never less felt than at this moment.

"Now if officials are very numerous, they are sure to have a predilection for initiating new measures. And if they have this predilection for initiating new measures, they are also sure to enjoy gaining distinction. If the Government then pays no attention to the capacity of the people, but devotes its energies to administration, and the officials are eagerly bent on initiating new measures and in distinguishing themselves, it is impossible to avoid neglecting genuine work for empty principles. Still more when a feeling of patriotism causes them to emulate the good government of those enlightened states, and to desire to rival them immediately. Under such circumstances measures will be largely initiated, and they fear lest the instruments of administration should be deficient. Consequently they denounce every thing that they think hurtful, and support every thing which is likely to prove advantageous. Some look out for chances of promotion, others seek favor for starting novelties. From all the departments and sub-departments of state down to the local administrations every one is greedy of distinction, and the number of officials in each gradually swells. The quantity of business increases, measures multiply until they interfere with each other at every turn, and the Government itself becomes unable to withstand the pressure of the evil. Besides, if there are officials, they must be paid. If measures are to be carried out, there must be expenditure. In this way business multiplies from day to day, and the outlay increases in a corresponding ratio. The annual revenue being insufficient to cover the annual expenditure, the necessary funds must be demanded from the people.

"The absolute necessities of government are naturally great, but in a time of activity like the present, the best counsel is the accumulation of money; for if that be neglected, then it will become impossible to provide for the necessary expenditure. If the necessary expenditure cannot be provided for, how can any thing be carried out? Under these circumstances taxation has to be increased, or forced labor must be demanded, and the people be subjected to burdens. The end of this will be that the people can no longer breathe in peace, and the country must inevitably decline in consequence. This has been a common trouble in all ages, and one which must cause the greatest alarm to the Government.

"A rough calculation of the total annual revenue of the whole country shows that it does not exceed forty million yen, while the expenditure for the current year may be estimated to reach the sum of fifty million yen, if no unforeseen trouble occurs. So that on comparing the revenue and expenditure of a single year, a deficit of ten million yen appears. Besides this, in consequence of urgent national affairs since the Reformation, the outlay which has been incurred from year to year, *i. e.* in excess of revenue, probably exceeds ten million yen. In addition to this the paper money issued by the Government departments and the former Han, and the debts due in Japan and in foreign countries, when added together, amount to close upon one hundred and twenty million yen. So that the total liabilities of the Government at this moment are one hundred and forty million yen, and no provision has yet been made for paying them off.

"Under these circumstances it behooves us at once to take immediate measures for gradually extinguishing them, for if this is not done the popular mind will henceforth lose faith, and should an unforeseen disaster befall us some day, we shall be overwhelmed with trouble and confusion. It will be then too late to regret.

"If then the Government still pays no attention to these matters, but, on the contrary, devotes its energies to all manner of reforms, still searching as before only for an 'enlightenment' theory of administration, how will it be able to protect the interests of the people? If the Government be unable to protect the interests of the people, how shall the people come to life again? Some advocate says: 'The people on unproductive land labor hard, while those who occupy fertile land live at ease. Ease begets poverty, labor begets wealth. If therefore you wish by developing their intelligence to make them wealthy, increase their taxes, and we shall find them at once on the level of European or American countries.'

"What an error! The people of European and American countries are for the most part rich in intelligence and knowledge, and they preserve the spirit of independence. And owing to the nature of their polity they share in the counsels of their government. Government and people thus mutually aid and support each other, as hand and foot protect the head and eye. The merits of each question that arises are distinctly comprehended by the nation at home, and the Government is merely its outward representative.

"But our people are different. Accustomed for ages to despotic rule, they have remained content with their prejudices and ignorance. Their knowledge and intelligence are undeveloped, and their spirit is feeble. In every movement of their being they submit to the will of the Government, and have not the shadow of an idea of what 'a right' is. If the Government makes an order, the whole country obeys it as one man. If the Government takes a certain view, the whole nation adopts it unanimously. In manners and customs, language, dress, furniture, even in the toys of every day use, every one is eager to be first, and afraid to be last in imitating the taste of the Government. But the lower classes are more exaggerated in their tastes than their superiors. For this reason the importation of foreign toys and trinkets is enormous, and the exports do not exceed six or seven-tenths of the imports. How is it possible to prevent the people from falling daily deeper into poverty?

"One of the ancients has said: 'He looked on the

people as he would on a man who was wounded.'*
But at present the Government is not only unable to
look on the people as it would on a wounded man.
On the contrary it restrains them with new laws, and
burdens them with new taxes. Every one must be
registered. No private companies can be formed
without a license. For their dwellings they must
have title-deeds. The men must be subject to the con-
scription. Then there are law expenses, fines for
violating petty rules, laws for the price of goods, for
their sale, for cattle, horses and servants. In consequence, whenever a new decree is put forth the people are stupefied. They are at a loss how to act, and
lose all confidence. If they are unsuccessful in trade
they try some kind of handiwork. If unsuccessful as
artizans they try agriculture. Cases of beggary and
ruin follow each other incessantly, and the number
of those who become paupers is double what it used
to be. The Government constantly advances its steps
into the region of enlightenment, and the people as
constantly satisfy their ignorance with barbarous
customs, so that the lower classes and their superiors are as widely separated as earth from heaven.
When the theory of administration is in contradiction
with the capacity of the people to such an extent as
this, the good and beautiful lose all their value.
We see what is to be grieved over and find nothing
to rejoice at.

"Every thing has its measure and the resources of
every country have their own limits. The essence of
good government is to be in accordance with the
spirit of the time, and a government, in order that
its measures may be successful, must be well ac-

* Mencius, B. K. IV., Pt. II. Cap. XX., § 3, Legge's version; i. e. he regarded the people with compassionate tenderness, ditto in note.

quainted with the limits of the national resources, and must understand the ideas and feelings of the people.

"The government of all European and American states determined their revenue after having estimated their expenditure, and as every one knows perfectly well that we cannot do this in the present state of the national resources, and of the ideas and feelings of the people we must for the present adhere to the old practise of determining our expenditure after having estimated our revenue for the year, fix our expenditure so that it cannot possibly exceed that revenue. The departments and sub-departments of the Government and the local administrations must consider what is the best order in which to carry out the various measures they propose, and when the expenditure for these has been definitely fixed they must not be allowed to exceed it one atom. As for our debts and paper currency, we must diminish our unnecessary expenditure, economize needless salaries, and apply the funds thus obtained to the gradual extinction of one and the redemption of the other. We must not advance except in proper order, nor initiate measures unless for solid objects. The people must be recalled to life, and the Empire be made to comprehend with clearness that the objects which the Government has in view are widely different from those of former times. This is the present condition of things, and our national resources and the ideas and feelings of our people are not fit for any thing beyond it.

"Should the principle be accepted, the chief functionaries ought to be assembled and be publicly made acquainted with its essence. They should mutually bind themselves to make it their duty not to lose sight of the aim intended. The comparative urgency of different measures, and the order of their execution, such questions as whether liberal appropriations should be made for the army and navy, if the expenses of legislation be curtailed, or a certain sum be devoted to public works, and the expenditure for education be cut down, whether the taxes on the agricultural population should be lightened, and the taxes levied on the trading classes be increased, should be fully debated by all, the best course be selected in each case, and the principle be adopted for the future that the theory of administration should be in harmony with the capacity of the people.

"If this were done, the people would before long regain confidence, and being able to devote their energies to the acquisition of wealth, they would make progress in enlightenment, in unison with the theory of administration.

"But if it be not done, then disasters will befall us from within and without at a moment when we least expect them, and the ruin will be so complete that nothing may avail to prevent it. Under such circumstances, how could it be said that the Government's measures had been right measures? In spite of our unfitness we have for a long time unworthily superintended the finances, and thus, although we have not accomplished any great exploits in the discharge of our duties, we cannot be said to be altogether ignorant of the subject, since we have had personal experience of the facts. When we reflect on what we see, we not only see nothing to rejoice at in the enlightenment of to-day, but find that subjects for grief are ready to make their appearance at every moment. It is quite clear that henceforward the question will depend, not upon the effect of natural causes, but upon the measures adopted by the Government.

"To know this and yet to be silent would be disloyalty. To say it without knowing it would be folly. Even if we should be rebuked for ignorance, we have no desire on the other hand to be disloyal servants. Although we have asked for our dismissal, because we are unequal to the duties of our office, our feelings will not suffer us to remain indifferent at this moment. These reasons have induced us to record our humble opinion, in the hope that it may receive a little consideration from the Government."

## ITO HIROBUMI.

HE was born in the province of Choshiu, about the year 1840, and was well educated in his native language as well as in English. During the troubles preceding the Restoration, he rendered important services by keeping down the hostile feelings against the Europeans, and while holding the position of Governor of Hiogo (or Kobe), he did much to protect the Imperial interests.

In 1868 while holding a position of trust in the Treasury Department, he was sent as a commissioner to the United States, to investigate the coinage system in operation there, and his report resulted in the establishment of the mint of Japan. His next position was that of acting Minister of the Public Works Department, and while holding it, he originated the idea, and, with his friend Okuma, consummated the building of the railroad between Tokio and Yokohama. He then became a member of the Iwakura Embassy, in 1871, and on their arrival at San Francisco, on their way around the world, he delivered an interesting speech, explaining the objects of the embassy, which attracted marked attention.

In 1873, when the Ambassadors returned from Europe, they found the people greatly excited about the affairs of Corea, and he was one of those who earnestly opposed every thing like aggressive measures; and when General Saigo and others of the existing cabinet resigned, because their war-like measures could not be carried out, Mr. Ito was promoted to a seat in the Cabinet as Minister of Public Works. He was also one of those who attended the famous meeting at Osaka, called for the purpose of discussing the measures for the organization of a Constitutional Monarchy, and with him were associated such men as Okubo, Kido, and Itagaki; and the plans proposed at that meeting were sanctioned by the Emperor of Japan, by a decree issued in 1875. It was about that time, also, that he took a decided stand against the too great freedom of the press in Japan.

In 1876 he accompanied the Prime Minister of Japan on a tour of inspection to the Island of Yesso, and made valuable suggestions for the welfare of the people in that province.

During the Satsuma Rebellion, he went to Kioto, where he had the control of various affairs connected with the suppression of the Rebellion, and for these services, on his return to Tokio, he was honored with the first degree of the Order of the Rising Sun. In the same year he was placed in charge of the Hosei Kioku, or Law Making Office. In 1878 he left the Department of Public Works, and became Minister of the Home Department; and in 1880 he was promoted to a position in the Cabinet as one of the Sangi; and is one of the most influential and industrious members of the Government.

## ITAGAKI TAISUKE.

HE was born in the province of Tosa, and educated for the military profession; was an aid-de-camp to the General of the Imperial army during the war for the Restoration; led the forces under his command to victory on several occasions, and took an active part in the subjugation of the Prince of Aidzu; and for his important services received the annual pension of one thousand kokus of rice. After the war he retired to his native province, holding a position in the then existing Han, but it was not long before he was appointed one of the Sanji or privy councellors of the Empire, which office he held for two years in Tokio, from 1871, when with his friend Saigo he resigned, because he advocated a war with Corea, and was in the minority; but he was re-appointed in 1875 to the same important position. He was one of those, moreover, who advocated the establishment of a national assembly; and he also favored various other measures, looking to the better management of public business. About that time he was honored by the formation of a political society whose principles were founded upon those which he had been foremost in advocating. In 1880, sound political opinions were generally disseminated throughout the length and breadth of the Empire; and at the present time Mr. Itagaki is looked upon as one of the most eminent leaders of the party of liberal principles.

## IWAKURA TOMOMI.

HE was born in the city of Kioto, province of Yamishoro, Japan, in 1835, and early received all the educational advantages afforded by his country. While yet a youth he was appointed one of the chamberlains in the Imperial household of Komei Tenno — the father of the reigning Emperor, in which position he acquitted himself with credit. In 1858 when Hotta, as an envoy of the Shôgunate Government visited Kioto, and requested permission from the Emperor to conclude treaties with the foreign powers, and thus to open the entire country, Iwakura brought his influence to bear against the proposition, and by his boldness won the respect of the Emperor. The advantages promised by this new movement he did not believe in, and he forthwith suggested that the forces of the Emperor and of the Shôgun should be united to expel all the foreigners from the country. While this was undoubtedly the result of a patriotic impulse, public affairs were so complicated that what was intended to be a service to the Empire proved to be detrimental to the prime mover. An alliance by marriage between the younger sister of the Emperor and the Shôgun then in power, having been consummated, this event was followed by a mysterious break between the ruling powers and Iwakura, which resulted in his banishment; and in token of his regret for the course he had thought proper to pursue in connection with public affairs, when in exile he performed the customary operation of shaving his head, and remained in strict seclusion at his residence for a number of years. At that time, according to the best authorities, he was generally looked upon as a supporter of the Bakufu Government, and therefore disliked by many of the adherents of the Court party. Notwithstanding this, several eminent men knew his real aims, and formed a means of communication between him and Saigo Takamori, Okubo Kido and other prominent leaders of the Southern Confederacy, to restore the lustre of the Imperial throne by the overthrow of the Shôgunite. All this was entirely unknown to the Bakufu officials, and it was therefore a great surprise to them, when, on the Restoration being accomplished, he was openly recognized as one of the chief leaders of the movement.

Soon after the formation of the Mikado's government in 1869, he was appointed *sanyo*, councillor, vice-administrator and vice-prime minister, all of which positions he resigned, and retired to private life. In the following year, however, he was again called upon to serve the Government; was appointed dainagon, receiving at the same time a pension of five thousand kokus of rice as an acknowledgment of his services. On a subsequent occasion he was sent by the Emperor on a special mission to Satsuma and Choshiu, where he was successful in conciliating two disaffected princes, and in causing them to return to Tokio. In 1871 he was appointed Minister for Foreign Affairs, and was first honored by a visit in person from the Emperor, on which occasion the latter made the following remarks: —

> Ever since the restoration of our Imperial authority to the pristine splendor of our ancestors, you have labored earnestly and successfully,

day and night, in the administration of the affairs of our kingdom. You have spared no toil and known no fatigue in our service, and it is to you, under the favor of the gods, that we owe the flourishing condition of our kingdom. As a special mark of our favor, we have departed from the usual etiquette and have visited you in person to thank you for your services.

Before the close of that year he was appointed *U-daijin*, and visited America and Europe as the head of the great embassy, numbering about fifty persons, in which mission he was assisted by not less than four of the leading men of Japan. The mission in question was successful, and Mr. Iwakura subsequently made arrangements to publish an account of his observations in foreign parts, which work was duly issued in five volumes, and illustrated with three hundred engravings. The first volume is wholly devoted to the United States, and exceedingly interesting.

On his return in 1872 he found the cabinet engaged in debating the question of invading Corea. He saw that financial ruin must inevitably result from a declaration of war, and opposed the project with all his influence. His Excellency Sanjo was at the time in ill health, and the Emperor sought advice in the difficulty from Iwakura. The result may be easily imagined. The war-cloud dispersed, and by skilful negotiation Japan obtained from Corea all the concessions desirable. The position taken by him in the Corean and other questions — notably that of the samurai pensions — raised against him a host of enemies, and on the 14th of January, 1873, a desperate attempt was made to assassinate him by nine ronins — eight from Tosa and one from Satsuma. Returning in the evening from an interview with the Emperor, his carriage was stopped outside the castle moat, close to the gates of the Akasaka palace. Instantly the coachman and betto were cut down, and the body of the vehicle pierced with sword and spear thrusts. Wounded, but, fortunately for the future of the Empire only slightly, Iwakura leaped into the moat and escaped under cover of the darkness. In a few days he was able to attend to his official duties, and also plead for mercy to be extended toward his would-be assassins. In commemoration of this narrow escape the Emperor conferred upon him the Japanese order of the junior first rank.

In 1876 he accompanied the Emperor on his progress through the northern provinces, and subsequently to Kioto, where he remained in attendance upon the Sovereign during the Satsuma rebellion, acting as his most trusted councillor while that grave crisis was pending. Peace having been restored to the troubled land Iwakura received the decoration of the Rising Sun of the first-class.

After the cold-blooded assassination of Okubo Toshimichi in 1878, Iwakura became, and is still considered, the most influential member of the Cabinet.

He is a most agreeable man in his manners, and has had three of his sons educated in the United States.

## KABAYAMA SUKENORI.

HE was born in Kagoshima, province of Satsuma, about the year 1837. After receiving a good education at the local schools, he entered the public service in a subordinate position, in which his knowledge of letters and public affairs generally was useful. In 1868, when the war of the Revolution commenced, he joined the army under General Kawamura, as a petty officer, and participated in all the battles to the end of the struggle, and his bravery was proven by the fact that he was twice wounded in battle — in one of his hands and one of his shoulders. After the war he returned to Kagoshima, and was appointed Governor of one of the districts or townships of Satsuma, where he remained two years, and was then made a general in the provincial army.

When the troubles with Formosa began to agitate the Government, he was summoned to Tokio, and assigned to duty in the expedition against the Island, having been connected with it until the end, and having visited China when the final settlement was made.

When the revolt of the discontented Shizoe or Daimios of Satsuma took place, in 1875, he was forthwith despatched to the new seat of war. On arriving there, he found but few soldiers ready or willing to stand by the Imperial Government, in defending the castle of Kumamoto, but finally exerted such an influence among them, that the tide was soon turned, and the soldiers declared themselves ready to do any thing and every thing for their country and to defend the castle to the bitter end. When attacked by the samurai, under the leadership of the elder Saigo, they fought with great desperation, but were triumphant. During this siege, Kabayama received a severe wound in his chest, and also in one of his feet; but fearing that this calamity might depress his soldiers, he would not let his injuries be known, and though compelled to retire, he pretended that it was for some special duty, and when he had reached a quiet place, he fell to the earth exhausted. He was subsequently taken to a hospital, and after a few weeks of suffering, recovered.

But the rebellion was not yet ended, and he followed in pursuit of Saigo, and continued to fight until the rebels were all vanquished.

After the close of this revolt, he returned to Tokio, and was assigned to new duties connected with the army.

In 1881 he was appointed to the head of the Metropolitan Police, in Tokio, which department had been organized originally by Kawaji, and the duties of which were afterwards filled with great credit by Oyama, who was his immediate predecessor.

Throughout his eventful life he has proven himself a brave, modest, able and silent man ; and although deeply attached to the elder Saigo, when he was loyal to the Imperial Government, he did not hesitate to fight him with all his might on the battle field, under the influence of his loyalty for the nation at large.

# KAWAJI TOSHIYOSHI.

HE was born in the province of Satsuma, about the year 1829; and although his family was somewhat obscure, he received a good native education, and early displayed abilities of a superior order. On becoming of age he attracted the attention of Okubo and the elder Saigo, and became their friend. When the latter came up to Tokio to support the Imperial Government, an agreement was made between him and Kawaji that they would remain there and not return to Satsuma. But when the Corean question came up for discussion, and Saigo became dissatisfied and was about to return to Satsuma, his followers called upon Kawaji to accompany him and them, but he refused to do so. He also reminded them of his own and Saigo's pledge made before leaving their native province, and said that he intended to stand by the Government at all hazards. In recognition of his loyalty, he was treated with the attention that his abilities deserved.

Having paid special attention to the business of local government, he was placed in charge of the police establishment of Tokio, and as this was in an unsatisfactory condition, he devoted all his energies — he devoted all his attention to a complete reform of the service then existing. His idea was to have a regular system of armed police similar to that existing in France, and there called *gens d'armes;* and in 1878 he was placed at the head of a commission of four or five competent men, who went to Europe for the purpose of collecting the desired information. For his services up to that time as the military protector of Tokio, he had been honored with the title of the third class. His sojourn in Europe lasted only a few months, when his health declined, and he was obliged to return to Japan, where he soon after died, in 1879. He was a man of fine personal appearance, modest and unobtrusive in his manners, a true lover of his country, and will long be remembered because of his honorable services in giving the Imperial city an effective police establishment.

## KATSU AWA.

HE was born in the province of Shidzruoka, but for the greater part of his life was known as a Tokio man. His family was one of influence and were devoted to the cause of Tokugawa. He was reputed brave and sagacious even from his youth, and was well read in the literatures of China and Holland, as well as of his own country. In 1855 he had much to do with the building of the first man-of-war ever built by Japan after a foreign model; and when another ship was assigned to the duty of taking an embassy to San Francisco, he was assigned to her command.

When the Tokugawa Government for the second time sent an army against Cho-shu, Katsu was the man who advised against the measure, and thereby only displeased the Tycoon, who accused him of insincerity; but his loyalty to the Emperor was firm; and after the death of the Tycoon he was made commander-in-chief of the land forces, and did much to restore peace to the distracted country. In these efforts he was assisted by Okubo to a great extent; and they not only did much to prevent the fiery young soldiers of the Tycoon from fighting the army of the Emperor, but were so successful in pleading the Imperial cause that this induced Saigo, who was then in command, not to make an attack upon the city of Yedo, as had been contemplated.

When Admiral Enomoto escaped from Shimagawa Bay with the vessels of war in which he had been fighting the Imperial forces, it was through Katsu's management that the fleet was overtaken and all brought back to the Bay of Yedo. He was subsequently assigned to the duty — with Okubo and others — of preserving the peace of the city of Yedo, and for a time did with great difficulty suppress the rebellious conduct of many of the retainers of the Tokugawa family, who called themselves *Sho-gi-tai*, or Soldiers of Righteousness, but could not prevent the shedding of blood, and on several occasions narrowly escaped with his own life.

In 1872 he was appointed Vice Minister of the Imperial Navy, and in the following year rendered important service at Kagoshima. When, soon afterwards, the question of making war upon Corea, arose, he declared himself against hostilities, entered the Cabinet, and was placed at the head of the Navy Department. In that position, as well as many others, he displayed rare ability, and won great popularity.

When the new Senate was organized he was at once made a member of that body by appointment, but foreseeing a difficulty between Saigo and Okubo in regard to their diverse politics for the welfare of Japan in 1874, he resigned and retired to private life. He next devoted himself to the study of literature and science, and especially of chemistry; he also did much for the welfare of the Commercial College of Tokio, and with his private means sent many young men abroad for purposes of study, and assisted in various ways many poor people living in the interior of Japan; thereby doing much good for his country, and bringing great honor to his name.

## KAWAMOORA SMIYASHI.

HE was born in the province of Satsuma, Japan, about the year 1835; received a good education at best schools of his country, and then travelled in foreign countries, making the tour of the world for the purpose of increasing his store of knowledge. During the late revolution in Japan he firmly espoused the cause of the Emperor, and rendered good service in various positions of responsibility, and was subsequently made Vice-minister of the Navy Department, holding the office until he became a member of the Imperial Cabinet, when he was placed at the head of the Navy Department, in which position he still continues. His knowledge of affairs is extensive, and his influence wide-spread and beneficial. The editor greatly regrets that he is unable to give a more satisfactory account of this eminent man. That he belongs to one of the oldest and best families in Japan; is an accomplished scholar; progressive in his views of public affairs, and popular with the people, are the only facts that can be added to what has already been stated.

In no department of the public service has Japan made better progress than in the building up of her navy; and the zeal of Mr. Kawamoora has been especially valuable to his Government. It was through his instrumentality, that so many young Japanese were educated at the Naval Academy of the United States.

## KIDO TAKAYOSSI.

THIS eminent statesman was born in Higo, the province of Chôsiu, about the year 1830, and belonged to the Negato clan. His father was a physician and in comfortable circumstances, but the boy had a severe struggle with life. According to a fashion of the time, he became an adept in the art of fencing, and fortified with a limited education in the Japanese and Chinese languages, he went to Tokio and there established a fencing school. He subsequently went to Osaka in the capacity of a porter, to carry the baggage of a prince, he going on foot while his employer rode upon a horse. The prince blamed the porter for want of speed, and the porter rebuked the prince for his lack of feeling, when a separation took place. The whilom porter entered a fencing school, soon became a leading scholar, and afterwards had charge of the establishment; and in which, by his honesty and boldness in directing his pupils, and preventing them from taking undue advantages, he became very popular.

The province of Chôsiu was among the first to raise the standard of revolt against the late Tycoonate, and having already won some reputation as a leader, he was one of the chief emissaries in organizing the army, and did much toward securing the victories which it accomplished. After the Tycoon had abdicated, and the Emperor Mutsu Hito had assumed his rightful supremacy, he was made a member of the Privy Council, serving in that capacity with such men as Iwakura, Okubo, Okuma, and the elder Saigo, who soon afterward went into retirement, and has since been so unaccountably associated with the recent rebellion in the province of Satsuma.

When, in 1871, the Emperor reconstructed his government, he retained the presence of Kido at the Board of Councillors, as he could not be dispensed with. Although he had not at that time been out of Japan, and was unacquainted with the English language, he was an earnest advocate of modern methods, and was one of the first to recognize the newspaper press as an element of civilization, and founded at his own expense, the daily journal called *Shinbun Zasshi*, or, *Miscellany of News*, which is still published with the title of *Akebono Shinbun*, or *Morning News*. He was a member of the embassy which visited the United States and Europe in 1872. When in Washington he made it his special business to collect information in regard to the judiciary, and had frequent and prolonged consultations with several noted lawyers. His questions on many delicate points displayed great ability, and the lawyers regretted that they were compelled to converse with such a man through an interpreter. He returned to Japan before the embassy had finished their mission; received soon afterward the appointment of Sangi, which he accepted and held for a time; was next appointed to a distinguished position in the Imperial household, and in the early part of 1875 was again elected to the rank of Sangi, and was in attendance upon the Emperor at Kioto at the time of his death, which occurred on the twenty-seventh of May, 1877.

In person he was above the average height of his

countrymen, and in his deportment dignified if not stern. If not as popular with the people as were some of his associates in the Government, he was nevertheless a man who commanded the highest respect and confidence of his sovereign as well as of his countrymen, and his presence was greatly missed from the councils of the nations.

A few months after Kido's death, a number of documents which he had laid before the Daijo-daijin and the U-daijin, were made public, and as these clearly expressed his opinions on the condition of public affairs at the time, the following synopses are worthy of consideration:

"Kido used repeatedly to say that it was yet far too early to attempt any reform of the land tax, or the capitalization of the pensions of the Kwazoku and Shizoku. The Government, however, was of a different opinion.

"A Chinese writer has said that 'when Government measures do not meet the requirements of the times, they should be reformed again and again until they do.' On such a principle our present Government seems to be acting, but the ancient sage did not mean that it would be wise to issue a law in the morning and repeal the same in the evening.

"The memorial addressed by Kido to the two Daijin, was to the following effect:

"Firstly, that the annual expenditure of the various Government departments should be diminished, in order that the taxation of the people might be reduced.

"Secondly, that local expenditure should be controlled by the local authorities, and not, as now, by the Government officials. It is well-known that each district has its own peculiar customs and privileges, which can only be properly understood by the local officials, who should have the power of so conducting local matters as to suit them to the special wants of the district under their jurisdiction.

"Thirdly, that laws should not always be considered as necessary because they appear to be good in themselves, but that such laws as meet the requirements of the people should meet with first consideration.

"Fourthly, that as the Government is now all under one head, no district should be allowed to enjoy special privileges owing to any superior power that it may be supposed to possess, as thus other districts which are debarred from the enjoyment of such privileges, are unjustly treated.

"Fifthly, that whereas since the demand for peoples' rights and liberties has made itself heard, the country has become divided into two parties, Conservative and Progressive, the Government professed to be the upholder of the former, whilst all its actions favor the policy of the latter. To the proper solution of these points the Government must give its most earnest consideration.

"The letter addressed by Kido to his friends was to the following effect:

"I have laid before the Daijin a memorial respecting the affairs of our country, but can not tell how it will be received. What I have to request of you is that you will coöperate with me in promoting the welfare of the Nation. Men who are swayed by patriotic motives should not retain their offices merely for the sake of the emoluments attached to them. If they cannot discharge the duties entrusted to them according to their conscience, they should at once resign their positions. For my own part I intend to resign my post, to return to my native province and teach the people there the true road to civilization. He who would assist others must deny himself. I therefore trust that you will work with me, selling your houses and unnecessary property, and endeavoring to act independently.

"As I have held high positions under Government for a number of years, I am possessed of abundant means, and if any of you need assistance from me, I shall be most willing to grant you whatever you may require.

"Though we return to our native province, it will be necessary from time to time to come to Tokio, and not remain in ignorance of what is transpiring around us in the world. I am now building a new house which will be available for our meeting in Tokio.

"There is another important point which I am desirous of bringing to your notice, and that is, that you will guard yourselves against indulging in any feelings of personal enmity. This has caused some of our friends to break the laws of the country and to turn criminal by opposing the authority of the Government. Such action is decidedly wrong.

"But when I say that I shall return home I do not mean that I shall entirely withdraw from all active participation in the affairs of my country, and trouble myself no more concerning them. When I see that matters are going wrong, I shall come forward and entreat the Government to change its mode of action."

While Kido lived he was the pillar of our country, and never lost sight of the welfare of the people. There can be no question of greater importance than the reduction of the taxation, and of the Government expenditure. The Imperial decree, issued on the third of January, 1876, was founded upon this memorial of Kido.

Some people accused Kido of duplicity, but judging from his acts he was a faithful patriot, and his untimely death was greatly regretted. "There are, however," wrote a Japanese editor, "one or two points of Kido's conduct upon which we are in the dark. He was in office at the reform of the land-tax, and the capitalization of the pensions of the Nobility and Gentry. Now if his views were entirely against the action of the Government in these matters, why did he not uphold them; and if after repeatedly urging them upon the administration, he found that it would not act in accordance with his representations, why did he not resign his post?"

Again in his letter the same writer says, "He speaks as though he intended immediately to resign his position. Yet this letter was written in December last, and he was still in office when death removed him in June following. It is true that he may have tendered his resignation, and that the Government refused to accept it; but we have never heard that such was actually the case. Had he but lived these things would doubtless have been made clear to us. Now we can only regret his untimely death.

"P. S. The two lawyers to whom the editor introduced Mr. Kido when in Washington, were the late Professor Samuel Tyler, and the present Judge Walter Cox (who presided at the trial of assassin Guiteau), and it was upon their suggestion that Mr. Kido caused the publication in Japanese, in eight volumes, of *The Spirit of Laws*, by Montesquei."

## KONO BENKAI.

HE was born in the province of Tosa, and while a pupil of one of the Retainers, he was one day sent on an errand to the house of the Minister Tomomi Iwakura, with whom he happened to have a conversation on public affairs. The impression made by his remarks was such that the Minister had him appointed to a position in the department of law. On a subsequent occasion when the Retainer alluded to above had been arrested for some improper conduct, and Mr. Kono was sent to look after the business, the Retainer was very indignant, whereupon Mr. Kono quietly informed him that while he was now a culprit, he himself was a judge, and the punishment of the law should be properly inflicted. He performed the duties of a judge for several years with great ability and discretion. He was also made a member of the Senate, where he remained until 1880, when he was placed at the head of the Educational Department; and in 1881 he became the minister for the newly established department of Agriculture and Commerce. In his political principles he is liberal and progressive.

The honorable career of this young man affords another illustration of the fact that, in Japan, in these progressive days, merit and ability, when supported by integrity, are certain to be fostered and protected by the leading officials of the Government.

## KURIMOTO-JO-WUN.

HE was born in Tokio in 1821, and during his earlier years suffered from continuous illness, so that he could not prosecute any studies of consequence; but as he advanced toward the period of manhood he was enabled to acquire a good medical education at the native schools. When in 1850 he offered his services to the captain of a Dutch vessel recently arrived in the bay of Yedo, he drew upon himself the ill will of his countrymen, and was obliged to retire for a time to private life. In 1851 he went to Hokkaido, or Yesso, where he conferred with the native physicians and established at Hakodate a medical school as well as a hospital; about the year 1857 he was appointed to an official position at Hakodate; subsequently called to Yedo, where he was promoted; devoted some of his time to teaching the Japanese language to foreigners, and especially to persons connected with the French and other legations then established in Yedo. It was through his influence that a French school was established in Yedo, and through whom the tactics of the French army were transplanted to Japan; he was also instrumental in establishing an iron factory for the use of his countrymen; he made a visit to France, from which he brought back much information that proved of value to his countrymen. During his sojourn in France he was earnestly invited to become a permanent resident in that country, but he scorned to heed such advice. On his return home he was urged to join the army of the Tycoon, then fighting against the Imperial Government at Hakodate, but he declined all such offers, and devoted himself to literature, compiling two extensive works out of the works of famous travellers in various parts of the world. Of late years he has been wholly occupied as a writer for the press, and as editor of the *Ho-chi-Shimbun*, or *Japanese Mail*, in which capacity he has won a brilliant reputation. He is a bold and fearless writer, but entirely loyal to the ruling government. As a specimen of his style of writing, we submit the following translation of an article from his pen on the subject of Education:

"Two great duties devolve upon parents, namely the rearing and the education of their children. The helplessness of an infant makes it absolutely dependent on its parents, and their care is willingly bestowed upon it. When of more mature years parents seek to secure for their children the blessings of education, so that they may grow up wise, happy and independent. All this is or should be a pleasure to parents. The making of a man is dependent on the education he receives when young; if carefully attended to, the youth becomes a good or wise man, but if neglected he becomes the reverse. It is thus clear that parents are equally bound to educate their children properly as to protect them when infants, and if they neglect either they fail in their duty as parents.

"At the present time schools are established in every part of the Empire, which are readily available for those living within the district, so that the children of the highest and the lowest, the rich and the poor, can all read and write. Education is, indeed, widely spread throughout the country. But as regards the parents we find that they only consider themselves bound to maintain their children and protect them in infancy, and quite lose sight of the fact that they are responsible for their education, as the present state of affairs leads them to suppose that it is the duty of the state to educate their children, and that they themselves are relieved from any obligation in this respect. If their reasons for holding such opinions are inquired into, they disclaim personal responsibility because they are obliged by law to send their children to school, and it is therefore no concern of theirs whether the master is competent to teach, or if the children receive a sound education. This indifference on the part of the parents conduces to carelessness and idleness on the part of their children, so that the education offered them is too often thrown away.

"For this reason, if we compare the present system of education with that in vogue during the Shôgunate, we cannot but come to the conclusion that the result only shows retrogression. Under the Shôgunate the extent of a child's education depended on the condition of his parents. The poor people placed their children under the instruction of either Shintô or Buddhist priests, while those who could afford it had their children instructed by competent masters at home, or sent them to good schools in the capital to study such special subjects as the bent of their minds or their capacity for learning showed was desirable. In short, at that time parents, high or low, rich or poor, fully recognized the duty incumbent on them of seeing that their offspring were properly educated, and their obligation to bear the cost of such themselves.

"But at the present time, though the country has

advanced in civilization and the people are intellectually improved, parents are gradually adopting the belief that the education of their children is the duty of the state, and the reason of this is that at present the cost of such education is borne by the Government, or is covered by local taxation which therefore but indirectly touches those who are naturally responsible.

"In every country and in every age the want of education has been a curse, as thousands of illiterate persons, whose good qualities have not had an opportunity of development, are led through ignorance to lead dissolute lives, and perhaps eventually lapse into crime to the great injury of society. For this reason it is perhaps as much the duty of the Government to enforce education among the people as it is to establish police and law courts in order to secure peace and order in the country. Now parents may have conveniently adopted this view, without taking a higher one of their responsibility, and therefore in the long run, beneficial as Government instruction may appear to be, we imagine it is conducive of harm. If it is the duty of the state to educate the children, why should they not at once be sent to the poor-house and there maintained and educated, without causing any trouble and anxiety to their parents? Yet no one would say that such a course would be right. Parents are naturally bound, if possible, to protect and maintain their offspring, and there is so close a connection between this duty and that of attending to their education, that the one can no more be set aside than the other, and the responsibility of the latter should not devolve on the Government. In Western countries parents are held responsible for the education of their children, and why should they not be so in this country?

"Although much of the present improved condition of the country is due to our enlightened Government, still much more of it is due to the march of time. And if in the unenlightened times of the Shôgunate parents recognized the necessity of properly educating their children, how much more will they recognize that necessity now if they are in no way relieved of their responsibility, especially as they really dislike the present system of forced education, are alive to the retrogressive result, and consequently place no reliance on the existing schools being able to effectually benefit their children. Even now there are parents who prefer to rely on private tuition as an addition to the instruction obtained at the public schools, and we are sure that benefit would result from education being left entirely to the free will of the parents. It would then be to the interest of parents to take care that the instructors of their children, whom they themselves would have to pay, were fully competent to perform the work they undertook, so that not only would the masters themselves be kept well up to their work, but the scholars under their care would receive wider and more exact instruction. Moreover, it would save a large outlay by the Government, which could be otherwise employed to the good of the country, and would encourage parents to faithfully perform the duties alloted to them by Nature.

## KURODA KIYOTAKA.

GENERAL KURODA is a member of one of the historic families of the great Satsuma clan, and has the reputation, proved on several trying occasions, of being a brave and upright leader, with but slight regard for pomp and ceremonial.

Prior to the Restoration, he allied himself with the opponents of the Bakufu Government, and loudly expressed his dissatisfaction with the arbitrary conduct of the Shôgunate officials, and their contemptuous disregard of the Imperial authority. In conjunction with Saigo Takamori, Okubo Tochimichi, and other able leaders, he acted a prominent part in the wars of the Restoration, and when peace was reëstablished received in recognition of his valuable services the appointments of Privy Councillor, Chief of the Colonization Department, and General in the Army.

General Kuroda then went to Yesso and energetically devoted himself to the colonization of the island. Under his auspices waste lands were brought into cultivation, roads and bridges constructed, and towns and villages sprang into existence with marvellous rapidity; so that whatever progress has attended the settlement of the Hokkaido, is in no small degree owing to his influence and example.

While he was engaged in this peaceful work, the Coreans insulted the Japanese flag by firing upon the *Unyo Kan*, at Kokwa bay. General Kuroda was chosen ambassador to demand satisfaction for the outrage, and his dangerous mission was crowned with complete success. The Corean Government apologized for the conduct of their officers, entered into a treaty of amity and commerce with this Empire, and opened Corea to Japanese trade. The valuable results of the General's embassy are now becoming apparent in the increasing importance of the mercantile relations springing up between the two countries.

In 1877 the formidable rebellion in the southwest found the subject of this memoir appointed to the command of a division acting against the enemy. Embarking with his soldiers in transports, General Kuroda landed at Yashiro, and at once assumed the offensive. He attacked the rebels, who fled after a sanguinary struggle, abandoning to the victorious troops all their arms, ammunition and stores. General Kuroda then raised the siege of the fortress of Kumamoto, which was closely invested by the rebels, and on the point of falling into their hands. His forces being augmented by the relieved garrison, General Kuroda marched upon the enemy and took part in the closing struggle at Shiroyama, when the great Satsuma rebellion was finally crushed with the death of its mainstay, the redoutable Saigo.

General Kuroda was not overlooked in the distribution of rewards which followed the restoration of peace. He received the honorable distinction of the highest rank of the Order of the Rising Sun.

The recent changes in the Cabinet have not effected General Kuroda, who still retains, with advantage to the Empire, his high offices of Privy Councillor, Chief of the Colonization Department, and General in the Army.

In January, 1882, at his own request, General Kuroda

was relieved of his functions as Privy Councillor and Chief of the Colonization Commission, and appointed Cabinet Adviser in the Imperial — one of the most honorable positions in the gift of the Government. In the meantime the Kaitakushi Department has been placed in charge of General Saigo (the younger), who would seem to have more than his share of public responsibilities.

# NEESHIMA JO.

HE was born near Yedo, in 1844, and is one of the samurai; studied navigation, and became assistant to a Japanese captain who had charge of an American ship owned by a Japanese prince. While this vessel was lying for several months at Hakodadô, he supported himself by teaching the Japanese language to a Greek priest, and at the same acquired the English language from the clerk of a commercial house.

He was early inspired, notwithstanding the opposition of his parents, with the wish to become a Christian teacher to his own people, and with that object in view, he secreted himself in the cabin of a ship, with an American captain, bound for China. He was discovered in this hiding-place after the ship was out to sea, and the captain allowed him to work his passage. He remained in China, where he sold his two swords, about nine months, and then sailed for America from Shangai, in a ship bound for Boston. On this voyage he taught the captain the Dutch language, and in other ways assisted him so as to obtain a free passage.

The captain became much attached to him, and on his arrival in Boston introduced him to his employer, who kindly put him in the way of obtaining an education.

Early in his career he translated the gospel of St.

John into Japanese, and dated his true conversion to the full appreciation of the thirteenth verse of the third chapter of that book.

When the Japanese Embassy were in Washington he was sent for by Mr. Mori, and became assistant to Mr. Tanaki on a tour to examine the educational institutions of this country. He went with the embassy to Europe in the same capacity, and when they left for Japan, he returned to Massachusetts and pursued a theological course for two years; after which he went as a missionary to his native land.

He took the name of Joseph at his baptism, his second Japanese name being *Jo;* and he is now known as the most influential and zealous native teacher of the Christian religion in Japan. He has established a school for young men in Kioto; is married, and lives in a pleasant home after the American fashion; teaches natural philosophy in the Kioto college, and spends much of his time in preaching the truths of the Bible to his countrymen. He has also written and published one or more books bearing on the history of Christianity, and edited several others. There was a time, in his early years, when he was disposed to become an atheist, but all such ideas were abandoned long ago; and in the eyes of the Christian world at least, he occupies to-day one of the most noble and honorable positions that could fall to the lot of any man.

## MIURA GORO.

MIURA GORO is a member of the Choshiu clan, his family name being Ando, which was changed, in accordance with Japanese custom, on his being adopted by his father-in-law, Miura, whose property he has inherited. The subject of this sketch was distinguished during his boyhood and youth for his fearless disposition and the extreme devotion which he paid to his studies, more especially those dealing with military subjects.

When the Bakufu Government despatched an expedition against the Prince of Choshiu, Miura joined the late Mr. Takugi, General Yamagata, and other influential leaders, in exhorting the members of the sept to show a firm front and oppose the threatened danger. Their exertions were crowned with success, and the men of Choshiu, fired with patriotic enthusiasm, determined to repel the invaders of their hearths and homes or die resisting gallantly to the last.

The result of the expedition is history. Miura, at the head of a detatchment operating on the Kokura road, contributed in no small measure to the frustration of the efforts of the assailants, who, beaten in several severe engagements, withdrew their shattered forces to a place of safety. Owing to the altered condition of political affairs the invasion of Choshiu was abandoned, the Bakufu authorities being engaged in a struggle for existence in the north against the constantly increasing power of the Imperial party.

Miura took a prominent part in the wars of the Restoration, and commanded the Imperial forces entrusted with the task of reducing the province of Echigo to submission. The fruits of early training matured in the stern school of later years were now made fully apparent. Miura gained a series of brilliant victories over the rebel army opposed to him, inflicting defeat so crushing that when the campaign closed the royal authority was firmly established, and the malcontents dispersed.

When peace was reëstablished Miura was appointed lieutenant-general in the army, and has since received the insignia of the Japanese Order of the fourth class.

In 1876 the standard of revolt was raised by Maibara Issei, and Miura, then in command of the garrison at Osaka, took the field at the head of troops hurriedly got together for the purpose of quelling the rising before it had time to attain formidable proportions. Miura executed a forced march to Higi and encountered the rebels in several engagements, the result being, that the armed opposition to the Government was first localized, and then stamped out.

Scarcely had this service been successfully accomplished than the Satsuma rebellion broke out, taxing all the resources of the Government and the utmost skill and energy of the Imperial leaders. Miura, at the head of one *corps d' armée* took a prominent part in all the momentous struggles of that eventful period. In Higo, Osumi, and wherever hard blows were struck and danger to be encountered, Miura was to be found in the forefront of the battle, leading his men with the most desperate bravery and a contempt of death which compelled the admiration of the foe and excited the emulation of his followers. At last the sanguinary struggle was closed with the crowning episode of Shiroyama, and the forces were enabled to rest after their arduous toils and painful sacrifices. Miura was not overlooked when the distribution of rewards for faithful services and dauntless courage took place. Promotion to the rank of general, and the Order of the Rising Sun of the second class, were allotted to the warrior who, in the full enjoyment of mental and bodily vigor, is now, as ever, ready to furnish with his victorious sword the material for another chapter in the history of his country, should the circumstances of the nation again demand his services.

## MORI ARINORI.

HE was born in the province of Satsuma in 1846, and, as a boy, enjoyed all the advantages pertaining to the retainers of the local Daimio. He was among the first of those students who were sent to England to be educated, and after residing in London for two years he returned to Japan. During the rebellion which soon culminated in the restoration of the Mikado, his sympathies were with the progressive party, and it was not long before he became a member of the newly-organized national legislature, and in which, notwithstanding his age, he made a decided impression. He introduced among others, a proposition to abolish the wearing of two swords by the privileged classes, and the opposition to it was so desperate as to endanger his personal safety, and the result was that he retired from public life for a time; and while in the seclusion of his country home, he subsequently had the satisfaction of being informed that his ultra proposition had been successful. Not only so, but several years afterward, when he was in Washington, he presented to the museum of the War Department, a sword which had been given to him by a Japanese gentleman, then travelling in this country, who had formerly been one of his bitterest opponents in the legislature, and who had voluntarily abandoned the wearing of his swords.

He was the first Japanese who, under the Restoration,

was appointed to a foreign mission, and in March, 1871, while bearing the title of Jugoi, he presented his credentials at Washington as *charge d'affaires*, where he remained two years. The duties which devolved upon him during that period were novel and arduous but performed with credit to himself and were beneficial to his country. Not only did he perform his ordinary diplomatic duties, but he was obliged to exercise a kind of supervision over the large number of students then in this country, and in one sense had charge of all the arrangements and ceremonies connected with the advent and the sojourn in this country of the Iwakura Embassy. In the meantime, but more in a private capacity than as minister, he greatly interested himself in the cause of education, and caused the publication, for the benefit of his countrymen, of a work on the *Resources of America*, another on *Education for Japan*, and several pamphlets on kindred subjects, one of them on *Religious Freedom in Japan*.

It was in the latter part of 1871 that Hamilton Fish, then Secretary of State, informed Mr. Mori of the existence in his Department of the Indemnity Fund, which the Secretary said really belonged to Japan, and should be returned: and, true to his instincts, Mr. Mori immediately replied: "If that money is returned, I shall propose to found a great library in the city of Tokio." There was much talk upon the subject at the time, and the press discussed the question in a friendly manner, but after the lapse of ten years the great Congress of the United States had failed to reach a settlement, thereby proving that the majority of our legislators were as mean and covetous in their manner of doing business as they were narrow-minded and ignorant.

Mr. Mori returned to Japan by the way of Europe,

and was thereby enabled to profit by further experiences in foreign lands. For a brief period after reaching home he took no special part in public affairs, but as was his wont at all times, he watched the course of affairs with interest. In 1874 he entered the office of Foreign Affairs as the First Secretary; his next position was that of Second Assistant Minister in the Foreign Office; he afterward went to China as Minister Plenipotentiary; returned home again and was made the First Assistant Minister of Foreign Affairs; and in the latter part of 1879 he was accredited Minister Plenipotentiary to Great Britain. By his friends this was considered a well-deserved compliment, and proved that his public career in various positions had won the approval of his Government. Before leaving Japan on his new mission he announced a change in the spelling of his name from what it had hitherto been, to that of *Maury*. What was his object is not known to the writer, but his right to make the change was not questioned. At the same time those of his countrymen who had ever been ready to criticise his acts as a public man, because of his advanced ideas, did not scruple to make a handle of the new name for their amusement. It would seem indeed that the more his facetious countrymen criticised his political opinions, or his tastes as a private gentleman, the more indifferent did he become to their carping criticisms; and when they found that they could not make him angry, the more angry did they themselves become.

## MOSHITSU OTSUKI.

THIS man, like Genpaku Sujita, mentioned elsewhere in this volume, was one of those whose labors as a scholar paved the way to the era of progress now enjoyed by Japan. He was a native of Sendai, and went to Yedo when quite young and joined the Translating Society which had been founded by Genpaku. In his plan of operations, he had in view a knowledge of medicine as well as an acquaintance with the treasures of Dutch literature generally. He made one or more pilgrimages to Nagasaki, in the hope of obtaining superior facilities for study in that city, and having returned to Yedo, he published a work entitled *Steps to the Dutch Language*, which was considered as an invaluable work for those who desired to know more about foreign lands. One of the results of this success was that many men of note asked the privilege of becoming a pupil of the successful Japanese-Dutch scholar. It was about that time — in 1807 — that the Tycoon was led to believe that Russia and England had some sinister designs respecting the invasion of Japan, whereupon Moshitsu was ordered to compile an account of those countries from the Dutch books, which duty he faithfully performed. For this labor he was regularly compensated for many years; until 1822; and it is said that this was the first instance of the Tycoon's Government directly encouraging Western learning.

The books of this author were numerous. He published a revised edition of the *Analytical Anatomy* first issued by Genpaku; also *Strange News of the Seas*, and many volumes of miscellaneous essays. He had a son named Genkan, who was also a fine scholar, and rendered valuable assistance to the Government by his pen.

## MUMETA GENJIRO.

MUMETA GENJIRO was a native of Wakasa. He was famous for his literary acquirements, and often went to Yedo, where he associated on friendly terms with Fujita Hio, Sakuma Shozan and Fujimori Kowan. When he was over thirty years old he removed to Kioto and opened a school. Afterward he visited Choshiu and became intimate with Takasugi Shinsaku, Hisazaka Gisuke and Miokoji Seikio. He was a very courageous man and constantly referred to the subject of the Son O Jo-i and framed a plan of his own for the defence of the seacoast. In the ninth month of the first year of Ansei, 1854, a Russian man-of-war arrived in Osaka bay, and the people residing in that neighborhood earnestly watched the behavior of the strangers. At this time the peasantry of Totsugawa, in Yamato, became much excited and organized a band of soldiers, appointing Mumeta Genjiro as their leader, for the purpose of driving away the intruder from the coast of Japan. But before they had made complete preparations for action, the ship departed of its own accord. Thus their intentions failed. Soon afterward, vessels of the United States of America, France and England frequently came between Musashi and Sagami, and their presence caused great irritation. Nevertheless the Bakufu Government could not prevent them from coming close to the shore. The Imperial Government frequently issued orders to the Bakufu, and instructed them to drive away the foreign barbarians from the borders of the Empire, but the authorities at Yedo took offence and instead of complying, made arrangements to negotiate treaties and carry on trade. Genjiro, on hearing of this intention, became anxious about the non-performance of the Imperial commands, so he gathered together a number of influential friends and addressed them as follows : If we depend upon the weak Bakufu to conduct our national affairs, it will be difficult to clear away foreigners and prevent them from coming into our waters. I have heard that Nariaki, the lord of Mito, is an eminent man and a patriot. He has designed a scheme of Son O Jo-i and prepared for the defence of the sea-coast, and his soldiers are superior to any others. He has often sent in his view of the situation to the Tokugawa rulers, and, on the other hand, he offers his loyal service to the Kioto court as well. Thus his conduct is honorable, and his action trustworthy, and we should unite in asking the Imperial officers to appoint him leader of a band of patriots, in order that measures may be taken to maintain our country in peace and tranquility for the future. Favor me with your views upon this subject." All the party quite sympathized with the proposal of Genjiro. Then they sent a document secretly to the chief authorities in Kioto, Seiren in no Miya, Konoye Tada-aki, Sa Dai Jin, Takatsukasa Sukeaki, U Dai Jin, Sanjo Sanchisa, Nai Dai Jin, Kuga Tatemichi, Dainagon, Ichijo, Saneyoshi, Dainagon and Nakayama Tadayoshi, Dainagon. The Imperial Government praised their loyalty and sent instructions to Nariaki to expel the foreigners on their appearance. At this time, Ii Camon no Kami sent Nagano Shujen, his retainer, to Kioto for the purpose of persuading the authorities there to agree to a treaty with the strangers. This messenger, hearing about the secret document of Genjiro, reported the particulars to his master. Then Ii became alarmed and privately directed Shujen to seek out the names of the members of Genjiro's party. Neither Genjiro himself nor any of his associates knew that their plans were thus discovered, so they proceeded with their purpose and continued to communicate with the authorities or the Kieto council.

Just then Tokugawa Yoshihiro, Dainagon, Matsudaira Yoshinaga, Chusho, Yamanouchi Toyonobu, Shosho, and Date Muneki, Totomi no kami, proposed to have Hitotsubashi Keiki, Kiobu Kio, summoned to Kioto castle and proclaimed as the successor to the Shôgunate, since it was expected that the actual Shôgun would shortly die and it was their desire to secure the office for one who, they believed, would carry out the law of prohibiting foreigners from coming to Japan. They sent Hashimoto Sanai and Kusakabe Isanji to Kioto to manage this business secretly. One day they told Kobayashi, Sab-dayu of Minbu, that the Bakufu, being afraid of foreigners, could not drive them away if they chose to come, and added: "We recommend Hitotsubashi Keiki, the seventh son of Nariaki, Daimio of Mito, an illustrious and popular man and one who has a formidable plan for the expulsion of the strangers, as a suitable successor to the Siagunate and a proper representative of the Tokugawa family in conducting the affairs of the nation." Kobayashi, on listening to the proposal of the two men, was persuaded to agree with them, and used all his influence to assist their design. Finally the Imperial Government sent a secret order to Hitotsubashi to come from Mito to Kioto castle. Ii Kamon-no-Kami, on hearing of this secret order, immediately nominated Tokugawa Iyeshige, lord of

Kii, as the immediate successor of the existing Shôgun. But this prince, being then but a child, did not understand public affairs, therefore Ii Kamon no Kami was enabled to selfishly wield the power which he held, regardless of popular opinion. Genjiro increased in anger on witnessing the conduct of the Tairo, Ii, and of the authorities of the Bakufu council. In the third month of the fifth year of Ansei, Ii sent Mabe Jensho, kakuro, to Kioto, as if to inquire after the health of the Emperor, and this messenger presented gold and silk to the sovereign and also to the high authorities and members of the nobility. Thus he laid his schemes for the purpose of getting into favor with them, and he gradually took opportunity to explain the benefits of foreign intercourse and trade. He also contrived the arrest of Genjiro and his comrades, numbering more than thirty, and threw Seirenin no Miya and several other ministers and noblemen into confinement. This proceeding was known by the name of the "Calamity of Bogo" (Bogo being another name for the fifth year of Ansei). Genjiro was imprisoned and addressed him thus: "You did not respect the Bakufu and participated in a secret movement by the name of Jo-i. You must have been beguiled into doing so by some other person. Acknowledge it without fail." The reply of Genjiro was that he knew nothing but a great principle in the Son O Jo-i. The officials examined him many times in a day, sometimes beat him unmercifully, and sometimes inflicted the punishment of compelling him to hold up for many hours a heavy stone. While he was almost exhausted and breath had nearly left him, he repeated that he knew nothing else but the principle of Son O Jo-i, and he had not uttered any thing else. The torture which he had undergone made him appear at the point of death, but the attendants took great care to revive him and so he gradually recovered his health. In the twelfth month of the same year he and the others of his party, more than thirty prisoners altogether, were sent to Yedo, and while he was imprisoned in a jail of Kokura Han, he died at the age of forty-four. This happened on the fourteenth of the ninth month, the sixth year of Ansei, 1860.

## NAGANORI ASANO.

THIS gentleman, who is still quite young, is a member of the nobility, and was born near Osaka. He was highly educated, and is recognized as a man of superior abilities. He was formerly a member of the Japanese Senate; received the order of the second rank for his services; is noted for his liberality; and in 1882 was appointed Minister Plenipotentiary to Italy. In his letter of credence, the Emperor of Japan spoke of him as "faithful and prudent, as well as diligent and exact in business," and had no doubt he would be kindly received by the Emperor of Italy. His predecessor in Italy was Nabeshima Naotake, who is also a member of the nobility. It is a hopeful sign for Japan that men of the stamp here mentioned, members of the nobility and wealthy, should be willing to serve their government as envoys to foreign countries; and the fact is in keeping with another custom, which has prevailed for a dozen years or more, of giving the most obscure men all the rewards of office to which their abilities entitle them.

The commercial intercourse between Japan and Italy has been far more intimate than is generally supposed, and the policy is a sound one which induces Japan to send to Italy men of practical experience and ability to represent her interests in regard, especially, to the culture of silk.

## NARUSHIMA KIUHOKU.

THIS distinguished journalist was born about the year 1837, in the city of Tokio, and his family had long been closely identified with the Tokugawa dynasty. He displayed extraordinary talents even in his youth, and rapidly became a master of the Chinese and Japanese languages and history. In his eighteenth year he was sufficiently advanced in his studies to become a regular instructor in the family of the Tycoon. It was not long after that time that he became dissatisfied with the policy and inaction of the Government, and boldly proclaimed his opinions. This course made him unpopular with the ruling powers, and he consoled himself by leading a free and easy life, and occasionally writing a satirical poem on public affairs; his official connection with the Government was severed, and he was for a time imprisoned for performing a part allied to the English Junius, only that he did not condescend to do any thing secretly.

He next turned his attention to the study of the Dutch language, and at the end of three years was quite a proficient; for this course he was severely criticised, and was even threatened with assassination, but he went on his own way rejoicing, and not caring for what people thought or said about his conduct.

In 1865, however, public opinion experienced something of a change, and he was placed in charge of a body of cavalry; in this position he acquitted himself so well, that when he petitioned to the Government that the tactics of the French army should be engrafted on the old Japanese policy, his prayer received a favorable answer. According to his sagacious mind, he saw that trouble was looming up in the distance, and for two years he dropped all his literary pursuits, and devoted himself exclusively to military affairs. He now perceived, however, that the fortunes of the Bakufu were waning, and he retired to private life. But in this position he was not permitted to remain, for he was forthwith called upon to perform the duties of a commissioner in the Treasury Department, as well as in a second position connected with foreign affairs.

When the Tycoon Keike had committed a certain act reflecting on the Emperor, he was advised by Narushima to visit Kioto and apologize to the Emperor, but the advice was not taken; and, subsequently, when the Imperial army came to Yedo, and the retainers of the Tycoon advised him to take his own life and thus save his followers, Narushima advised against this, and finally the retainers agreed with him. From that time, however, he never visited the Court of the Tycoon, and again retired to private life, begging his friends to consider him thereafter as one of the common people. Then it was that he not only resumed his literary studies, but, after travelling extensively over his own country, he made a protracted tour through Europe and America, returning to Japan fully supplied with important knowledge of public affairs throughout the world. He was next called, after the Restoration, to an honorable position connected with the Senate, but declined the office; not long afterwards he became the editor of the *Chôya Shimbun* (Daily News), in Yedo, which acquired an extensive circulation; he also published a number of valuable books, and did much to promote the cause of literature. During the Satsuma Rebellion he went to Kioto, where he wrote many important letters which were printed in his journal. Among his countrymen he is reputed to be a very eloquent writer, a man of uncommon sense and sagacity, a true patriot, and an able poet. As to his newspaper, it is to Japan what the *London Times* is to England — an institution of superior power.

And here, by way of giving the reader a taste of his quality as a writer, we append the following translation of an article which appeared in his paper in August, 1876, on *Class Privileges:*

"We have already published articles applauding and commending the step which our Government has determined upon — namely to abolish the paying of hereditary pensions to the nobles and samurai, and, instead, to issue to them in bonds during the space of thirty years, such sums of money as will serve as a capital whereby they may acquire a livelihood; and we have at the same time given some advice to these two classes. We will to-day carry our argument further than we have hitherto done, and see whether or not both nobles and samurai will henceforth be on a perfectly similar level with us commoners.

"The chief impediment which has hitherto existed to prevent a standing of equality as between the nobility and samurai on the one side, and the commoners on the other, is the payment of these hereditary incomes. The system under which these payments were made has, however, now been altered, and public bonds will be issued in lieu of them. These bonds can be held by the humblest commoner, and they cannot, therefore, be regarded in the same light as were the hereditary pensions. Even granting that it has been forbidden for the present either to pledge or mortgage them, what has given rise to this prohibition is simply the apprehension that the thoughtless nobles or samurai would recklessly squander or dispose of them and thus bring themselves into straits for their future livelihood. We would venture to say that the present bonds cannot be considered as being in any way different from those previously issued by the Government, or as being a hereditary source of income. The chief distinction which has hitherto existed between the nobles and gentry and us commoners has thus been removed.

"The second distinction is the rank which attaches to the former. Careful consideration shows us that no rules authorizing this rank have existed from antiquity, and it was owing to the absence of such that even confectioners assumed the names of Yamashiro Daijo and Yamato Daijo, and sword-makers those of Kaga-no-kami and Musashi-no-kami. At the time of the revolution the false assumption of these names was forbidden, and we see no difference between the case of those who then took them and that of the nobles and samurai at the present day. We earnestly hope that henceforth the rank that the unofficial nobility and samurai now hold will be taken away from them, that they will be reduced to a level with the commoners, and that the justness of equal rights to all classes will be made known throughout the Empire. If, however, our Emperor, on account of very kindly feelings which he entertains toward the nobles and samurai, cannot bring himself to deprive them of their rank, we will allow this subject to lie over for the present and make it our object to beg for reform of the third distinction which exists between us.

"What is this third distinction? A most serious one; to wit, the system of 'intercalary punishment.' This system was devised as an indulgence on the part of the Government towards both nobles and gentry, but when viewed by us commoners it seems to be an act of partiality limited to those two classes. Just let us see. When a member of either commits a crime his rank is taken away from him and he is made a commoner. To make commoners who have been guilty of no crime, and who can look both towards heaven and upon earth without any sense of shame, associate on equal terms with samurai and nobles who by their disgraceful conduct have outraged decency, should this be called oppression or not? Within recent years commoners have been permitted to ride on horseback and to assume surnames, the nobles and samurai not being, at the same time, deprived of these privileges which they alone had previously enjoyed. These precedents should now be followed and the intercalary punishments to which nobles and samurai are liable abolished, the same punishments ordained for them as commoners and the infliction of corporal punishment entirely done away with. If these steps be taken the feelings of the nobles and samurai will be assimilated to those of the commoners, all will become equally industrious and all equally watchful over their conduct; both the former classes would for these reasons regard such a step with feelings of rejoicing instead of as a grievance, and, as regards us commoners, we should be freed from the injustice of having to associate on equal terms with nobles or samurai who had for disgraceful conduct been thrown into our ranks. This is but what strict justice demands, and is it not besides gaining two ends by one action?

"Every one knows that in savage countries, such as India, there are many distinctions of class between people of the same country, and that the bad custom of separation of high from low cannot be got rid of, a matter which affords great ridicule to the civilized countries of Europe and America. Now when our Empire is advancing with such rapid strides towards the attainment of public justice, is there one of us would rejoice at seeing the custom of the barbarians maintained among us for a single day? There may, however, be some who may advocate a procrastinating and dilatory policy — who may say that though the pensions of the nobles and samurai should be abolished, their rank should be left, or that though their rank be taken away, intercalary punishments shoud be preserved. If the Government approves of such a line of argument as this and extends its principle a little, the conclusion will be arrived at that the pensions should never have been abolished, and that the feudal system should still be maintained — a very startling and deplorable one. We are, accordingly, eagerly desirous to see the securing of like privileges with all speed to all classes of people. What say ye, ye learned men?"

As bearing more directly upon this editor's own experiences, we also append the following paragraphs on the subject of Progress in Japan:

"Who can accuse the Japanese Government of being harsh and despotic, or the people subservient and ignorant? Experience and observation have proved that the contrary is now the case, though formerly there may have been grounds for the accusation. At present it is clear that the chief aim and desire of the Government is to turn the needle of administration in the right direction, to pay attention to public opinion, to consolidate the foundations of national liberty by judicious reforms, and finally to secure lasting peace and prosperity to the country by the firm establishment of a constitutional monarchy. It is, therefore, the duty of the people to assist the Government in the advance of the country in civilization.

"About two years and a half ago the writer was imprisoned for an offence against the press laws, and so cut off from the knowledge of what was being done in the country. But on the fourth of November the Government kindly permitted the introduction of newspapers into the prisons, so that after a dreary blank of nearly two years we became acquainted, by means of the public journals, with the wonderful changes that had taken place, which led us involuntarily to exclaim, Ah! the advancement of the country is as the rising sun! No one can now reasonably bewail the curtailment of national liberty, or regret the want of influence attached to public opinion. Among the most important changes that attracted our attention were the revision of the laws, the establishment of local assemblies, the advancement of national education, the growing love of national liberty, the due appreciation of rights and obligations by the people, and the recognition of the power of public opinion. Had not the Government fostered public opinion, and carefully guarded the rights and liberties of the people, the country could not have reached its present state of civilization.

"In glancing back at the condition of the country prior to our imprisonment, we are at a loss to know when the first steps in liberty were taken. It is as if one were following a narrow and uncertain footpath across a vast plain, not knowing when the broad and safe high road would be reached. Some years ago the love of liberty and the appreciation of public rights and duties were as dim as the stars in the morning, the people were destitute of patriotism or courage to express their desires, and were content to remain in ignorance, thus giving no indication to the Government of the direction in which the needle of administration should be pointed in order to secure their liberties.

"In the course of a few years the advancement of the people in knowledge has been as a strong wind or a flowing tide, and nothing checks the progress of civilization. Newspapers are everywhere published and debating societies are everywhere met with. The love of liberty is increasing and the due appreciation of rights and duties daily extending among the people, who show an eager desire to take part in the administration. The Government carefully observing the advanced condition of the people, notified in November, 1876, that local assemblies would be established in the future, and have since given effect to this announcement and extended the franchise to the people of every Fu and Ken. The great advantage of this reform has been that a sympathy has been established between the Government and the people, disorders which were previously rife have ceased to exist, and the people have learned to take a lively interest in politics. Furthermore, the Chihô-kuan Kuaigi was opened this year, and the foundation of a representative government has been laid by the establishment of Fu and Ken assemblies. A great change in the administration has thus been brought about by transferring some of the burden from the central to the local governments, and the extention of the franchise to chô and son. The Government has thus clearly shown that it does not desire to grasp arbitrary power, and the condition of the country is consequently greatly benefited.

"Many desirable reforms have taken place in our laws, the most notable of which are that the guilt of the accused must be established by witnesses (June, 1876); the prohibition of the arrest of those against whom a civil action is brought (September, 1876); the abolition of torture and the admission to bail (February, 1877); a revision of the laws of evidence leading to more perfect and careful judgments, and nondetention of prisoners in prison while awaiting their trial (December, 1877). All these commendable measures have had the effect of dissipating grievances, and confirming the happiness and prosperity of the people. In addition, new criminal codes have been compiled and will soon be carried into effect.

"In the draft of the new press laws that the *Akibono Shimbun* lately published there are one or two clauses which we cannot suppose were framed by our enlightened Government, and therefore do not stop to criticise them, but hope that when the revised laws are issued they will not contain the obnoxious clauses.

"The great changes we have enumerated were gradually brought about while we were undergoing imprisonment. They are sufficient to prove the benevolence of the Government and the improved condition of the people.

"For two years and a half our life was a dreary blank in a darksome prison, but our restoration to freedom has afforded us the gratification of contemplating the wonderful changes that have been effected in this country, and we are now glad to have an opportunity of freely congratulating our countrymen on the improved state of affairs. We trust the love of liberty will continue to increase, and that every man will do his utmost to serve his country truly and faithfully, so as to advance her steadily in the path of civilization."

As there is hardly a single feature in the history of modern Japan which better illustrates the prevailing spirit of progress than its newspaper press, it affords the editor special pleasure as an appropriate sequel to this sketch, to print the following account which he has received from a friend in Osaka:

"In reviewing our past history, we find that the first newspapers were published in Japan in the first year of Manyen (1860). They were such as *Chiugwai Shimbun*, *Moshio-gusa* and *Noriai-banashi;* but were, however, much more like magazines than newspapers.

"The first daily paper was the *Mainichi Shimbun*, of Yokohama; this was followed by the *Nichi Nichi Shimbun*, published at Asakusa, Tokio, on the twenty-first of February, 1872. On the eleventh of March of the same year, an Englishman issued a paper called the *Nisshin Shinjishi*, which was followed by the *Hôchi Shimbun*, the *Kôbun Tsûshi* (now known as the *Chôya Shimbun*), the *Shimbun Zasshi*, (since changed to the *Akébono Shimbun*), *Kiôgi Shimbun*, and *Kiôkai Shimbun* (which has been changed to *Meikiô Shinshi*), all of which are issued every day, every other day, or weekly.

"In 1873 Mori Arinori, Katô Hiroyuki, Tsuda Shindô, Mitsukuri Rinshô, Nishi Shu, and other equally prominent men formed a society and published a paper called *Meiroku Zasshi*. This journal stood first among all similar magazines. Shortly before this Fukuzawa had published a paper called *Minkan Zasshi*, but it was completely eclipsed by the latter publication.

"Although at this time so many journals were published, they bore little resemblance in form to those of the present day. The paper on which they were printed was either of Chinese or European make: the type was large, and the only newspaper whose columns would admit of a leading article was the *Nisshin Shinjishi*. The people were also ignorant of the power of journalism. The higher classes did not care to read the frivolous and often obscene items of news of which most of the newspapers were made up, and therefore almost exclusively patronized the *Meiroku Zasshi*.

"As it was found necessary to institute some regulations for the conduct of the various newspapers as they came into existence, in October, 1873, the Government issued laws regarding the native press. The newspapers from this time commenced to be more and more extensively patronized by the people, and consequently became greatly improved in form, being printed on large paper with fine type. All kinds of interesting news were published, and as the number of their correspondents increased, the various journals were unable to find space for the mass of matter. In the same year the minds of the people became exercised on the question of sending an expedition to Korea, and of people's rights, which topics were discussed with great vigor in the native papers. At this time Bajô Daijiro, of the *Nisshin Shinjishi*, Tachibana Mitsuomi, of the *Hôchi Shimbun*, and Neko-o, of the *Nichi Nichi Shimbun*, were the most prominent writers. Before this the mass of people had looked upon newspapers in much the same light as the colored pictures sold in shops, but they now commenced to see that they were wrong in holding such views. Thus the reading of newspapers greatly increased, and the journals themselves commenced to exercise considerable influence over public opinion.

"Just at this time several writers who held extreme views of progress, commenced to write articles denouncing in strong terms the actions of the Government and its officials, even going so far as to attack the reputation and honor of certain of the Kuwazoku, Shizoku and Heimin. In consequence of this the Government, on the twenty-eighth of June, 1875, repealed the press laws, and issued in their stead others, including the law of libel, the violation of which was to be punished by the severest penalties, such as three years' imprisonment, a fine of five thousand *yen* and confiscation of type and printing machinery.

"On the promulgation of this law the writers were thunderstruck, finding themselves debarred from expressing their views with that freedom which had hitherto characterized their productions. But these repressive measures were instituted in order that the minds of the people might not be too much excited by the utterances of newspapers, and that the authority of the Government might thereby be overthrown. They were also necessary in order to prevent attacks on personal character and reputation, or the publishing of matters which should be kept secret. It was not with the view of closing the mouths of the people that such repressive steps were taken, and the writers at last understanding the intention of the new laws, saw that they could without infringing them, find ample space to express their views upon politics, political economy, religious and popular customs. Still, many writers who held extreme progressive views upon the subject of peoples' rights and national assemblies, expressed themselves in violent terms, and thus overstepping the limits prescribed by the laws, were punished for so doing.

"Among other rules laid down it was especially stated that all proprietors, directors and editors of native papers must be Japanese. The Englishman was therefore compelled to cease all connection with the *Nisshin Shinjishi*. In December, 1875, he issued a new paper called the *Bankoku Shimbun*, and it was expected that some trouble would arise therefrom with regard to its being an infringement of the press laws. The British Minister therefore gave an order that its publication should be stopped, and the paper thus ceased to exist.

"The *Osaka Nippô* issued its first number on the twentieth of February, 1876. Previous to this there had been the *Naniwa Nichi Nichi Shimbun*, and the *Naniwa Shimbun* published at Osaka, but they both came to an end. After the Tokio newspapers, the press of Yokohama and Osaka stands foremost in Japan.

"Since the commencement of its career the circulation of the *Osaka Nippô* has greatly increased in various Fu and Ken. This arises from the fact that the people have found newspapers to be aids to progress, and thus they have flourished in spite of press and libel laws.

"The number of those newspapers who have been carried away by their zeal and whose editors have been punished by fine or imprisonment has been very large. Some of them not being content with the judgments rendered at the ordinary courts went so far as to appeal to the Superior Court (*Daishin-In*). But even then the more progressive among them refused to change their tone, and kept up their arguments most vigorously, so that the Government was induced to issue a notification to the effect that any newspaper or magazine which might be considered obstructive to the observance of peace in the country should, by order of the Naimusho, be suspended from further publication. This notification was issued on the sixth of July, 1876, and on the eleventh of the same month, the *Sômô Zasshi*, *Hiôron Shimbun*, and *Kokai Shimpô* were suspended. These were followed by the suspension of the *Chiugai Hiôron*, *Môsô Zasshi*, *Sômô Jijô* and *Bummei Shinshi* in Tokio; in Osaka *Gakumin Shinsei* and *Tôyô-kiji Shimpô*, and in Kioto the *Minkai Sankôron*, all of which were prohibited from publication, one after the other.

"The newspapers publish particulars of all events of interest which may transpire, sending reporters to the scenes described in order that the real facts may be ascertained. This was the plan pursued with regard to the Korean and Formosan Expeditions, the trouble with China, and the disturbances which occurred in Saga, Kumamoto and Hagi. The editors expressed their views upon these questions, and published the letters from correspondents relating thereto.

"Reporters even followed troops to the seats of war and when the Emperor went to Oshiu to open the railroad, and also on the occasion of the opening of the Uyéno Exhibition, special seats were set apart for the representatives of the press.

"When the recent rebellion broke out in Satsuma, the press without exception condemned the movement as a wrong one, and thus they and the Nation were in perfect accord in the opinion held with regard to it. Many of the more ignorant of the people, not being aware of the manner in which their confessions had been forced from Nakahara Hisao and others, imagined that such a man as Saigo Takamori would not have risen against the Government without some rightful cause, and it was not until they had read the opinions of the press and the correspondence from the seat of war, that they were convinced that there was no just cause for the movement. Owing to the influence exercised by the representations of the press, the people were induced to come forward from all parts of the country, and volunteer to fight againt the insurgents. Thus the power of the press in overcoming an enemy is greater than a regiment well armed, and the capture of fortifications.

"Newspapers sent special reporters to the seat of war, and even in such desperate engagements as those which took place in Tawara and Uyeki, they braved the bullets and never for a day omitted sending reports to the papers. When communications were opened with Kumamoto, and when the Imperialists made their attack upon Mifune, the reporters suffered very severely, and some were even captured by the rebels. Fukuchi, the editor of the *Nichi Nichi Shimbun*, who returned to Kioto for a short time, was called before the Emperor and H. E. the Prime Minister, and gave a description of events of the seat of war. This is indeed an honor to be conferred upon the editor of a newspaper. At this time the attention of the people was concentrated on Kiushiu, and thus the newspapers became of great necessity to the people, and their circulation in consequence immensely increased. On some days it was even necessary to publish extras, which were distributed after the ordinary daily issue. Thus the papers enjoy the full confidence of the people."

## OKI TAKATO.

HE was born in Saga, province of Hizen, and received a liberal Japanese education. At the time of the Restoration he was called to become one of the Sanji in Yedo, and was also associated with the office for Foreign Affairs; he was afterwards connected with the War Department, and was chairman of the new Senate; and on relinquishing all these positions, he became the head of a communion, composed of Samashima, Mori and Kanda, whose province it was to make certain examinations connected with the organization of a legislative body and the municipal affairs of Tokio. In 1870 he was appointed Vice Minister of the Home Department, and shortly afterwards full minister of the same; and it was about that time that he took a leading part in the establishment of the Educational Department, in which he had long taken a special interest. In 1872 he was transferred to the Department, having charge of religious affairs; in 1873 he was placed in the Cabinet as a Sanji; and while still holding that position, he was, a few months afterwards, placed at the head of the Department of Justice.

When the revolt took place at Kiu-Shu in 1876, he was sent to that locality as a peacemaker, and was successful in his efforts. In 1877, with Okubo, Okuma and other men of note, he received the first degree of the Order of the Rising Sun, for his long-continued and patriotic services as an official in the various positions which he was called upon to fill.

When we consider the large number of his public positions, which were all of great responsibility, we cannot but be surprised to learn that he is a great lover of books and a very extensive reader of them in various languages.

## OKUBO TOSHIMICHI.

OKUBO TOSHIMICHI was born in the province of Satsuma, on the island of Kiusu, a region long renowned for the bravery and heroism of its people in the cause of Japan, about the year 1829. He belonged to the higher class of "Retainers," a term which in Japan is allied to that of knighthood in Europe during the Middle Ages. His early education was the best that the country afforded, and from his youth until he attained the age of about thirty years, he participated in the public affairs of his province, and was a faithful friend and special adviser of the ex-Prince or Daimio of Satsuma. His early service was rendered to the late or most famous Prince, the predecessor of the ex-Prince. That Prince, by the way, who died about the year 1857, at the age of fifty-four years, was the foremost leader in steadily advocating the restoration of the ancient Imperial dynasty, and the adoption of the new order of things abroad. He was one of the most profound scholars in the Chinese classics, as well as those of his own country, and fully informed in their general history and literature; and he was also well acquainted with Western civilization, including its philosophy and science, and is asserted by many to have been the corner-stone of the new government.

Not only did Okubo as a young man do what he could to help the administration of his province, but he early became interested in the welfare of the whole Empire. He took sides with that small but more patriotic body of men who, about twenty-five or more years ago, began to grow restless under the corrupt and despotic reign of the Tycoon dynasty; and when in 1868 the great questions arose as to the immediate restoration to power of the legitimate Emperor, and of opening the port of Kiobe to foreigners — as was stipulated in former treaties with other powers — Okubo was among the foremost to advocate the preservation of the national dignity, and was supported in his views by Iwakura, Sanjio, Kido, Saigo, and many others who have also become famous in the recent history of Japan.

At this point we may turn aside for a moment to mention two or three of the most singular measures which the successive administrations of the hereditary Tycoons were in the habit of employing for the maintenance of their power and for keeping their country in the old paths. For no less a period than two hundred and seventy years they compelled all the Daimios of the Empire to leave their wives and children in Yedo, where their principal homes were ordained to be, and where they — the wives and children — were held as hostages, or as a check upon the possible disloyalty of the Daimios, who were allowed to reside in their own provinces in alternate years. The Tycoons were also in the habit for many years of intriguing to give a fictitious and semi-divine elevation to the position of the true Emperor of Japan, so as to remove him from all participation in the affairs of state. There was still another measure, born of the spirit of cunning, and employed in the early part of the Tycoon administration, about two hundred and fifty years ago, and ever since continued until the new era dawned, namely, that no vessels larger than those employed in the coasting trade and fishing in the seas of Japan, should be built, as they would inevitably bring the people in contact with foreign nations, thereby causing them to become more enlightened, and inclined to throw off the yoke arbitrarily placed on their necks. These, with other measures looking to the same end, excited the apprehensions of many of the thinking and patriotic men of Japan; they were the cause of the local dissensions which afflicted the country for many years; and it was inevitable that they should culminate either in the forced or voluntary abdication of the Tycoon — voluntary, because it could not morally be sustained any longer — and the restoration to power of the true Emperor or Mikado. The truth is, that for centuries there was a spirit of progress permeating Japan through all its length and breadth, which was unfortunately crippled by sundry checks of despotic legislation: and we all know that a civilization, however peculiar to themselves, was found among the Japanese when that country was first introduced to the world. But there seemed to be no heroic leaders of opinion until the forced abdication of the Tycoon led to the restoration of the Imperial Government, when such able and patriotic men as Okubo, Kido and Saigo came prominently upon the stage of public affairs. The rapid progress that Japan is now making is, therefore, no longer to be wondered at when we carefully and logically compare the principles of the old and the new government of Japan — the one "compulsory, restrained," the other "free progress." In other words, it is but the natural law of things exemplified, the reaction from absolute coercion.

In the hostilities which soon followed and resulted

in a change of government, Okubo participated with energy, not so much as a military man, but as a counsellor with the Prince of Satsuma and others. As soon as the Tycoon abdicated, in 1868, he was appointed a counsellor in the national Government, a capacity in which he remained until 1871, when he became the Minister of Finance, a position in which he exercised a paramount influence ; and he was also a member, with his friends Iwakura, Kido and Ito, of the embassy which visited America and Europe in 1872. The last-named of these visited this country several times in an official capacity, and is remembered by many as a man of superior ability.

On the return of the embassy in 1873, the questions bearing upon Corea and Formosa were both attracting much attention, and for many months there was much said about local insurrections, and Okubo took upon himself the task of trying to throw oil upon the troubled waters. His argument was that nothing should be done on the Corean question until more important and pressing matters had been properly dealt with — such as the proposed revision of treaties with sundry powers, the settlement of the tariff question, the establishment of a new system of internal revenue, as well as the questions bearing upon Saghalien and Formosa.

These were undoubtedly all sound and wise considerations, and as there was no war with Corea, of which so much had been said, as threatening the Empire, the presumption is that Okubo's advice was heeded. It so happened, however, that in October, 1873, there was a split in the Cabinet on this question, and the men who resigned were Saigo, Soyeshima, Goto, Etagaki and Yeto.

About the middle of February, 1874, news reached

Yeddo that an insurrection had broken out at Saga, in Hizen, and at once Okubo with a detachment of the army, was despatched to the theatre of war, and by his sagacity and firmness the leading insurgent and ten other ringleaders were captured and promptly executed by court-martial — an event which very decidedly put a stop to the scheme of going to war about Corea. For this important service Okubo was congratulated by the Emperor and greatly applauded throughout the Empire.

It was also during these exciting times, just one month before Okubo's departure for Saga, that the cowardly attempt was made to assassinate Iwakura Tomomi, on his way home from the Imperial palace, by the partisans of the insurgents in Saga. Having failed in this wicked deed, the assassins had run away, and in vain tried to hide their bloody hands in obscure corners. They were soon arrested, however, nine in number, tried, found guilty, and sentenced to death. If to American minds that punishment seems severe, here is what the *Japan Mail* said on the subject :

> The ruffians who attempted to assassinate the Udaijin in January last have by this time paid with their lives for their crime. And it is well that it is so. If men are to resort to assassination, or to threats of it, in order to prevent the rulers of a country from following the course on which they have determined, after mature deliberation, as the course best for the country, or to force them into some course of which their judgment disapproves, all government, or the possibility of it, is at an end. We trust the apprehension and execution of these men will give a sound lesson to the undisciplined spirit which is one of the worst signs of the condition of the country, and we congratulate the Government on its success in bringing them to justice.

When the Formosa question became so formidable as to attract universal attention, Okubo seems to have taken to himself the burden and responsibility of carrying out the plan, in regard to this question, which had been adopted by the Cabinet; and it also appears that it was his policy first to settle this question so that the proper title to the islands of Loochoo, which were partly claimed by China, might be determined. Finding that an immediate expedition to Formosa was inevitable and expedient, he gave his hearty support to the cause. He, together with Okuma, who, we are told, had been appointed president of this expedition, looked after the operations of the army and the departure of troops, which took place from Nagasaki.

Soon afterwards a complication was apprehended with the Chinese Government in regard to the expedition. In order to avoid any further misunderstanding on the part of the Chinese Government, he was commissioned an ambassador plenipotentiary to that Empire to negotiate with it in regard to a proper and peaceful arrangement for both Empires. He left Yokohama for Nagasaki on the sixth of August in the Pacific Mail steamship *Costa Rica*, and at the latter port took a man-of-war belonging to the Japanese Government for China. After his departure one of the leading journals of Yedo spoke of him in these terms:

> Okubo is now the man to whom the country looks to steer it clear of danger; but there is a predominant feeling that it is better to fight China, at whatever risk, than yield in the smallest degree to menace.

Another of the native newspapers, while discussing the question between China and Japan, made these remarks:

> The two Empires have long been very intimate: therefore Okubo has been sent to China by the Mikado. It is not known what his orders are; but it is supposed they are to make known its faults to the Chinese Government, and that we, after getting a proper indemnifica-

tion from it, shall continue as intimate as before. If China opposes Okubo's words, he will soon be succeeded by our forces. Okubo is the pillar of our Empire, and its safety or danger depends only on him. Now, we ask all patriotic men, Shall we carry arms against each other, like Prussia and France, or shall we be intimate, as before? Which of these will Okubo prefer?

Okubo reached Pekin on the twenty-seventh of August, and immediately entered upon important negotiations. How, by his wisdom, lofty bearing and boldness, he succeeded in effecting an honorable peace with China and securing an indemnity, is already well known to the world. On his return to Yedo on the twenty-seventh of November, the people throughout the Empire were most enthusiastic in their congratulations to him and the Nation. Escorted by several regiments of troops and high officers of the Cabinet, he went to the Department of the Interior, instead of going home, after which he went to the Imperial palace, where he was warmly received by the Emperor, and congratulated on the great success he had achieved, and his safe return. The newspapers were enthusiastic, and spoke of his mission as one that would stand high in the annals of the Nation and place him among the benefactors of his country, and for several days there were continuous festivities throughout the capital and Yokohama.

His skill as an envoy, the firmness of the Japanese Government and its proud attitude before the world, were facts which filled the Empire of Japan with rejoicing. The questions settled by the successful mission of Okubo are various and of great importance, but this is not the place to enlarge upon them.

Aside from the rightful settlement of certain territorial lines, the fact has been demonstrated that Japan will hereafter be to China what the Western nations have hitherto been to the Asiatic nations generally, and the success of Okubo was simply a grand illustration of the wonderful advance which the "Empire of the Rising Sun" is now making towards civilization.

With regard to the personal character of Okubo, it was in keeping with his high position as a patriot and statesman. He could not speak the English language, but he was a profound scholar in the history and literature of both Japan and China; his ideas were those of the most advanced of his countrymen; he was an advocate of education and agricultural improvement throughout the Empire; was long Minister for the Interior; a leader in the National Council, popular with the people, and the governors of the kens or provincial divisions, and the man who was looked to for the future welfare and growth of Japan.

As not inappropriate to the foregoing account, it is hoped the reader will be interested in the following:—

"When Mr. Okubo was in Washington, in 1872, I saw more of him than I did of the other ambassadors, and remember with great interest the incidents of that intercourse. Wherever he went he was accompanied by a secretary, who acted as interpreter, and he was constantly taking notes of what he saw and heard. The medical museum with its curious and horrible specimens of splintered and dead humanity greatly excited his feelings; and when his attention was directed to the bones of a human leg, whose proprietor was at that time the American Minister in Spain, and 'walking Spanish' undoubtedly, his amazement was profound. If I had been a political prophet, I might have told him, what actually came to pass, that the mate of that museum leg would, in less than ten years, be carried by a Democrat, as the first had been by a Republican.

"But an interview that Mr. Okubo had with Professor Joseph Henry, at the Smithsonian Institution, was particularly agreeable and instructive to both parties. When the conversation happened to be on the national foods of Japan, and Mr. Okubo had said that animal food was not popular in that country, Professor Henry immediately turned to a large globe, and pointing to the island Empire, said that the Japanese, notwithstanding their religious prejudices, could never become a beef-eating nation, for the reason that the area of their country was too limited to afford pasturage for sufficient numbers of cattle; and he made the further remark that the customs of all nations were always influenced by geographical characteristics. This suggestion seemed to impress Mr. Okubo, and he made an elaborate note of what he had just heard. On passing a glass case where were displayed a large number of Indian arrow-heads, Professor Henry said, 'I suppose you have nothing of that kind in Japan!' but Mr. Okubo replied in substance: 'Yes, these things are very common in Japan,' whereupon Professor Henry was quite as much astonished as his visitor had been a short time before. And thus, for an hour or two did these two representative men from the two sides of the globe entertain each other, as well as their listeners; and in view of a little lecture on electricity, when Mr. Okubo left the Smithsonian building he quietly remarked, 'That is one of your greatest men, I am sure.'

"Apropos to the Indian arrow-heads, the following circumstance is perhaps worth mentioning. A collection of photographs of a large number of arrow-heads and other Indian relics, with many original specimens having come into my possession early in 1878, I sent them to Mr. Okubo, in Japan, who acknowledged their receipt and disposition in the accompanying letter:

TOKIO, May 11th, MEIJI, 11th.

DEAR SIR:—I have received your kind letter dated February 20th, 1878. When, several years ago, I had occasion to visit the Smithsonian Institution under your guidance and saw the Indian arrowheads and other stone implements, I stated the fact that similar relics of the past were found in our country. It is in remembrance of that fact that you have sent to me the plates and photographs of the relics in question, and I now express my sincere thanks for them. These pictures will be at once arranged in our museum, and they will be of the greatest interest to our historians. And now as my sincere recompense for the above I have ordered the director of our museum to copy in photograph the collection of our ancient stone and earthen implements, and I will send them to you when they are finished.

With compliments,

OKUBO TOSHIMICHI,
Minister of the Interior Department.

In May, 1878, only a few days after this letter was written, the news reached Washington by wire that Mr. Okubo had been assassinated, and the particulars of the sad event as subsequently obtained, are as follows:

On a pleasant morning he started from his house for the Mikado's palace, where he had an engagement. He was in a carriage drawn by two horses, and was preceded by a running groom. While passing through a picturesque dell, he saw two men by the roadside with flowers in their hands, and before he could cast a thought upon the cause of their appearance in that place, they drew their swords from under their garments and rushed upon the passing carriage, when they were immediately joined by four other men. They first mutilated the horses, then killed the coachman, and in the most barbarous manner murdered the minister; and throwing away their weapons, the six assassins went immediately to the gate of the Imperial palace, and proclaimed themselves the destroyers of Okubo. Before committing their dreadful deed they wrote to two of the Tokio papers, proclaiming their intentions, and those letters were being read at the very moment the murder was committed. These men were from the province of Kaga, and the chief reason assigned by them for the murder was, that they wished to revenge the death of the elder Saigo, for whose death, during the Satsuma Rebellion, they most unjustly considered Okubo indirectly responsible; and it is a remarkable fact that the man who found and took the body of Okubo to his place of residence, was the younger Saigo, brother of the famous Satsuma General, and now holding a high position in Tokio. In due time the assassins were beheaded.

The grief of the Nation on account of this unjustifiable assassination was universal, and Okubo was buried with almost Imperial honors. Among the acts performed at the funeral was one wherein the friends of the departed were permitted to go up to the altar alone, and place upon the bier some leaf or twig of a favorite tree, as a token of affection, and of their belief in immortality; and it is said that when Iwakura Tomomi, who had visited America with Okubo, and had himself a year or two before nearly lost his own life by an assassin, went up to deposit his tribute, he was affected to tears, and so were many others in the vast concourse.

"In 1879, a Tokio paper called attention to the photographs and specimens which I had long before sent to Japan, stating that similar pictures of the arrow-heads of that country had been made to be placed in the Imperial Museum by the side of those from America; and the editor added the pleasant words, moreover, that the present writer had been remembered by Mr. Okubo, as one of his most attentive American friends.

"The very interesting collection of pictures which I have mentioned, reached me in June, 1881. The specimens depicted, number one hundred and fifty-four. So far as the Japanese arrow-heads are concerned — in size, shape, and variety of stone — they are precisely like those which are common in the United States, and this single fact, it seems to me, is one of great interest to the students of ethnology. The descriptive list, or 'explanatory index,' as it is called, which accompanied the photographs in question, gives the localities where the relics were found, and as a taste of their quality, I submit the following brief descriptions:

Stone Hammers: Taken from an ancient tomb.

Stone Swords: Taken from an old fortification at Hakodati in Yesso.

Stone Axes: Found deeply imbedded below the surface of the ground.

Magadamas: These stones are all similar in shape, generally from one half to four inches long, and beautiful. They are among the most ancient of Japanese relics; were worn as ornaments in the hair, and around the neck; and chiefly by members of the Imperial family. It is also said that they were sometimes used as money, and are at this time considered valuable; they are found only in the most ancient tombs; and the materials from which they are made are rock-crystal, agate, carnelian, ruby, and other precious stones, and are of many colors — red and blue predominating.

Sexangled Beads: These are of rock-crystal and quite small.

Kudaishi: These are of stone, in shape and size like the stems of the common clay pipe, and are strung upon a thread similar to the old Indian wampum of the United States, which was made of shells.

Stone Arrow-heads: These are numerous, of many sizes, and made from various kinds of stone. Found everywhere and precisely like those of America.

Bronze Arrow-heads: These vary in shape, and are especially interesting on account of their novelty. They prove how the Stone was followed by the Bronze age, even in Japan.

Sword ornamented with Gold: Very old and greatly worn by rust and rough usage, and found broken in three pieces. About two and a half feet in length.

Sword ornamented with Silver: About four feet long.

Old Iron Helmet: Found in a tomb at Higo.

Old Armor: Found in the same province and place.

A Gilt Shoe: Found in a tomb, and about thirteen inches long.

Bronze Bells: Very small, and from the province of Shimodzuke.

Iron Bits: Taken from a tomb in Higo.

Iron Stirrups: From the same place.

White Bronze Mirrors: From the same place.

Earthen Horse: About two and a half feet high, and supposed to have been made fourteen hundred years ago. In those times it was customary to bury such images in the tombs of famous men.

Bronze Spear: This is without a handle, and is nearly three feet long.

Stone Image: This is of a man, and nearly five feet high. It was made in the time of the Emperor Kuitaiteuno, A. D. 530. In those days there was a man named Iwai, who was extravagant, cruel and violent, and who revolted against the Emperor. When he came to build the tomb in which he expected to lie, he surrounded it with images of men and horses and shields, all made of stone. Soon after this work was completed, the Emperor sent a military force to punish this rebel for some of his disloyal conduct; to escape death he fled to another province, whereupon the army demolished the greater part of the images, of which there were sixty, and they were chiefly used, with other materials, in building a wall near an Imperial castle; of those images, only two were preserved, one of which is now in the museum of Tokio.

"It will be remembered by many that Mr. Okubo was the chief official to whom was assigned the duty of directing the Japanese arrangements at our Centennial Exposition in 1876, although not in this country at the time; and I record the fact with sadness, that the accomplished young man, Hatakeyama, who acted as his secretary in 1872, and was officially connected with the Exposition, returned to Japan only to die. He had been educated in this country, and in various capacities had rendered important services to his native land.

"Before concluding this paper I desire to emphasize the fact that while I take an interest in ancient relics generally, I have not one iota of respect for those people who are perpetually digging into the earth for the purpose of finding something that will disprove the records of the Bible. Of that brood of dreamers — when we consider his antecedents, his limited experience and audacity — I would assign the post of distinction to the man whose exploits are chronicled in the following extract from one of the newspapers of the day:

Infidelity — in Japan — is vigorous and aggressive, clothed in the garb of culture. An ex-railroad clerk from Massachusetts, at one time strangely associated with the Tokio University as a scientist, was a pronounced skeptic, and exhibited the zeal of a ranter against the Christian religion, and by working upon the minds of the young men who came under his influence did great harm to evangelical faith. He not only recommended the publication of infidel books, but frequently went out of his way to ridicule the Christian doctrines and the people of the United States.

"I have no personal acquaintance with this man, but the testimony is extant which fully endorses the above paragraph."

## OKUMA SHIGENOBU.

HE was born in the province of Hizen, Kiusiu, in 1837, and having had the advantages of the best local schools, he soon displayed abilities of a superior order. He studied the Dutch language as well as English, at Nagasaki, and proved himself competent to serve his country in any capacity, but did not accept any public position prior to the revolution of 1868. In that year, however, he was appointed Chief Assistant in the Department for Foreign Affairs; in 1869 he was made Secretary of the joint departments of the Interior and Finance and acquitted himself with discretion and ability; in 1870 he was made a Sangi or Councillor of State, still having charge of the Finance Department, which had been separated from that of the Interior; in 1871 he was superseded as head of the Finance Department, but still held the position of Sangi. When the Exposition took place at Vienna, he was made President of the Commission which represented the Japanese Government at that place; and from the superb display which Japan made on that occasion, may be traced the remarkable interest which has since been felt by the Western nations in the art productions of Japan. When the Expedition to Formosa was inaugurated, Mr. Okuma took a prominent part in directing the affairs of the Government, having been the President of the Commission sent to that island. In 1872 he was again placed in charge of the Finance Department, and since that time has borne a conspicuous part in all the commercial as well as financial affairs of the Empire.

By way of illustrating the character of Mr. Okuma as a member of the Government, while at the same time giving an insight into Asiatic methods of doing business, the subjoined translation is submitted of his address to the Emperor of Japan, in January, 1875, as President of the Formosa Commission :

"In the month of January, 1874, the said Shigenobu and others, in accordance with the confidential instructions they had received, laid before Your Majesty a project for the chastisement of the savages. In April the Formosan Commission (literally board of affairs of the savage land of Formosa) was instituted, and Shigenobu was appointed its Chief to superintend all business belonging to it. In May the Commander-in-Chief Saigo Yorimichi departed to the land of the savages at the head of a force, exterminated the wicked, pardoned the submissive, and remained there a long time encamped. During the same month the Minister Plenipotentiary Yanagiwara Sakimitsu was despatched to China, and in August the High Commissioner Plenipotentiary Okubo Toshimichi also was sent to the said country. Toshimichi and the others worked diligently and devotedly in the discharge of the important trust committed to them. In October a convention was exchanged with the said country, and in November Toshimichi and the rest reported the fulfillment of their mission. In December Yorimichi returned in triumph. From the Institution of the Commission up to this date a period of eight months had elapsed. Hereupon the wrongs of the sufferers were for the first time redressed, the position of a subject han for the first time cleared up, security restored to the mariners of all countries for the first time, and the dignity and influence of the State consequently vindicated.

"After our troops had started and were on their way, foreign public servants remonstrated; the Chinese Government hastily despatched an envoy, sent letters and manifested a wide difference of opinion. Some persons not comprehending the views of the Government, began to doubt whether it was justified in the course which it was taking. Others discussed the want of funds, and rumor became so noisy that the state was again imperilled.

"Shigenobu and the others nevertheless accepted the responsibility, but day and night they were so busily employed that they feared lest their strength might be unequal to the task. Fortunately, the wise resolution of His Majesty the Tennô never wavered, and the councils of the Government became still more resolute. Great military preparations were made, and the mind of the people, both in the towns and in the country, learnt to recognize the purpose of His Majesty. Some desired to cast away their lives and to die for the national cause, others offered to contribute towards the army expenditure. The civil and military officers united all their efforts, and the great work of chastising the savages became an accomplished fact. We have nothing to be ashamed of before foreign nations concerning this measure, and its glory will not pale before the deeds done in ancient times.

"If, while public rumor was clamorous, we had hesitated or drawn back, the injuries done to the sufferers would not have been redressed, the position of a dependent han would not have been cleared up, the mariners of the world would never have known security, and a land of cannibals would have been established forever.  Had such been the result, we should not only have been disgraced in the eyes of the world, but it would have been a sign that the dignity and influence of the state were about to fall prostrate.  Consequently important interests were involved in the chastisement of the savages.

"I humbly pray that His Majesty the Tennô will eagerly carry on the work and carefully ponder ; that by reflecting on the past he may be enabled to think out the policy of the future so as to exalt his wise work to the highest pinnacle and glory, and that he will not stop with the chastisement of the savages.

"Shigenobu reverently begs that the name of Formosan Commission be now abolished, and himself relieved of the title of President, so that he may attend to the duties of his proper office.  As for the collection of the documents of the Commission and the audit of the accounts, this he hopes may be completed by the officials of the regular service in about a month, and a report can then be made, together with a detailed account of all that has been done since the institution of the Commission."

## OTORI KEISUKE.

HE was a retainer under the Tokugawa Government, and after completing the ordinary education of his class turned his attention to the study of military affairs in which he became a proficient. Prior to the year 1861 he published a book on the subject of Infantry Tactics, and soon afterwards another on fortifications, gleaned chiefly from French authorities; and those two productions were the first ever printed in Japan from metal types, and are said to have exerted an important influence on the military affairs of the Empire.

At the time of the Restoration he had command of a large military force in the eastern provinces; and although he displayed ability in their management, he was defeated, and then joined the army of Enomoto in the island of Yesso. After the capitulation at Hakodate he was sent as a prisoner to Yedo, where he remained in confinement for two years, having been liberated in 1871. As was the case with Enomoto, he was treated with kind consideration by the Imperial Government, and was appointed to several honorable positions, among which was that of an under secretary in the Treasury Department, in which capacity he accompanied Yoshida Kinyonari to England when that gentleman made his important loan. In 1875 he was made an officer of the fourth rank in the Public Works Department, then went upon a mission to the Government of Siam, and on his return published an interesting account of his travels. He is greatly respected for his talents and character, and as late as the year 1881 he was still connected with the Public Works and Engraving Departments of the city of Tokio.

## OYAMA IWA-O.

OYAMA IWA-O is a member of the Satsuma clan, which has furnished so many of the typical heroes who flourish in the pages of Japanese history "to point a moral and adorn a tale" :— at once guides and examples to future ages. General Oyama is a relation of the celebrated Saigo Takamori, a leader in the movement which restored the Imperial authority to the position it had been deprived of for over three centuries, and who subsequently raised the standard of rebellion in the southwest, expiating his error with his life on the fatal field of Shiroyama. General Oyama bears a high reputation for gallantry in action and iron resolution. He is well educated, possessed of an extensive knowledge of strategy, and particularly careful of the wants and comfort of his soldiers.

At the time of the Restoration General Oyama associated himself with Okubo and the rest of the patriotic party, and throughout his whole career has devoted himself to the best interests of Japan. After the Restoration was accomplished he received the appointments of lieutenant-general in the army and Assistant Vice-Minister of War. He also received civil promotion to the senior fifth class. When the rebellion in the southwest occurred, the General was despatched to the scene of operations in charge of a division of troops, and rendered brilliant service in quelling the rising. After the conclusion of peace he was decorated with the Japanese Order of the second class, and since then upon the death of General Kawaji, received the appointment of Assistant Home Minister and Chief of Police. When the changes of the time took place he became Minister for War.

# OYANO IWAO.

THIS well-known and influential man was born in the province of Satsuma, and is about forty years of age. He became interested in the affairs of his own country and of the outside world while yet a mere youth; participated in the late revolution with great zeal; and having visited Europe, spent several years in Paris as a student. While doing all in his power to have the late Tycoon relegated to his proper sphere, he espoused the cause of the Mikado, and did much to promote the prosperity of the Empire as a loyal adherent to all its interests.

He was a cousin and devoted friend of the elder Saigo, and greatly mourned over the disaffection which resulted in rebellion. After making himself useful in various ways, he was appointed to a position in the army; then made Assistant Secretary of the Interior Department; and while holding that office he was also called upon to take charge of the Police Affairs of Tokio, after the death of Kawajai; and for those and his other services he was presented with a medal of the second class and honored with the title of the second rank in the Government. He also rendered important services during the Satsuma Rebellion, where he had command of a division of the army, and was compelled to do all in his power to overthrow his kinsman and friend, General Saigo. In 1880 he was appointed Secretary of War, and is still in charge of that Department. His habits are those of a student, and his acquired tastes have induced him to live in a house built after the European style and to indulge in all the household conveniences and luxuries associated with modern progress. He is reputed to be a man of superior natural abilities, and has made the very best use of his advantages of study in foreign countries. It should be added moreover, that Mr. Oyano has been elevated to the position of Sangi ; and that, according to late intelligence from Japan, had been offered the mission to France.

## RAI MIKISABURO.

RAI MIKISABURO, the third son of Rai Sanyo, was born in Kioto. He was very clever from his childhood and was the beloved son of his father. When he was eighteen years old he went to Yedo and entered a school called Shohei Ko, and there became intimate with Saito Issai, Kikuchi Gosan and Riosen Seigan. He remained about one year, and afterward visited various provinces, viz., Hidachi, Kotsuke, Shimotsuke, Awa, Kadzusa and Shimosa. When he was in Yedo he paid a visit to the Kuwanyei temple. Perceiving the extravagance displayed in that edifice, he said sighing, " This temple, which is very beautiful, was founded by the Tokugawa Siogun, but Tokugawa squeezes the fat and blood of the country from the provinces and spends them in such useless buildings as this. Ah, Tokugawa is a great sinner and robber. Who shall not execrate his name ? " While he was on his way home he noticed a crest of the Siogun's family carved on a stone lamp post. This he threw down, and trampled upon the emblem, saying, "Awoi (the hollyhock) is the sign of the Tokugawa house ; it delights my heart to tread upon it." His companions endeavored to check him, but he persisted, their efforts only increasing his anger. Hearing the disturbance, a party of Government officers appeared and arrested Rai Mikisaburo. But this offence was soon overlooked and he was released. Afterward he returned to Kioto, and then commenced a journey through the Western and Southern provinces. One day an exhibition of pictures and famous writings was held at Maruyama, in Kioto. Many celebrated artists assembled there, and Rai Mikisaburo also attended. He fell into a quarrel with one Ikenouchi and spat in his adversary's face. Ikenouchi tried to throw him on the floor, but Rai drew his sword to defend himself, whereupon Ikenouchi also drew his sword and the two began to fight. The people of the exhibition interfered and stopped their quarrel. Rai often drew his sword in this way, but he never hurt any one.

In those days the American envoy arrived at Uraga, in So-shiu, and presented a letter to the Tokugawa Government, asking for the negotiation of a treaty. The authorities did not know what they should do, and they contemplated acting in opposition to the law of the country. Now Rai turned all his attention to the means of getting the foreigners away from the shores of Japan. About this time Riosen Seigan removed from Yedo to Kioto, and Rai concocted a plan with him and collected a band of faithful and loyal samurai from various provinces. Mumeta Genjiro on hearing this was pleased, and joined with them. One of the results of their schemes was to secure the issuing of an Imperial order by the Kioto Government to the lord of Mito, upon the subject of the expulsion of foreigners. But this plan was discovered by the officers of the Tokugawa Government, and the conspirators were arrested. Rai being sent under guard to Yedo, he was examined in court. He stated that he had indeed laid plans on the principle of Son O Jo-i, with his faithful friends. He believed that a man who, in this crisis did not take steps toward the necessary end, committed a great crime toward his country and should be considered a slave of the barbarians. Who, he demanded, would wish to be thus branded as a criminal and a slave of barbarians? And he declared that he would have nothing to say on any other subject. The officers did not press their inquiries further, but caused him to be imprisoned for a long time, at the expiration of which he was executed in Yedo.

# SAIGO TAKAMORI.

BY the name of Saigo, the people of Japan have hitherto recognized one of their most famous soldiers and statesmen. He was born about the year 1825, in the province of Satsuma, at the southern extremity of the Empire, and belonged to the class of samurai, or Retainers. He was well educated in the Japanese and Chinese classics, particularly in history, and from his boyhood was an acute observer and enthusiastic admirer of the patriotic heroes of all countries. He became a leader, but not in a boisterous manner, in all the liberal movements of his province and of the Empire, and he was the bosom friend of many men who sacrificed their lives in the national cause, and especially of all those who were anxious to emancipate their countrymen from the rule of the Tycoon, who had oppressed them for nearly three centuries. He was one of the most trusted subjects and special favorites of the famous Prince of Satsuma, who died about the year 1858, and whose younger brother became the second Minister of State in the Empire, and he served his prince most faithfully in carrying out his enlightened policy.

It was the policy of Saigo to promote such measures as he conceived would save the Empire from the despotism of the Tycoon's Government, and at the same time from foreign aggressors, and to this end he repeatedly manifested his willingness to sacrifice his possessions and even his life. The Prince of Satsuma shared his desire to set aside the Tycoon and restore to the Mikado the supreme rule of the Empire, and sought to counteract the cunning intrigues of the Tycoon and his followers, who, for centuries, had exalted the Mikado to such an apparently high position that it was thought condescending in him to meddle with the temporal government; hence had invested him with the name Spiritual Emperor. By a restoration of the only rightful ruler of Japan to the full measure of his authority, Saigo perceived that one central government would be established in the stead of nearly three hundred provincial governments under the administration of the Tycoons; and by the concentration of the governing power in the person of an Emperor who was the focus of the reverential respect and devoted affection which all the Japanese of every grade cherished for the Imperial lineage, he believed that the greatest good could be done for the greatest number of the people.

About the year 1857, while Saigo was thus zealously engaged in the pursuit of this patriotic cause, the Tycoon's Government issued a secret warrant for his arrest, because of his supposed hostility to the existing administration. It became impossible, therefore, for him to remain in Yedo, and he departed from the capital to his home in Satsuma. A large force of police was soon sent to apprehend him and his associates; and as it was found unsafe for him to remain on any of the large islands, he was ordered by the Prince of Satsuma to assume a fictitious name, leave Satsuma and take up his residence on a remote islet belonging to the Prince, which was named Ohsima, and lay in the Pacific Ocean, near Loo Choo. There Saigo passed more than three years in exile. In 1861, when the political storm had blown over, he was summoned to his home again. During his absence the Prince of Satsuma had died, but Saigo found in his younger brother, Prince Shimadzu, an equally zealous supporter of his political policy. His zeal for the national cause had only been strengthened by his long confinement, and he proceeded at once to take an active part in the political movements of the time.

In 1862 Prince Shimadzu, accompanied by a large number of leading patriots, among whom Saigo and Okubo were the foremost, proceeded to the national capital, Saikio, then called Kioto, where the Mikado then resided, and presented to the Emperor a memorial, which afterwards served as the " Declaration of Independence" of the recent Revolution in Japan. Thereupon Saigo was again banished to a remote island. He was conveyed thither in a small Japanese junk, and was made as uncomfortable as possible on the voyage, but he endured his sufferings without a word of complaint. When the sailors offered him some relief he declined to receive it, saying that as the state had ordered him thus to suffer, he would submit. The cause of this second exile was, therefore, somewhat different from the former one. That was reported and believed to be in consequence of some difference in political opinions between the Prince of Satsuma and Saigo, although some persons think that the difference was more apparent than real. The prince certainly seems to have listened to men who immediately surrounded him, and who were the bitter opponents of Saigo, and they, perhaps, misled him to the belief that his own views and those of Saigo were irreconcilable.

In a few months after his arrival on the island to which he was now banished the second time, Saigo was transferred to another and a smaller island, avowedly to add to his sufferings. Three weary years thus passed away, and at last, in 1866, it was found that the services of Saigo were again required by his country. Messengers were despatched to liberate him, and he again returned to his home. But a terrible change had been effected in his physical health. When he was taken out of the cage in which he had been confined, and which was so small that he could not stand erect in it, he could not stand at all, and a considerable time elapsed before he could walk even with the support of two men. In this plight he made the voyage of nearly fourteen days from the island of his imprisonment to Kagashima, a city of Satsuma.

The reception he met with from his compatriots and relatives upon his return was extraordinary. Its enthusiasm, probably, never was surpassed in any country. In due time strength and health were restored to him, and then he again began to take a lively part in the affairs of his nation. In the Revolution of 1867 and 1868 he was a prominent leader, and was of course an earnest advocate of the policy of abolishing the Tycoonate and restoring the Imperial Government to its full functions, which was finally accomplished by the combined efforts of several patriotic hans, or principalities, and their Retainers. The Tycoon's abdication took place at Osaka in November, 1867, at a time when all the representatives of foreign powers were assembled at the port of Osaka for the negotiation in regard to the opening of the port of Kobe. But the Tycoon's party or followers considered the abdication a forced one, and rose in arms. Led by the Idsu han, or the Retainers of the Prince of Idsu, the disaffected army, composed of nearly thirty thousand men, began a march upon

Kioto. Perceiving the motive of this movement, the Mikado ordered the Imperial troops to oppose their entrance into the city. But the Imperial army numbered only about four thousand men. Nevertheless it did not shrink from an open combat. Early in January, 1868, many skirmishes took place between the opposing forces at places between Osaka and Kioto. At last two days of hard fighting decided the fate of the rebellion, and the thirty thousand insurrectionists were routed and retreated to Osaka. The Tycoon soon afterward embarked at Osaka on a foreign vessel, and betook himself, with many of his adherents, to Yedo.

Among the foremost officers whose heroism inspired the victorious army to its extraordinary success, were Saigo, Okubo and Kido, and the names of all three of them are familiar in the subsequent history of Japan. Although Kido was not present in Kioto, his influence with the loyal party and the soldiers was very great. Immediately after the overthrow of the rebel forces, the Imperial army was swelled to an immense strength by voluntary enlistments throughout the Empire, and within two months after the events that have been recounted, it marched towards Yedo under the command of an Imperial prince, Saigo acting as lieutenant-general and aide-de-camp. On the day of its entrance into the great city Yedo, it was met by Mr. Katz, a civil dignitary of the deposed Tycoon. An interview took place between Saigo and Katz, at Shinagawa, four miles from the Tycoon's palace, and the result of their negotiation was the unconditional surrender of the Tycoon. Thus peace was nominally restored on land. It was the general belief that no other two men could have been found capable of adjusting this negotiation. Katz was loyal to the

Emperor, although he belonged to the Tycoon's clan; and he is at the present time Secretary of the Navy Department of Japan.

Another, and the last, demonstration made by the Tycoon's adherents, was headed by Enomoto, the Tycoon's admiral. He took command of a squadron (although his proceedings are not supposed to have been approved by the Tycoon), and went to Hakodate, as if to capture and retain possession of Yesso. His plans were, however, all frustrated by the zeal of the Imperial forces. Numerous fights occurred at several points between Yedo and the northern extremity of the Empire, and finally the rebels all withdrew to the fortress of Hakodate, where they defended themselves skilfully by land and sea with the aid of three Frenchmen, who were formerly employed by the Tycoon as military instructors. Their military leader, General Otori, it is said, displayed great skill and fortitude. But they were compelled at last to surrender to the Imperial army, in April, 1869, and with their surrender the civil war came to an end.

The leading rebels, at the time of the capitulation, implored, it is said, that they alone should be subjected to severe punishments, and that the minor officers and the common soldiers should be pardoned. We do not know whether their petition had any influence; but we are informed that in fact only seven or eight of them were imprisoned, and that after the lapse of three years, even these were unconditionally released by the Imperial pardon. It is an interesting circumstance, in view of our own appointment of Mr. Orr, of South Carolina, to a similar embassy, that the principal leader of the rebels is to-day the Japanese envoy to the Court of

St. Petersburg. The magnanimity thus manifested by the Imperial Government towards Enomoto and his followers was unparalleled in the annals of Japan, if not in the history of mankind. Many of the rebels are now in office, and enjoy the confidence of the Government.

Saigo has been more or less connected with military affairs all his life. During the Revolution he was, as we have related, appointed lieutenant-general, and afterwards he became the field marshal of the Empire.

When the new government was fully established in 1869, Saigo returned to his home in the country. He was soon appointed Chief Minister or Secretary of the province of Satsuma. In this capacity he accomplished many important and wholesome reforms, particularly in respect to the development of industry and education, and his measures of reform were so wisely framed that they were copied throughout the whole Empire. In 1870 it was generally considered that Saigo's immediate coöperation in the Imperial administration was grearty needed, and the Emperor sent his well-known ambassador, Iwakura, to consult with him on affairs of state, and to invite him to take a portfolio in the Imperial Cabinet. To this appeal he listened favorably. He accompanied Iwakura and Okubo to Yedo, and he was appointed Councillor of State, with the title of Shosammi — the third rank in the Empire.

He held that office when the embassy returned to Japan from America and Europe, but when the Corean question came up, which caused a dissolution of the Cabinet or Privy Council, he, with several of his associates, withdrew again into private life.

One of the most significant features of Saigo's

character is indicated by the fact that, reared though he was amidst the most tumultuous factions, and entreated by some of the most dissatisfied and influential men to take active part against the existing Cabinet in Japan, he never displayed the slightest inclination to become the leader of a faction, but, on the contrary, inculcated among his associates and followers the doctrine of entire and peaceful withdrawal from political strife. He felt that he had done his full duty while he remained in active discharge of the administration of affairs, and when he was defeated in his liberal policy by a majority, he considered that it was his part to keep quiet and to wait for a reversal in popular opinion and in the existing order of the state, as became a loyal citizen. In this condition he remained for several years in solitude at his country home, indulging himself in hunting, shooting, and other rural pastimes.

In the early part of 1877, however, the astounding news went abroad that the province of Satsuma, long considered without a rival in power and influence, had rebelled against the Imperial Government of Japan. The precise cause of this open hostility was for a long time inexplicable; and while it was asserted that the instigator and leader of this rebellion was General Saigo, neither the masses of the people in Japan, nor the officials of the Government, could believe that the charge was true. It must be confessed, however, that there were people in Japan who believed that he had really been anxious to see established in Japan a military despotism, of which he should be the head under the Mikado.

Even his brother (who is a general in the Japanese army, and who visited this country as Chief Commissioner to the Centennial Exposition) could not understand the meaning of the strange intelligence which reached him in this country.

As the new Rebellion proceeded, however, and especially when it began to feel the force of successful military operations under the national flag, the elder Saigo was found to be the ruling spirit among the insurgents, he was proclaimed an outcast and a rebel, a decree issued depriving him of his rank, and a price was set upon his head. The astonishment that filled the hearts of the loyal people throughout the Empire was something quite unprecedented, as he had always been known as a man of peace and order. It was in September, 1877, that the Rebellion finally collapsed, and the event was commemorated by the suicide, within a short time, of Saigo and some half dozen of his leading supporters.

That this noted man will take his place in history as an extraordinary character is most certain, and the difficulty will be to fix his position, for he must be remembered as a great partisan and chief, a hero, a patriot, a statesman of integrity, and a rebel. He had much to do, as already shown, with the extinction of the Shôgunate in 1867, and was behind no man in his devotion to the Emperor. In 1868 he received the highest encomiums of that sovereign, and, as we have seen, was offered one or more of the highest positions in the Government.

In 1873 he suddenly left the public service because of the refusal of the Government to organize a war upon Corea, and from that time would seem to have devoted himself in his retirement to the establishment of a so-called military school at Kagoshima, upon a scale that proved that his real object was the creation of an armed force devoted to himself. At that place he made his first stand as a rebel chief, but was defeated there as well as at other points where he and his forces appeared in hostile array. He was also influenced in his hostility against the legitimate rulers by the edict against wearing two swords, the yielding up of Saghalin to Russia in exchange for the Kurile Islands, and the capitalization of the pensions of the samurai. He took up arms, not against the Mikado, but against the managing men of the Government; and while willing to welcome to the shores of Japan what is popularly termed modern civilization, he ended his days as if he had been living in one of the older centuries. Aside from the ignominy that must rest upon him as a rebel, he will be remembered as a gallant Japanese gentleman and a grand type of the old school of statesmen in that Empire.

"If we all had known at the beginning," said one of the Japanese papers, "the treason that was in his heart, instead of loving Saigo so greatly, we should have hated him enough to have eaten all his flesh off his bones." Another also said: "This treason is not of human origin, but is a supernatural dispensation." And still another: "His heart was as clear as the bright moon above and his conduct as high as a lofty mountain. But the great works performed by him have passed away like a wave of the Southern sea."

The man of all others who most earnestly coincided with Saigo in promoting the restoration of the Mikado, was Kido Takayossi, and they were attached friends. During the progress of the Satsuma Rebellion, Kido was taken sick at Kioto, where he died; and it is said that during his entire illness he was constantly talking about the affairs of the Nation, and among his last words were the following, apparently addressed to his old friend: "Ah, Saigo! are you still doing that? Stop your course. Don't act in that way against the true welfare of your country!" In due time by a mutual friend, this incident was repeated to Saigo in Satsuma, and his reply was to this effect: "Kido is gone, and it will not be long before I shall follow him."

The universal popularity of Saigo when in his prime, was something quite remarkable, and was chiefly due, according to the testimony of those who knew him, to his personal character and qualities. He was in person a large, well-built and powerful man, and notwithstanding his dark bushy eyebrows, his face wore the expression of kind simplicity and frankness. He was a good swordsman, and, as already stated, fond of field sports, both fishing and hunting; he was not partial to study, and when in office always found his public duties irksome; morally, he was considered intrepid and courageous to the last degree; he scorned the accumulation of money, and was always ready to help the needy with his purse; in his home habits he was sober, frugal, self-denying and unostentatious; by the people of Japan he was considered at one time the beau ideal of a samurai; and it is strange that, while he lived the life of a true patriot, he died with the blight of traitor resting upon his name. He wanted his native province to continue forever the ruling force of the whole Empire, and cherished the dream that the governing element in all the departments of the public service should be the samurai.

With regard to the manner of Saigo's death there is some doubt, but the following is positively asserted:

During the principal battle of the campaign he received what was considered a fatal wound from a bullet, whereupon one of his lieutenants, as an act of friendship, proceeded, with his sword, to sever the head of the General from his shoulders, in order to spare him the disgrace of falling alive into the hands of the Imperial forces. This done, his head was delivered to one of his servants for concealment, and the officer who had decapitated him then committed suicide. And with this tragedy the Rebellion came suddenly to an end.

Since writing the foregoing the compiler has received some further particulars of Saigo, which are as follows :

During the years of Kaiyei (1848–53), while in Kioto, he formed a friendship with a priest of the temple called Hôshô-In, at Kiyomidzu, by the name of Gessho, who, like Saigo, was an ardent upholder of the Kinnô (literally, duty toward the Emperor) cause, and who was a favorite of Kinnoye, a kuge of high rank.

In the autumn of 1858 Saigo was induced, against his judgment, to make a journey to Mito as the bearer of a message from Kinnoye, delivered to him through Gessho, to the Daimio of that province, who was confined in his Yashiki by the Bakufu (government of the Shôgun). The Imperial court had expressed a desire that the Daimio of Mito should be appointed one of the advisers of the Bakufu, as he was known to be a staunch upholder of the Kinnô cause, and the message that Saigo carried was an official notice of the desired appointment. But he failed to carry out his mission as he had expected, and came to Yedo. After remaining there a short time he returned to Kioto, where he resided with Gessho, Umiyeda, and Yechiji, all adherents of the Emperor's cause, and with whom he consulted as to the best steps to be taken for the overthrow of the Shôgunate.

In the meantime the Bakufu had commenced a rigorous persecution of all partisans of the Kinnô cause. Saigo and his friends were especially the objects of its hatred, but for some time no severe measures were taken against them, probably through a wholesome fear of the Satsuma party. At length, however, Gessho was threatened, and his life being in great danger, by the advice of Kinnoye he escaped in a kago to Osaka, closely pursued by the officers of the Bakufu. Saigo and Umiyeda together managed to protect his flight, and to get him safely into hiding at Osaka. Saigo then went back to Kioto, but after a short stay, finding that Gessho's life was still threatened, he hastily returned to Osaka and induced Gessho to attempt flight into Satsuma. Accordingly, accompanied by Umiyeda, they procured a junk and set sail for the south. They were chased by their enemies, and narrowly eluding pursuit arrived at Shimonoseki. Leaving Gessho behind, Saigo proceeded to Satsuma to procure a hiding place. Gessho, however, was compelled to fly, and came to Fukuoka, in Chikuzen, and after many narrow escapes, by the assistance of a certain samurai named Hirano, managed to make his way to Satsuma, where he took refuge in a temple. In the meantime Saigo was urging the Satsuma authorities to afford protection to Gessho; but owing probably to fear of the Bakufu, assistance was refused. Meanwhile the Bakufu authorities were endeavoring to procure spies at Fukuoka who would undertake to go to Kagoshima and capture Gessho.

On the fifteenth of October, in the dead of the night, Saigo came to the temple where Gessho had taken refuge, and found him and Hirano sleeping. He silently roused them, and Gessho at once comprehended from the anxiety visible in his friend's countenance, the imminence of his danger and the necessity for immediate flight. Taking with them the priest's servant Insuke, they entered a junk and set sail to the east. The boat was amply provided with food and *sake*, and a feast was prepared and partaken of. Suddenly without a word Saigo rose, and embracing Gessho, plunged with him into the sea and disappeared. After a few moments they reappeared on the surface, and were at once seized by the bewildered occupants of the junk and dragged on board. Both were found to be senseless. Saigo, a robust, powerful man, after a time revived, but all efforts to restore life to Gessho were in vain. Saigo's motive for this action has been accounted for in various ways, but the most probable solution is that, despairing of saving his friend, he resolved to perish with him.

Saigo now changed his name to Kikuchi Genjo, but the Satsuma authorities, dreading the vengeance of the Bakufu for permitting the escape of its intended victim, banished him to Oshima, where he again changed his name, taking that of Oshima-Sanyemon, in consequence of his having three times visited this place of banishment. In spite of the bodily hardships that he had to endure during the years of exile spent on this island, he continued to cultivate his mind, and never wavered in his firm resolve to overthrow the Shôgunate and restore the Mikado to legitimate power.

In 1863, when the struggle between the Imperial Court and the Bakufu grew more open and bitter, Shimadzu, lord of Satsuma, pardoned Saigo, and recalling him, placed him at the head of the administration of affairs in his province. In 1865, when the Bakufu and Choshiu clan were in open warfare, Saigo arranged an alliance offensive and defensive between this clan and his own. In 1867 he attended the great meeting at Kioto and profoundly impressed the assembly by the truth and shrewdness of his counsels. In 1868 he was appointed adviser to the Commander-in-chief of the Imperial forces.

When the Mikado's troops advanced as far as Shinagawa in the final struggle with the Shôgun, Katsu Awa in an interview with Saigo begged him to cease hostilities, as Keiki, the irresolute and effeminate head of the Bakufu, was willing to surrender. This was at midnight, and Saigo straightway asked to be furnished with a proof of submission. Katsu Awa said that on the following day the castle at Yedo should be surrendered. Saigo at once replied, "If to-morrow, why not to-night? There is no need to wait." The terms were made and the castle was given up.

After this Saigo accompanied Arisugawa, the present commander of the Imperial forces, to Echigo, in an expedition against a number of rebels who had not yet thrown down their arms. After subduing these, Saigo was ordered to reduce to submission the retainers of the Shôgun's cause who had made their way to Yedo, which he undertook to do in thirty days, and he accomplished the task, giving proof of excellent judgment and great valor. For this the Government at once wished to appoint him to the office of sangi, but he declined the distinction and returned home.

On the second day of July the Mikado acknowledged his services in the following terms:

You have been the strongest upholder of my cause, and you have for years been zealously endeavoring to secure my restoration. Owing to your skill as military commander, in obtaining possession of Yedo Castle, in gaining the victories of Echigo, and by your diligence in all affairs connected with my service, you have gained for me the peace I to-day enjoy. I honor your actions, and as a reward therefor decree to you an income of two thousand kokus of rice per year.

This Saigo likewise declined to accept, but on the Mikado's ordering him to receive it, he complied.

In 1871 Saigo was recalled by the Emperor and elevated to the office of sangi, with the rank of *jussami*. In May, 1873, he was appointed general of the Imperial army, still retaining the office of sangi. In October of the same year arose the Corean question which led to a disagreement between Saigo and some of the other members of the Cabinet, unfortunately resulting in Saigo's withdrawal and return to Satsuma. Since that time the Government has made frequent overtures to him, and the Emperor has more than once ordered the return of the man most influential in effecting his restoration, and whose firm devotion to the throne he re-established still, we thoroughly believe, remains unchanged. But from dislike to some of those who surround the sovereign, and who, he has reason to suppose, seek to advance their personal power instead of laboring for the dignity and welfare of the Empire at large, he has remained in retirement, devoting his time to the direction of a system of "private schools," or, as we now know, military academies established by him, and supported to some extent by the pension decreed to him by the Mikado as a reward for his faithful services.

## SAMESHIMA NAONOBU.

THE Japanese minister, Sameshima Naonobu, who died in Paris, in 1880, was, in many respects, an interesting character. He was born in Satsuma, Japan, about the year 1845; was educated in the local school of that province, and studied Dutch and English at Nagasaki. In 1865 he was one of fifteen Satsuma students who went to Europe to prosecute their studies, almost all of whom subsequently became useful to their Government, and among whom were Mr. Yoshida, minister to Washington, Mr. Mori, minister to London, and such other well-known men in Japan as Hatakeyama, Machida, and Matsmura. On his return from Europe, Sameshima travelled extensively in the United States. He reached Japan just as the new era was beginning in that Empire, and became very useful in public affairs on account of his foreign experiences. His first official position was that of Chief Clerk of the Foreign Office in Tokio, and he was next made Secretary of the Municipal Government, and greatly interested himself in visiting and caring for the poor of the city. When the ironclad *Stonewall*, which had been purchased of the United States, reached Yokohama, there was much difficulty in having her delivered to the proper authorities, and when H. E. Iwakura called at the American Legation to secure the steamer for the Mikado, Sameshima and Mori were the interpreters. After she had been duly delivered to the Imperialists, she was sent to Hakedota, and did efficient service against the forces of the Tycoon until the final triumph of the Imperialists.

After his services as a local officer he was sent as Chargé d'Affaires both to London and Paris; held for a time the office of Assistant Secretary of State; was next made Resident Minister at Paris, and subsequently Minister Plenipotentiary at the same place. His influence as a man and an officer was extensive, but it was due more to his innate goodness of heart and personal popularity than to extraordinary abilities. His health had been poor for many months, and he died of consumption, leaving a wife and one child.

## SAIGO TSUGUMICHI.

THE subject of the present memoir is a younger brother of the late Saigo Takamori, formerly marshal in the Japanese army and leader of the Satsuma Clan, one of the promoters of the Restoration, and finally the head of the Satsuma Rebellion. Saigo's earlier life was devoted to the study of literature and military science. During the war of the Restoration he acted a prominent part, and fought battles in almost every part of the Empire, from the commencement to the end of the struggle, always gaining splendid victories, and thus greatly distinguishing himself. After the conclusion of the war he was appointed general in the Imperial army, and nominated a junior noble of the fourth rank, and commander of the Tokio garrison. Shortly afterwards, when the invasion of Corea had become a great question for discussion in the Cabinet, his views were opposed to those of his elder brother, who strongly insisted upon war, an idea which was ultimately abandoned. The two brothers then parted, the elder retiring from the Cabinet, while the younger remained in the Government ; and it is said that from that time there was no real friendship between them. In the Formosan expedition in 1874, Saigo Tsugumichi was appointed commander-in-chief, and led the Japanese fleet and army to the island, where, after fighting several battles, he successfully subdued the brave and aggressive savage tribes. The expedition was thus terminated, and a war indemnity of five hundred thousand taels was paid to Japan by the Chinese Government. In 1876 when the Philadelphia Exhibition was held, the General was appointed Vice Commissioner for the Japanese Section. He therefore went to America, where he honorably, and to the satisfaction of all, represented the interests of his country at the great International Exposition. When the Satsuma revolt broke out in 1877, he wished to take up arms against his rebel brother, but the Government would not allow him to do so. However he remained in Tokio in control of the War Department, during the absence of the then Minister of War, General Yamagata, at the seat of strife. Although Saigo did not take part personally in the campaign, his services in supplying the Imperial forces in the field with provisions and ammunition from Tokio without interruption, was worthy of praise, and greatly contributed to the termination of the war in September of the same year. The assassination of His Excellency Okubo, late Minister of Home Affairs, perpetrated in May, 1878, occasioned some changes in the Ministry. The subject of this sketch was then nominated Privy Councillor and Minister of Education, which latter office he left when he was appointed Minister of War, and Commander of the Imperial Guard, in place of General Yamagata, who was transferred to the control of the Staff Office. In consequence of the changes effected in the Ministry at the commencement of the present year, General Saigo remained Sangi, having to devote all his attentions to the duties of that post. His portfolio for the War Department was confided to General Oyama, and the command of the Imperial Guard was assumed by His Imperial Highness, General Prince Higashi Fushimi.

## SANJO SANETOMI.

THIS distinguished man, formerly known as Fujiwara no Saneyoshi, is the second son of Sanjo Sanekazu, the late U-daijin, and one of the kuge or Court nobles, descendants of former occupants of the Imperial throne. It was therefore only natural that Sanjo Sanetomi should desire the restoration of the authority of the Emperor; and to that end he accordingly devoted himself from his youth, with all the tact and ability for which he is so distinguished. In January, 1863, matters being considered ripe for the contemplated change, Sanjo and Anè-nô-Kôji Shosho, were sent as envoys to the Shôgun by the Mikado. They informed the Bakufu officials that all old abuses must be cleared away, the constitution reformed, and the anxiety of the Emperor respecting the troubles brooding over the country, removed. The Shôgun was also ordered to present himself at Kioto during the coming spring, and, in the meantime, to make preparations for the expulsion of foreigners. This decided step appears to have aroused the Shôgunate supporters to their impending danger, and they made a supreme effort to recover their lost influence at Court. On the thirtieth of September, in the same year, a coalition was formed, with the object of removing Sanjo and his friends, whose growing power, zeal and ability, the Shôgunate recognized and feared. The Emperor was induced, under various pretexts, to order the punishment of Sanjo and six others of the Court nobles, but, after receiving timely warning, these withdrew to Choshiu before the storm burst, taking with them the present Emperor. Here the fugitives remained in safety until 1865, when they were forced to take refuge in Chikuzen. In 1866, however, the clouds of adversity passed over with the death of the late Emperor and the ascension of the present occupant of the Imperial throne. Recognizing the folly of further resistance to what was inevitable sooner or later, Tokugawa Keike, the reigning Shôgun, restored the administrative authority to his Imperial master, and thus came to an end the Bakufu Government, which had ruled Japan with a rod of iron for nearly three centuries. With all the faults of the Shôguns, the Tokugawa have one proud boast: "We preserved Japan from internecine warfare for two hundred and fifty-three years."

After the retirement of Keiki, the subject of this sketch was appointed Vice-Administrator and a member of the Senate. During the wars of the Restoration, Sanjo was constantly in attendance upon the young Emperor, and administering the affairs of state in those trying times when error meant disaster, and disaster ruin irremediable. Peace being at length restored, Sanjo was chosen to superintend the affairs of the eastern portion of the country, and also received the appointment of commander-in-chief of the "left hand" division of the Imperial guard.

In 1868 the attitude of the adherents of the Bakufu Government excited the apprehensions of the Imperial authorities, and Sanjo was entrusted with the arduous task of inducing the malcontents to submit to the new order of things. This delicate mission was successfully accomplished; and His Excellency was then appointed U-daijin, as a recognition of his services. Subsequently he received the office of Sa-daijin, and in 1870 that of Daijo Daijin, or Prime Minister, which he still holds. It is needless to say that the early prejudices of His Excellency respecting foreigners, have long since been entirely removed by intercourse with the Western strangers. No member of the Government is more keenly alive to the vast benefits derived by Japan from entering the comity of nations, and following in the paths of civilization and progress, than His Excellency Sanjo Sanetomi.

By way of giving the foreign reader an idea of Sanjo when communicating his ideas to the public, we submit the following translation from a letter which he wrote to the assembly of nobles, in July, 1875:

> Last year you bound yourselves by a common vow to establish your Assembly, to take deeply to heart the kindness of the Imperial instructions to you, and to discharge to the utmost of your ability your duties as nobles. This was truly a matter for congratulation, and if the nobles had striven zealously to realize the practical results of such a resolution, it would have been indeed fortunate for our country.
>
> Since that date, however, the meetings have been but scantily attended, and I have not learnt that any definite plan has been formed for accomplishing these results. Some, while agreeing with the objects of the Assembly, have gone elsewhere, others who agree equally with them, stand by almost like mere spectators. It does not seem as if any notice were taken by them as to whether the Assembly was in a state of prosperity or decay, or whether it was being established or abandoned. If such indolence and negligence continues, what is, after all, the good of your Assembly? Saneyoshi's former rejoicing is turned into sorrow. He is prevented by the pressure of his important duties from attending the Assembly frequently himself, but he cannot forget it by day or by night. He hopes that the members will commit to writing, and communicate to him, their plans for discharging the functions of the Assembly, together with their views as to the means of increasing its activity for the future. He will aid you in your endeavors. Do ye all give due consideration to these words. (Signed) SANEYOSHI.
> To the Assembly of Nobles.

## SANO TSUNETAMI.

HE was a retainer of the Saga han and born in 1823; and after the usual education of his class, he went to Nagasaki, where he acquired a knowledge of medicine. His abilities having been brought to the knowledge of one of the local princes, he was for a time employed in an important position under the Saga han. About the year 1862 he was sent to Holland by the General Government, where he superintended the building of a man-of-war, and on his return was employed by the authorities of the Navy. After the Restoration, he was invited to Yedo, and placed in charge of the Lighthouse Department, and did much to advance the usefulness of that branch of the public service. In 1873 he was sent to Austria in the capacity of *chargé d'affaires* and was also Vice President of the Japanese Commission to the Vienna Exposition, remaining in that city about two years. During his previous visit to Europe, he took occasion to visit the Paris Exposition, and his experiences in that city were of great service in Vienna.

The very gratifying impressions which were made upon the whole world by the Japanese exhibits sent to the Austrian Capital, were owing in a great degree to the sagacity of the chief official in charge.

After his return from Austria, he was made a member of the Japanese Senate, and in 1880 he was again promoted and made the chief minister of the Treasury Department.

While a love of art is quite common among all the educated classes in Japan, with Mr. Sano Tsunetami it is allied to a passion, and his influence has been great in making his countrymen acquainted with beautiful and antique productions from foreign lands; and through his personal efforts, there has been established a society called *Riuchi Kawai*, or Society of the Fine Arts. He is also the author and promoter of a Humane Society, of which he is President, and which has accomplished much good. From Austria as well as his own country, he has been the recipient of various honors.

## SATO SHUNKAI.

HIS native place was in the town of Sakura, province of Shimo-o-sa, and in early life was known by the name of Yaniaguchi. After acquiring a complete knowledge of Chinese, he turned his attention to the Dutch language, and, after going through a course of studies at Nagasaki, in the science of medicine, took high rank as a physician and surgeon.

In 1861, and on several other occasions, he was invited to take part in Bakufu Government, but declined all such offers. His mind having become deeply imbued with a desire to elevate the healing art in Japan, he devoted his whole attention to that object, and one of his first exploits was to build and endow a private hospital for the use of his countrymen; and with this he connected a medical school for beginners. In 1868 he visited Prussia, and added to his stock of information, his talents having been highly appreciated in Europe.

In 1869 he was invited by the Educational Department of the Empire to take charge of the medical branch of the Tokio University, and received the highest title attached to his profession. In 1874 he resigned that position, and devoted all his influence to the establishment of a large hospital in Tokio, and was made Inspector General of the army. His practise as a physician is extensive, and in influence is without a superior in Japan.

## SHIBUSAWA EICHI.

HE was born in the province of Zo-Shu, in 1840, and was the son of a farmer. When Tokugawa Akitake went to France for study in 1867, Mr. Shibusawa was his companion; and on his return to Japan, he was appointed to a subordinate position in the Treasury, but was soon promoted to the head of the Department as its Secretary. He was also called upon to manage the affairs of the printing bureau of the Government, and soon promoted for his services in that direction. In 1873, in conjunction with his friend Mr. Enouye Kaoru, he presented a memorial to the Government on the condition of public affairs, which document was signed by both of the gentlemen, and will be found embodied in the notice of Mr. Enouye in this volume. The views they held met with some opposition in the Cabinet, which induced them both to resign their positions under the Government.

During his residence in France, he had devoted special attention to the study of finance, and after his return to Japan, he exerted himself to establish a banking institution, of which he became President — the First National Bank — and which proved to be very successful. When, on a certain occasion, the financial affairs of the city of Tokio had become involved, he was called upon to look after them, and was successful in rendering the public an important service.

Still anxious to do all the good for his country, he

conceived the idea and carried it out, of establishing an extensive paper factory after the American plan.

As one of the results of his ability, he was made Chairman of the Tokio Chamber of Commerce, which he now holds, and is of course a very high authority on all matters connected with finance and commerce. He is said to have acquired considerable wealth, and it is known to everybody in Japan that his charities are in keeping with his wealth. During the Chinese famine in 1878, he was one of the first to send relief to the sufferers. When General Grant was in Japan, he was chairman of the committee delegated to pay the honors to the distinguished American.

By way of illustrating Mr. Shibusawa's style of thinking and writing, we append to our brief notice the substance of a speech that he delivered in Yokohama in 1877, from which it will be seen that his views are not merely speculative, but eminently practical; the speech was as follows:—

"Bankers should pay attention to the increasing of their production of the country.

"Bankers are the intermediaries between borrowers and lenders, and thereby aid the circulation of money. In a few words, the duty of banks is to receive deposits, lend the money received to those who may require it, issue bills of exchange, and buy and sell Government bonds and bullion. If proper care be devoted to the conducting of business, there is no reason why certain profits should not be obtainable. Those bankers who are desirous of doing only a safe business, should confine themselves solely to such transactions as the above, not seeking to do any other. Such at least are the views of steady-going men of moderate wishes. I shall say nothing against them. But for my own part in reflecting on the past and looking forward to the future, I have discovered a fact in connection with foreign trade which may end in great evil, and indeed affects our whole commercial prosperity. This is nothing else than that there is no proportion between the import and export trade of this country.

"I wish you would carefully look at the Custom House returns. In reviewing these reports from the first to the tenth year of Meiji, the imports balanced the exports only in the first and ninth years. In every other year the imports have been greatly in excess of exports, sometimes being twice as great. Now this is equivalent to so much money being sent out of the country, which is indeed a deplorable state of affairs, and calculated to cause grave anxiety. Now if we bankers who play so important a part in the financial condition of the country, leave such questions unconsidered, our business would soon cease, neither could we keep our establishments going, for the banks derive their profits not so much from the wealth that depositors entrust to their keeping, as to their commercial constituents. Now should the productions of the country gradually decrease, and trade languish, merchants would find themselves unable to carry on their business, because their losses would be greater than their profits, and before many years had passed, the resources of Japan would become exhausted. In such times even the wealthiest men are ruined. Now, under such circumstances, with whom would bankers be able to do any business? There would be nobody left, and that is therefore why I say that we must begin to look out for the future.

"As long as this present order of things remains, however, in accordance with the banking laws, banks may not concern themselves with the opening of mines, or developing the resources of the country in such wise. The Government does not overlook the fact that a development of its resources is the roof of the country's prosperity, but assists in such enterprises to a certain extent. But as the banks have so large an interest in the productions of the country, they must do all in their power to aid the development.

"The question then arises, what is to be done? The system of lending on personal security must be established.

"Japanese merchants — or at least a great many of them — up to the time of the Restoration, traded under license, and were granted monopolies of their several businesses, thus possessing special privileges. These rights have, since the Restoration, been done away with, and any one is now at liberty to undertake any branch of trade he may select. Owing to the abolition of monopolies, not a few of the solid houses of former days became bankrupt. Others again formed companies with officials who resigned their appointments and embarked their capital in trade. But most of their transactions were only reckless speculations, and without due regard to their operations, or knowing where to stop, thinking they could make a fortune in an instant, advanced their capital to dishonest men. Others who were entirely conservative, clung to the idea that they must act in such and such a manner only because their ancestors had done so. Thus if they fortunately — or unfortunately — possessed any money, they would let it lie in their vaults, so that it did no more good to them or to the public than if it had been so much mud. When such is the condition of the trading community, it is no wonder that failure has been the almost invariable result. New establishments sprang up only to decay like weeds, and merchants lost all confidence. Money could be borrowed without security, and therefore production could not be stimulated. That is why we have made no headway in this respect.

"Recently times have changed somewhat in this respect, and some establishments carrying on business on true trade principles have commenced to exist. But the great drawback is lack of capital, and it is to be greatly deplored that the country generally is so poor that they cannot effect their desired objects.

"The regulations with regard to banks are so severe, and the Government is so strict in enforcing them, that they have carried on their business in a quiet way, incurring no losses. But if banks commence to be led away with the idea that regardless of the character of their promoters, they can carry out any schemes that may be presented to them for the development of the production of the country, they must not expect to last long, for they cannot.

"Some system ought to be introduced whereby money might be lent at a low rate of interest, not looking so much to the security offered, as the character of the borrower. If his business be a sure one, he should thus be assisted, and entering upon any thing that does not look safe, should be protested against. Thus may we aid in extending the productions of our country, and if we succeed in doing this we have all done our duty. I am anxious to hear what you think of my ideas."

# SHIMADZU HISAMITSU.

HE was born in Satsuma, and was the second son of the Prince of that province. After receiving a good education, he began to take an interest in public affairs, and was among the first to advocate the restoration of the Emperor to his legitimate power. In 1862 he went to Kioto, where he did much to preserve the public peace in connection with the invasion of foreigners, and for his services at that time, the Imperial Court gave him the name of Sabro, by which he was afterwards known. From Kioto he went to Yedo as an assistant envoy from the Emperor to the Tycoon, the object of his mission being to have the foreigners expelled and the peace of the Empire preserved; and it was while returning to Kioto with his retinue, that the Englishman Richardson rudely interfered with the passing of his retinue, and for which conduct he was immediately killed by some of the retainers of Shimadzu. Following this event the British Government forthwith made a demand upon the Bakufu Government to deliver Shimadzu to them for punishment, and to pay a large indemnity; whereupon the Satsuma envoy sent a letter to the Bakufu Government, in which he said that the Englishman had offered an insult to him and his followers, and it was for that conduct he had been killed. He also said that if the English Government wanted any satisfaction from him, he was ready for battle. In process of time, however, the Bakufu Government paid an indemnity of four hundred and fifty thousand dollars, and so, as it was supposed, settled the difficulty. But the British Government, true to its tyrannical instincts when dealing with feeble powers, in the Orient as well as elsewhere, sent seven men of war to Kagoshima, where Shimadzu was fortified with a limited force of troops, and after making another demand for money, proceeded to hostilities; several severe battles were fought, and the English were whipped; but in the end the civilized Englishman obtained the additional gold thus wanted, and peace was secured.

When the Bakufu Government made its demonstration against Choshiu, Shimadzu was one of those who opposed hostilities; and for this, he and his second son and Prince of Satsuma, were rewarded with one hundred thousand kokus of rice. After this he retired to private life at Kagoshima, and though frequently importuned by the Imperial Court to go and help the Government in Yedo, he declined to do so.

In 1872 he submitted to the Emperor an elaborate document on the policy which should be pursued in the affairs of Government, whereupon a special messenger was sent to bring him back to Yedo, when he was appointed a counsellor to the Emperor, as well as a Sadai-jin. In 1875 he made a demonstration against one of the members of the Cabinet, and because the Emperor would not take his advice and remove the offending minister, he resigned his connection with the Emperor and retired to his native town in Satsuma.

When not engaged in serving his country as an official, he took a special interest in promoting the education of the common people in his province, spending much of his money as well as time for their benefit.

## SOYESHIMA TANEOMI.

HE was born in Saga, province of Hizen, and early acquired the best education afforded by the local schools. Having early turned his attention to the study of law, in 1868 he was made a commissioner for framing certain laws, and after performing that task most satisfactorily, he was promoted to be a Councillor of State. In 1871 he was sent on a mission to Russian Siberia, to settle certain boundary difficulties connected with the Island of Saghalien, and was successful. His next position was that of Minister for Foreign Affairs, and one of his exploits in that capacity was to cause the release and the return home of certain Chinese coolies, who were found on a Peruvian vessel, in the port of Yokohama. In 1873 he was sent as an Envoy Extraordinary to China, and was the first official of that character ever received in person by the Emperor; the chief reason for success having been the earnest arguments of the Japanese envoy. It is said that while in Peking one of the ministers said to him:

"Why do you wear the European dress, when you are a representative of Japan?" to which he replied: "I have not time to discuss such trifling matters as this."

On his return to Japan he was again made a Councillor of State, or Sanji; but having adopted the policy of General Saigo, to make war upon Corea, and the majority of the Cabinet being against them, he, with Saigo, resigned, and retired to private life. But his influence continued to be felt throughout the Empire, and he it was who, with Itagaki and Goto, petitioned the Government to establish a national assembly; and although they were not successful at the time, the prospects are that their hopes will yet be fully realized. After the Emperor had issued his decree to establish a constitution, it is said Mr. Soyeshima was invited to enter the Cabinet again, but he declined the honor.

His public mission to China having been successful, he visited that country in 1876 in his private capacity, where he made many personal friends, and astonished them by his remarkable knowledge of the Chinese language, and by the unpretending character of his deportment.

In 1879 he was invited to become a member of the Imperial household, and has latterly been devoting his time to study and the assistance of the Emperor in his private library, deserving and receiving the highest praise for his services from people of all parties.

# TANAKA FUJIMARO.

HE was born in the province of Owari, Japan, in 1843; received a superior education in the Japanese and Chinese classics, and was at one time the Secretary of the Board of Imperial Counsellors. When the Iwakura Embassy went abroad in 1871, he was attached to it as a commissioner, and after making many careful observations in the United States, connected with educational affairs, he went to Europe to continue his observations. On his return to Japan, he manifested increased zeal in the cause of education, and was subsequently appointed Vice Minister of the Department of Education.

When the International Exposition took place at Philadelphia, in 1876, Mr. Tanaka was of course placed in charge of the Educational Department on behalf of Japan, and the admirable display of his Government was greatly assisted by his management of its affairs.

He also rendered the public an important service at that time, by compiling and publishing *An Outline History of Japanese Education* which had a wide circulation in the United States, and is a work of very great interest to men of culture everywhere.

The annual reports which have been submitted by Mr. Tanaka to the Emperor, on educational affairs, since 1875, have all been distinguished for their judicious opinions and recommendations, and have been of very great value in helping on the enlightenment of his countrymen, and they have been published both in the Japanese and English languages. In 1881 he relinquished his position in connection with educational affairs and became identified with the Sangin, or new Parliament, as its Vice President.

## TANI KANJO.

HE was born in the province of Tosa, and has since his youth been remarkable for his brave, calm, and thoughtful disposition. His father was renowned for an extensive knowledge of literature, and being naturally anxious that the subject of this sketch should enjoy the advantages derivable from culture, he sent him to Yedo when a boy, to study under the celebrated Yasui, who was famous for his knowledge of Chinese, and had written many works in that language, which attracted much attention.

Yasui, perceiving the generous impulses and noble aspirations of Tani, bestowed great pains upon fitting him for his career in life; in fact, he became the old man's favorite pupil. An affection altogether dissimilar to the relationship usually existing between master and pupil, and not unlike the love David bore for Jonathan was the result, and continued not only without abatement, but increasing in strength until the death of Yosui plunged Tani into the deepest grief.

An active life was considered the best remedy for the state of despondency into which Tani had now fallen, and his feudal superior, the Prince of Tosa, accordingly appointed him a Censor and ordered him to visit and report upon different localities in his domains. This duty Tani executed in such a manner as to give great satisfaction, and thus led to more important employment.

At the commencement of the war of the Restoration, Tani was placed in command of a detachment of the Tosa army, and marched on Osaka, accompanied by Itagaki Taisuke (an ex-member of the Privy Council), and other prominent persons. After the occupation of Osaka he was appointed Inspector General, and entrusted with the command of the advanced divisions of the army. In March, 1868, he captured the castle of Kofa, and fought the battle of Katsunuma, in which the rebel forces, led by the brave Kondo Isami, were signally defeated. Tani followed up this victory by a rapid advance, and engaged the enemy at Shirakawa, Miharu, and Yasuzuka, in all of which combats he routed the adversaries opposed to him. Flushed with success the victorious army pushed on to Aidzu and routed their opponents on several occasions, and at last crowned their triumphs by the capture of the great fortress of Wakamatsu, the stronghold of Aidzu. The campaign being thus happily terminated, Tani led his forces back to his native province, and in recognition of his services was appointed a lieutenant-general in the army Imperial, and entrusted with the command of the castle of Kumamoto.

When the expedition was despatched to Formosa Tani was made an inspector-general and sent to assist the Commander-in-chief, General Saigo (the younger brother of the rebel leader), and, after the objects of the expedition were achieved, he returned and was unemployed for some time.

In 1876 the Jimpu party rose in rebellion in Kumamoto, and Tani was re-appointed to the command of the garrison upon the death of General Taneda.

In 1877 the great revolt of the Satsuma Clan occurred, and the stronghold of Kumamoto was for weeks the point to which the fears and hopes of the contending parties in the mighty struggle were turned. Never, during the brightest days of chivalry in Japan, were braver feats of arms performed than at the siege of Kumamoto ; the possession of that fortress being looked upon as of vital importance to both belligerents. Again and again the flower of the Southern forces, fighting under the eye of their beloved Saigo, rushed to the assault and as often recoiled, shattered and decimated by the stubborn valor of the defenders encouraged by the dauntless Tani, who exposed his life with the most reckless bravery. At last the siege was raised by the main body of the Imperialists ; and shortly afterwards the formidable rebellion was crushed, and peace restored to the distracted country.

Tani was rewarded for his extraordinary achievements with the Order of the Rising Sun of the second class, and promotion to the rank of general in the army.

## TERASHIMA MUNENORI.

HE was born in the province of Satsuma, in the year 1830, and was well educated in the provincial schools until his thirteenth year, when, because of his superior abilities, he was sent to Tokio, and went through a medical course of studies under a prominent physician in that city. He next turned his attention to the study of the Dutch and English languages, and acquired uncommon proficiency in both; so that when the Perry expedition reached Japan, he occupied a high position as a scholar, which he immediately applied to practical purposes. When the embassy of 1861 was about to leave for America, he was invited to become a member, and made himself very useful as an interpreter; in 1865 he was sent by the Prince of Satsuma to England, as a commissioner in charge of several students, and remained in that country about two years; at the time of the Restoration in 1868, he took an active part in public affairs, and was made a councillor in the new Government; in 1869 he was appointed Governor of Kanagawa, and at the same time acted as Assistant Secretary of the Foreign office, and exerted great influence as a diplomat; in 1871 he relinquished the position of Governor, and became the Senior Vice Minister of Foreign Affairs; in 1872 he was sent as Envoy Extraordinary and Minister Plenipotentiary to Great Britain, but his health prevented him from continuing in that position for more than one year, when he resigned. On his return to Japan, in 1873, he was appointed a Privy Councillor, or Sangi; and was then made the Minister for Foreign Affairs, the duties of which he performed with ability and dignity until the appointment of his successor, Mr. Enouye; and of late years his very extensive experience in national affairs has made him a useful member of the Government as President of the Genro-in, or new Senate.

Recent advices from Japan announce the fact that Mr. Terashima has been appointed Minister Plenipotentiary to the United States, to succeed Mr. Yoshida Kiyonari, transferred to the Foreign Office. There are few men in Japan who have seen as much of the world and had so much experience in public affairs as Mr. Terashima, and as he is understood to have a most interesting family, their presence in Washington will be warmly welcomed.

## TOYAMA MASAKAZU.

THIS well-known and successful Japanese scholar was born in the province of Satsuma, and belongs to a samurai family; and the present writer greatly regrets that it is out of his power to speak of him excepting in the most general terms. He was the Secretary of the first Japanese Legation accredited to Washington, and while making himself eminently useful to Mr. Arinori Mori, the *Chargé d'affaires*, he devoted the most of his time to study, with which he became infatuated. When the famous Japanese Embassy arrived in Washington he resigned his position as Secretary, although strongly urged not to do so, and resolved to enter an American college. A movement was then made to have him educated as a Government student, but he preferred to accomplish what was possible at his own expense. He then entered the University of Michigan, where, at the end of a regular course, he graduated with all the honors, and returned to Japan. During his sojourn in Washington, as well as at the University, he wrote many essays on various important questions then occupying the public mind, in which he displayed a knowledge of men and affairs, and a grasp of intellect which attracted very marked attention. When some of them were re-published in the volume entitled *The Japanese in America*, they were complimented in the highest terms by many of the leading reviews of

England and the United States; while some of them could hardly believe that such able writing on the affairs of the Western nations, could have emanated from an Oriental scholar.

Very soon after Mr. Toyama's return to Japan, he was appointed to a professorship in the University of Tokio, where he has continued to labor with unremitting faithfulness to the duties of his responsible position. The departments of learning to which he has been chiefly devoted, have been those of Philosophy and English Literature.

## TSUDA SEN.

HE was born at Sakura of Shimo-o-sa, in 1837, but while yet a mere youth he removed to Yedo, where he acquired a knowledge of the Dutch language, and was connected with the Tokugawa Government. In 1867, with his friend Fukuzawa, he visited the United States on a special mission for the Tycoon, but did not remain any great length of time. In 1873 he went to the Vienna Exposition as one of the commissioners from Japan ; and while there he was made one of the judges who were to pass upon the merits of the exhibits ; and for his services received a medal from the Austrian Government. During his stay in Europe he devoted special attention to agricultural affairs, and on his return home published a book in which were fully set forth the foreign methods of fertilizing lands. He not only wrote and published many papers on the various phases of agriculture, but exerted himself to found an agricultural school in Tokio, and established on a good foundation a periodical devoted to the science and the practise of agriculture. Although printed in Japanese, the motto of his journal was a sentiment taken from George Washington, and which, strange as it may seem, was copied from his magazine by the Agricultural Department of the United States, and placed over the door of the American Section for Agriculture, at the last Paris Exposition. Mr. Tsuda is a good English scholar, and by way of giving an idea of his style and at the same time an insight into some of his experiences connected with Vienna, we submit the following letter which he sent to the editor of the *Japan Mail*, on the seventh of August, 1876:

"DEAR SIR :—I notice in your issue of the eighth ultimo some erroneous statements about "a certain Mr. Tsuda," coming from the Kenrei of the Chiba Ken — one Naruto Yoshitomi — and the Kangiorio.

"As one of the many farmers of the country, on my return from the Vienna Exhibition, where I held the post of one of the Vice Commissioners of Agriculture, I attempted to teach my countrymen to develop some of the neglected agricultural resources of Japan, and introduce some of the new methods of scientific agriculture, such as I found being taught by the learned professors of the universities and colleges of Europe and America, and adopted by the farmers there.

"Since my return to Japan I have published several agricultural books, also the *Agricultural News*, wherein I have attempted, as far as my limited education and means will permit, to show our farmers how to develop many new agricultural industries, among which was Hooibrenks' method of using an artificial fertilizer for wheat, barley and rice, which, as I introduced it into Japan, is known in this country as the Tsuda-nawa.

"This process was used in many of the sheltered fields of France, as well as the Indian colonies, and is also described by His Excellency Mr. Rochusan, a Cabinet Minister of Holland, as a decided success. Mr. Hooibrenks received furthermore from the hands of the Emperor Napoleon III., a decoration for his introduction of the system.

"Now this method of cultivation is peculiarly adapted

to this country, where wheat and barley are sown in rows, and may therefore easily be fecundated by the Tsuda-nawa.

"Most of the arable land in Japan is too much sheltered and does not get the needful advantage of the breezes, so that the use of the Tsuda-nawa is beneficial, especially as the cost of same is small, say from yen one, twenty-five hundredths to yen five, and can be used for many years. Farm labour is cheap also, so that the use of the Tsuda-nawa does not entail any cost which is not fully compensated for by the return. Experiments have been made with it in nearly every ken in Japan, and while in some cases the result has shown an increase in the crop of forty per cent., the average may very fairly be stated at fifteen per cent. I can authenticate this statement by reports from ken officials and farmers, now in my possession, which are the result of hundreds of experiments. The unfavourable statements made by the Kenrei of Chiba ken, are based on a trial made under direction of the Kencho officials, which in some cases indeed showed a loss, but taken together showed an average improvement of four per cent., while experiments made in the same ken by farmers who were skillful in the use of the Tsuda-nawa, showed an improvement of twenty per cent. This will prove that the Kenrei was wrong in advising the people not to use the Tsuda-nawa, and his statement that it is not a success is opposed to facts as borne out by actual experiments.

"Such statements have caused me personal loss. Before they were made I could hardly fulfil the orders for the Tsuda-nawa which I received from the farmers in the various kens in Japan, but after the publication of the remarks of the Kenri of Chiba ken, the farmers, naturally, were chary of trying the experiment.

"It is my opinion, based on the result of numerous careful trials, that if the system I advocate were generally adopted as regards only one half of the grain crop in Japan, it would be increased annually to the value of eleven million yen.

"Now, if such is the case, those officials who through jealousy, do all they can to prevent the introduction of the system, are preventing the advancement of prosperity in the country and deserve punishment, or deprivation of their office.

"Mr. Naruto Yoshitomi, who through the medium of the press also attacked my agricultural improvements, asserts that the system which I have also advocated, namely that of the inclination of the branches of fruit trees, has never yet been tried in Japan. This assertion is incorrect, as this method of cultivation, which is in great favour in Europe and America, has been tried in many parts of this country with undoubted success, and to my certain knowledge the growth and bearing of apple, pear, mulberry and persimmon-trees, and the grape vine, have greatly benefited by it. In the province of Ise some fruit trees which had not borne for a whole generation, produced large quantities of fruit when so treated.

"By the increased knowledge of the art of agriculture to be derived from acquaintance with the methods adopted in foreign countries, particularly by more attention to proper drainage and subsoil ploughing; by a more careful cultivation of cereals, flax, tobacco, sugar-beets, alfalfa clover, grasses and fruits, and by the raising of stock, I hope to see the resources of this country in a fair way to be doubled within the next generation, and it will be a source of great pleasure to me to think that any efforts of mine have tended towards such improvement. The true progress of this country is to be looked for in this direction. In conclusion I would beg to thank the Government officials, the press and the people of my country, for the attention which has been paid to my endeavors to improve agriculture in Japan, and for the kindness and assistance rendered me; and I feel confident that my endeavours for improvement will ultimately result in benefit to the Government and the country.

"Yours faithfully, S. TSUDA."

While commenting upon Mr. Tsuda's career as an agriculturist, the *Japan Mail* says as follows:

"Mr. Tsuda, who had been trying to introduce into Japan the system of artificial fertilization of cereals as recommended by Mr. Hooibrenks, has published a pamphlet purporting to prove that the system has been fairly successful where a proper trial has been given to it. Mr. Tsuda says that his system has been tried in about one hundred different places in the Kanagawa ken, and that the result is an average increase of twenty per cent. in the crops. From various other parts of Japan have favorable accounts of the process been received, so much so that Mr. Kido, the Minister of Agriculture, has himself written a preface to Mr. Tsuda's publication, recommending a trial of the system. Mr. Tsuda further says that the labour of fertilizing growing grain is but one third that of clearing it from weeds, and the cost of materials required is trifling, so that the extra outlay in cash and labour is amply compensated for."

Notwithstanding the difficulties here commented upon, Mr. Tsuda has worked himself up to a most exalted position as an authority on agricultural affairs, and he has also frequently assisted the Government in its efforts to circulate valuable information for the benefit of the people.

Mr. Tsuda, moreover, was one of the first among the higher classes of Japan to adopt the Christian religion. His zeal in that direction is quite as great as it is in behalf of agriculture. Among his noble acts as a Christian was to hire or purchase one of the abandoned temples in Tokio, where a Methodist clergyman of high character and ability has preached the Gospel regularly on every Sunday, for several years; while during the week days a flourishing school has been maintained in the same old temple, and wholly at Mr. Tsuda's own expense. Like himself, all the matured members of his large family are communicants in the church of their adoption.

In his style of living and the adornments of his house, Mr. Tsuda has adopted many of the ideas gathered by him in foreign lands; and the extensive garden which surrounds his dwelling is said to be one of the most beautiful in the city of Tokio. Nor will a more interesting flower be seen there in the coming years, than the form of his daughter Ume Tsuda, who has for the last ten years been receiving a judicious education in the city of Washington, which was given to her by the Japanese Government as a tribute of respect for her distinguished father.

It may also be said of Mr. Tsuda that he has a habit of taking an interest in all the literary, scientific, and benevolent affairs of Tokio, and he did much to secure the establishment of an asylum for the blind, and the deaf and dumb of the city. And when General Grant visited Tokio, Mr. Tsuda was called upon to assist in doing the honors of the day, and he it was who planted the memorial tree for the ex-President and his wife.

# YAMADA AKIYOSHI.

THE subject of this memoir, although still young, — not yet forty years of age — has passed through stirring scenes of strife and peril which fall to the lot of few to experience even in the longest lifetime. General Yamada Akiyoshi is a scion of the Choshiu Clan, and was originally known as Ichi-no-suke. From his first admission into the ranks of manhood, he was a staunch and persistent advocate of the restoration of the Imperial authority. He also, we regret to record, favored the expulsion of foreigners; but his opinion on this subject has long since been changed; and the political errors of youth, when subsequently redressed, are, in his case, no more fit subject for animadversion, than would be a Liberal's condemnation of Mr. Gladstone for commencing his public career as a conscientious Tory.

In 1863 General Yamada visited Kioto with the object of assisting in the formation of a league to carry out the patriotic objects upon which his mind was fully bent. In the ancient capital he became intimate with the leaders of the party with which he had identified himself, and when the seven Imperial ministers (among them was the present Prime Minister, Sanjo Sanetomi) fled from Kioto to Choshiu for safety, taking with them the reigning Emperor, then the heir apparent, Yamada accompanied the party on their journey, until immutiny from all danger was secured to them. He then returned to Kioto and remained *perdu* in the dwelling of a secret sympathiser, watching the progress of events, and keeping the other leaders of his party acquainted with every thing of importance that transpired in the Imperial city.

At length concluding that the time for decided action had at last arrived, the subject of this memoir left Kioto in 1863, and returned to Choshiu, where he organized a large military force, and assuming the command, raised the standard of revolt against the Tokugawa dynasty. Nothing decisive following, he again visited Kioto in the ensuing year (1864), and there learned that Takeda Kôunsai had also refused further obedience to the Shôgunate authorities, and was in armed opposition to them in the province of Yashiu at no great distance from Yedo.

Yamada was anxious to throw in his lot with Takeda, but was prevented from doing so by various unexpected obstacles. However, in the autumn of 1864 his desire for active service was gratified, a detachment of the Choshiu army being sent to Fen-no-zan, whither he at once hastened. In conjunction with the celebrated leaders, Hisasaka Michitake and Maki Idzumi-no-kami, he warred with varying success against the armies of Aidzu and Yechizen, which were opposed to the Imperial forces.

Before this campaign was decided the allied expedition of the English, French, Dutch and American fleets sailed against Shimonoseki, and Yamada returned to Choshiu to assist in the defence of his native province against the assaults of the foreigner. In the winter of the same year the Shôgunate Government determined to send an expedition against Choshiu, which caused the seven Imperial ministers to withdraw to Chikuzen, as many of the Choshiu samurai were in favor of the Tycoon's Government and opposed to the reëstablishment of the supreme Imperial authority. In January, 1865, Yamada took the field against the malcontents, and in conjunction with Takasugi Shunpu, Ota Nawokata, and other loyal subjects, he completely defeated the partisans of the Tokugawa usurpers.

In the following year the Shôgunate authorities despatched a strong force against their stubborn opponents in Choshiu, and great preparations were made to give the assailants a warm reception. Yamada was appointed to the important position of commander of the Choshiu artillery, and took an active part in the operations which followed. Prominent among his many services may be mentioned a night attack by sea, which was ably designed and brilliantly carried into execution, and also a flank march towards the frontier of Geishiu, which resulted in the enemy being cut off from his base of supplies, out-manœuvred and defeated.

When the final war of the Restoration broke out at Fushimi in 1868, Yamada was appointed Head of the Staff under Prince Higashi Fushimi, the Commander-in-Chief, and after participating in the campaign he returned to Choshiu on board the man-of-war *Teibo Kan No. 1*. Leaving Choshiu he took part in the operations against the rebels in Yechigo, and distinguished himself at the stoutly contested and sanguinary battles of Idzumo-saki and Niigata, and indeed throughout the whole campaign, which resulted in the total defeat of the rebel forces.

While the operations in Yechigo were in progress, Enomoto Kawajiro (now Admiral Enomoto Take-aki, the recently appointed Naval Minister), who held a command in the Shôgunate fleet, sailed from Yedo to Hakodate with a rebel squadron, Yamada was placed at the head of the land and sea forces sent to reduce Hakodate to submission, and succeeded in accomplishing the object of the expedition after a series of hard-fought engagements, in which large numbers of men were killed and wounded.

Returning to Tokio in May, 1868, Yamada was appointed Daijo of the War Department, and in the following year he was rewarded for his eminent services with a pension of six hundred kokus of rice.

Early in 1870 Yamada was entrusted with the task of establishing and organizing the arsenal, military school, hospital, etc., at Osaka, and met with that success in this new field of labor which skill and energy always command. In July, 1871, he was appointed a lieutenant-general in the army, and afterwards to the suite of His Excellency Iwakura, with whose embassy he visited America and the various countries of Europe. While abroad Yamada attentively studied the military systems of the West, and returned to Japan in time to take part in the campaign against the Saga rebels in 1873. In command of a strong column of troops Yamada greatly distinguished himself, and the desperate valor for which he is celebrated was never more conspicuous than when he rallied his wavering troops under a tremendous storm of bullets in the decisive battle which crushed the rebel rising.

In February, 1877, the brave and popular, but misguided Saigo Takamori, the leader of the powerful Satsuma revolt and field-marshal in command of the Japanese army, yielded to the representations of false advisers and raised the standard of revolt in the southwest. Yamada had to take the field against his old superior officer, and took his usual prominent part in the sanguinary operations which resulted in the total defeat of the insurgents.

The return of peace to the country so long distracted by the horrors of war, brought new and well-merited honors to the subject of this too brief memoir; he was decorated with the Japanese Order of the second class and succeeded His Excellency Inouye Kaworu (now Foreign Minister), as Minister of Public Works.

# YANAGIWARA SAKIMITSU.

THIS accomplished nobleman was born in Kioto, and is not yet forty years of age. After acquiring a first-class native education he devoted himself to the study of Japanese and Chinese literature. During the troubles with China about Loo-Choo, he went to that country with Okubo, and assisted in the diplomatic negotiations which resulted so favorably. He was afterwards connected with the Gen-ro in, or Senate, holding two of the highest positions therein; and in 1880 he went as Minister Plenipotentiary to the Court of Saint Petersburg, where he still continues. The intercourse between Russia and Japan has always been most cordial and friendly; and as the Russian ministers sent to the Island Empire have always been men of high character, it is quite natural that the Japanese ministers accredited to Russia should be worthy representatives.

It is a singular coincidence that while Russia and China are, in their areas, the two largest empires in the world, and Japan one of the smallest, that they should both have gone into history as having added to their domain at the expense of Japan — Russia in purchasing Sagalin, and China in claiming jurisdiction over Loo-Choo. But it is a comfort to know that so long as Japan maintains her high character as one of the family of nations, she need not apprehend any trouble from foreign encroachments.

## YOSHIDA KIYONARI.

HE was born in the province of Satsuma, in 1845, and was educated by private tutors in his own language and Japanese history, and in the Chinese classics, at the Government College of his native province. In 1865, with Arinori Mori and other students from Satsuma, he visited Europe and went through a course of studies at University College in London. During his residence of two years in that city he kept his eyes wide open in regard to all the public events of the time, and among the results of his frequent attendance on the debates of Parliament was a feeling of special admiration for Mr. Gladstone, which has only been increased by the subsequent history of the great statesman. What Mr. Yoshida saw of the United States, on his way to Europe, induced him to reside in this country for a while before his return home, and while prosecuting a course of studies under private tutors in Massachusetts and New Jersey, he acquired a knowledge of the American people and of public affairs.

On his return to Japan he was made by Cabinet appointment one of the chief clerks of the Finance Department, having always had an aptness for that particular study. His next position was that of commissioner of Internal Revenue, which came to him in his twenty-sixth year by Imperial appointment, and he originated several important measures. In

When Mr. Yoshida was in Japan, in the enjoyment of his furlough, ex-President Grant arrived in that country, and it was the most natural thing in the world for him to be selected as the chief man to do the honors on that occasion; and that he performed the agreeable duties assigned to him in a highly creditable manner has passed into history; nor can it ever be forgotten that his accomplished wife did her full share in making the sojourn of Mrs. Grant all that could be desired.

While Mr. Yoshida has been quite willing to serve his country as a diplomat, the favorite bent of his mind is in the direction of finance, in regard to which his reading has been extensive. But aside from his many other duties as a diplomatic representative of his country, he negotiated at least one treaty which will ever remain a monument to his abilities, discretion and high sense of honor. When there was hardly a man in Japan who could speak a foreign language, a lot of foreign ministers put their heads together and made treaties with that Empire which were designed to help the pockets of the foreign powers at the expense of the simple-hearted Orientals. And their unhallowed intentions were fully realized. As time progressed it became a question of the greatest importance that the old treaties should be revised, and to the accomplishment of that task Mr. Yoshida bent all his energies from the moment of his accepting the mission to the United States. He tried his hand with Secretary Fish, but in vain; he did the same with Secretary Evarts, and was successful. The treaty was negotiated and promptly ratified by the Senate; and, to speak in general terms, all that was required from our Government was the recognition of the fact that Japan was a free and independent member of the family of nations, and had a perfect right to conduct all her internal affairs according to her needs and desires. As this was intended to be the first of the new series of treaties, and believing that all the powers of the world would be entirely willing to follow any just and proper example which might be set before them, Mr. Yoshida submitted a clause in his treaty to the effect that it should not go into operation until all the powers had adopted a similar revision of their treaties with Japan. This was the conception of an honest and high-toned man, wholly divested of any thing like the trickery which too frequently obtains in matters diplomatic. But what was the result? Because of the sordid selfishness of England there has not as yet been expressed by her Government a single word of manly, just, or generous recognition of the treaty made by Yoshida and Evarts. As we are thus reminded of the arbitrary and grasp-

It may also be mentioned as an evidence of Mr. Yoshida's quiet and unobtrusive influence in Washington, that Congress should have made and treated with the most friendly consideration the proposition to return to Japan a certain sum of money known as the Shimonoseki Indemnity Fund. Of course, as this is altogether an American affair, Mr. Yoshida, has had nothing to do with it excepting so far as the giving of information on the subject when required to do so; but while his ideas of propriety have prevented him from discussing the merits of the question, he took pleasure in manifesting to those concerned his warm appreciation of all that had been uttered in debate, published in the papers, or been done in Congress in regard to the proposed restoration.

The large and handsome building occupied by Mr. Yoshida as the Japanese Legation in Washington is the property of his Government, and on a beautiful lawn adjoining, the bright-eyed and happy children of the Minister were frequently seen frolicking with their nurses. The oldest of these children was a sweet little girl, and a great pet with the many people who visited Mrs. Yoshida; and the third child was a boy bearing the name of Grant, in honor of the ex-President and his visit to Japan. Although

Mr. Yoshida still keeps up his old habits of study, and is devoted to the higher branches of literature, he is fond of company, and his private entertainments in Washington were numerous and his public receptions among the most popular in the city. He is also devoted to the study and practise of art, and as an amateur well deserves to be classed with Sir John Crampton and Sir Saville Lumley, who were formerly associated with the British Legation in Washington. In the latter part of 1881 he was recalled from Washington and returned to Japan to become as was supposed, a member of the Imperial Cabinet.

## YOSHIDA TORAJIRO.

HE was born in the province of Chosiu, about the year 1830, and early became a superior scholar in the languages of Chinese and Japan. At the time of Commodore Perry's arrival in Japan, he went to Yedo and became a ronin, or feudal outlaw, or one of those who was willing to do any thing to produce a new state of affairs in the Empire, and where he was instructed in the Dutch language, and also supported by one of the retainers of the Shôgun's Councillors, named Sakuma Shozan. Hearing that a Russian ship had arrived at Nagasaki, which he desired to see, he went to that port in disguise, supporting himself by writing poetry; but finding the ship gone he returned to Yedo. Again hearing that Perry was on the coast and had arrived at Simoda, his vague desires received a new impulse, and he hastened to that place; there boarded the Commodore's ship for the purpose of making himself useful or of escaping into a foreign land; but the newly-made treaty stipulations caused him to be returned to the shore, when he and his friend Sakuma suffered a long captivity. In spite of all these troubles he succeeded in making converts to his ronin theories. We next hear of him as a school-teacher, but pursuing the calling under the surveillance of the Government. As time progressed, his hostility to the Shôgun's Government knew no abatement, and in his zeal to restore the Mikado to power, he went to Kioto in 1859, made an attempt upon the life of one of the Shôgun's ministers, but before leaving Tokio he wrote the following letter to his father:

MY DEAR FATHER :— I, Yoshida Torajiro, have been guilty of great errors, and have offended against the law of my country, yet still my life has been preserved. In looking back upon the last twenty-nine years I find I have frequently passed through great dangers; in fact, my very existence has often been in peril, and I know that I have caused great trouble to you all, my dear father and brothers. I have been a great offender and a bad son; but if I remain silent at the present crisis of our Empire, the result might be the destruction of the Imperial Government. Behold, how viciously the Bakufu authorities conduct their business! They discredit the commands of the Emperor and have entered into a treaty with a set of barbarians. Moreover when the Tai-ro (regency) and San-ke (heads of three great Tokugawa families) were summoned by their monarch to Kioto, they did not obey, but sent Mabe Jensho in their stead, upon the errand of imprisoning noblemen and arresting the gentry and common people. The Siogun being young, he is not personally able to administer affairs, consequently Ii Kamon no Kami decides every question, and Mabe Jensho assists him. Thus the management of the Yedo officials is growing worse and worse every day. Their guilt is very great, because at the same time that they oppose the will of the Emperor they also bring injury upon the house of Tokugawa. But there have been none who would complain of their crimes to the Government. I have been very angry with them and desired to eat their flesh. I have heard that the samurai of Owari, Mito, and Yechizen have conceived a plan for putting an end to Ii Kamon no Kami, and when this came to my knowledge I leaped up and danced three hundred times. Rejoiced as I was, I reflected that if I were to join in the execution of the plot people would laugh at me because I simply followed the lead of others. Therefore I arranged with a few of my own friends and am going to Kioto with the object of killing Mabe Jensho. It is our desire to cut off his head and impale it on a bamboo, and thus manifest our resolution to serve the rightful cause. But if we unfortunately are not successful in our project, and are arrested, we shall bravely declare our views without fear of keeping any thing back, and shall not cause any trouble to our lord of Choshiu. The reason why we do not obtain permission to travel from the Choshiu officials is, that we do not wish to give any embarrassment to the Daimio. We shall take all the blame of every thing that follows upon ourselves. Lately I sent a few memoranda of my opinions upon certain subjects to Riyosen Seigan. He presented them to the Emperor, and I have been honored with an acknowledgment from our Imperial master. There is nothing more glorious for me than to be distinguished in so honorable a manner, and I must prove my gratitude and loyalty without paying the slightest attention to the preservation of my life. I am not mindful of my duties to you, but I wish you to understand me that I have felt as if I were dead for a long time. I cannot write all I could wish, owing to the sorrowful state of my heart."

Having failed in his mission to Kioto he was again imprisoned. But he was not left without friends and supporters. The closing scenes of his life, given by one who knew him well, are as follows:

"In the next cell lay one Kusákahé, a reformer from the southern highlands of Satsuma. They were in prison for different plots indeed, but for the same intention; they shared the same beliefs and the same aspirations for Japan. Many and long were the conversations they held through the prison wall, and dear was the sympathy that soon united them. It fell first to the lot of Kusákahé to pass before the judges, and when sentence of death had been pronounced he was led towards the place of death below Yoshida's window. To turn the head would have been to implicate his fellow-prisoner; but he threw him a look from his eye and bade him farewell in a loud voice, with these two Chinese verses:

> It is better to be a crystal and be broken,
> Than to remain perfect like a tile upon the housetop.

So Kusákahé passed out of the theatre of this world.

"A little after, and Yoshida too must appear before the court. He seized on the opportunity of a public audience, confessed and gloried in his design, and, reading his auditors a lesson in the history of their country, told at length the illegality of the Shôgun's power and the crimes by which its exercise was sullied. So, having said his say for once, he was led forth and executed, in the thirty-first year of his age, having acquired fame as a poet, a patriot, a schoolmaster, a friend to learning, and a martyr to reform. He was not only wise and provident in thought, but surely a hero in execution. During the course of his trial the judge said: 'While Mumeta Genjiro was travelling in Choshiu, you joined him and sent a secret document signed with fictitious names, and otherwise planned to destroy the Bakufu Government. Your wickedness is great. Behold! when you offended before, the authorities liberated you with unmerited mercy. Why do you thus continue your enmity toward those who have treated you leniently?' 'You are mistaken,' replied Yoshida, 'I am a stranger to Mumeta Genjiro, and I do not know any thing about the secret document you refer to. But I must state that the true reason why I have been imprisoned is because first, I sent a communication expressive of my feelings on the subjects of Son O Jo-i to Ohara, saisho, and I have tried to induce the people of Choshiu to adopt my ideas. This communication has brought the suspicion of the authorities of Choshiu upon me. Secondly, I joined a few friends and went to Kioto for the purpose of killing Mabe Jensho. I do not know any thing further than this.' Thus he boldly avowed his deeds to the Bakufu officials, who had not expected such frankness. It is hard to say which is most remarkable, his capacity for command, which subdued his very jailers, his hot, unflagging zeal, or his stubborn superiority to defeat. He failed in each particular enterprise that he attempted; and yet we have only to look at his country to see how complete has been his general success. His friends and pupils made the majority of leaders in the final revolution, and many of them are, or were, high placed among the rulers of Japan. And when we see all round us these brisk, intelligent students, with their strange foreign air, we should never forget how Yoshida marched afoot from Choshiu to Yedo, and from Yedo to Nagasaki, and from Nagasaki back again to Yedo; how he boarded the American ship, his dress stuffed with writing material; nor how he languished in prison, and finally gave his death, as he had formerly given all his life and strength and leisure, to gain for his native land that very benefit which she now enjoys so largely. It is better to be Yoshida, and perish, than to be only Sákuma, and yet save the hide. Kusákahé, of Satsuma, has said the word: it is better to be a crystal and be broken.

"I must add a word," continued the narrator, "for I hope you will not fail to perceive that this is as much the story of a heroic people as that of a heroic man. It is not enough to remember Yoshida; we must not forget the common soldier, nor Kusákahé, nor the boy of eighteen, Normura, of Choshiu, whose eagerness betrayed the plot. It is exhilarating to have lived in the same days with these great-hearted men. Only a few miles from us, to speak by the proportion of the universe, while I was droning over my lessons Yoshida was goading himself to be wakeful with the stings of the mosquito; and while we were grudging a penny income tax, Kusákahé was stepping to death with a noble sentence on his lips."

# BIOGRAPHICAL ADDENDA.

THE foregoing collection of Japanese biographies is the first that was ever submitted to the foreign public; and as the editor was obliged to collect his facts and do his work thousands of miles away from the homes of the men he wished to write about, the reader will readily understand the difficulties he has had to contend with. Many men of high character, wide reputation and great usefulness have undoubtedly been omitted in this collection, whose very names are not known to the writer; and there are some who have done the public good service, in regard to whom his information was too limited to be of any use in the present publication. Among the latter, however, it affords him pleasure to mention the following:

Giro Yano, who had charge of the Washington Legation as *chargé ad interim* after the recall of Arinori Mori; Nabashema, Prince of Hizen, now Minister to Italy; Takaki Samro, at one time attached to the Japanese Legation in Washington, and subsequently Consul at San Francisco and New York; Tomita Tetsunosuke, who held precisely the same position, in addition to that of Consul at London; Yoshida Djiro, formerly Secretary of Legation at Washington and now in the Foreign Office at Tokio; Wooyeno Kagenori, Minister to England; Asada Yasunori and Amano Koziro, formerly in Washington and now in the Foreign Office; Takahira Kogoro the present *Chargé d Affairs* at Washington ; Kio Kawamoora, who relinquished his student life in America to become a painter, and who, after a long residence in France and Italy, returned to Japan with a brilliant reputation ; Kawase Matasaka, late Minister to Italy ; Tanaka Yoshio of the Interior Department in Tokio ; Riokichi Yatabe, who carried off all the honors of scholarship at the Cornell University and is now Professor of Botany in the Imperial University, of Japan ; Shiuichino Saito, the translator into English of the *Loyal Ronins*, by Tamenaga ; Hiboyuki Kato, the President, and Ichizo Hattori, Vice President of the Imperial University ; Masakoto Kimura and Tatsuo Kishmoto, professors in the University ; Noriuki Gah, and Yaskazon Tanabe, formerly of the Foreign Office and connected with the Iwakura Embassy ; and Giobu Neero, who was one of the first of the Satsuma Clan to espouse the cause of modern civilization in Japan, and who took charge of sixteen students during their residence in Europe, a large proportion of whom have since been honorably identified with the public interests of their native land. The editor also regrets that he has also been unable to give a sketch of the lives of Kei Sai Yei Sen and Watanabe Shoka, who take the lead among the painters of Japan, the last of whom possesses the wonderful skill of painting with both hands at the same time.

## PART SECOND.

# THE EMPIRE OF JAPAN.

AS the marvellous story of the Empire of Japan may be traced through more than twenty-five centuries, all that can be done in a single article is to touch upon the more important points of its geography and history. Whilst we look with amazement upon the recent developments in that highly favored land of the Orient, we shall also find that there has always been something allied to the wonderful in its career, whether we consider its physical characteristics, its people, or its government.

This Empire lies in the northwestern part of the Pacific Ocean, and consists of four large islands and a great number of smaller ones. It is separated on the west from Corea by a strait which is about five hundred miles wide; at its northwestern extremity is the island of Tisima, or "the Thousand Islands;" and at the north is the island of Krafto or Saghalien, which has long been held jointly by the Japanese and Russian governments, but now, according to a recent agreement, is held by Russia alone. The largest of the islands which compose the Empire is commonly called Nipon or Niphon — which name in reality belongs to the whole country — and contains about 94,000 square miles. The second is Yesso, with about 30,000 square miles; the third is Kiusiu, with 16,000 square miles; and the forth is Sikok, with an area of 10,000 square miles. The total length of the

Empire is 16,000 English miles, its greatest breadth a little more than 200, the number of islands 3850, and the entire area is estimated at about 150,000 square miles — all these figures being gathered from the latest official statistics. The sea-coasts are generally bold and rocky, and indented with very numerous bays forming spacious and secure harbors. The poetical title by which the Japanese designate their country is "The Land of the Rising Sun," which well describes its location as the most eastern of all the Asiatic empires, and their national emblem represents the sun rising out of the sea. The theory that America was originally peopled by Japanese, who were driven by stress of weather across the Pacific Ocean, is not only interesting, but claimed by many to be sustained by historical facts and traditions. That much of what passes as authentic history among the Japanese is mythical cannot be questioned, but there seems to be no reason to question the truthfulness of the statements which, with the help of Japanese scholars, the present writer has been able to cull from their history.

The cities of Japan are numerous. Two of them have become famous because selected as capitals — Miako or Saikio, the western capital, and Tokei, commonly called Yedo, the eastern capital. The first, which has never been open to foreigners, lies in latitude 35° 05' N., and longitude 4° 10' W., and was the ancient seat of government, dating its origin from A. D. 794. It stands on a plain, is surrounded with mountains, and directly through the centre runs the river Kano, noted for the purity of its water. It contains 374,000 inhabitants, and, though small when compared with the modern capital, is a place of great interest. It is entered by six principal roads. Its streets are clean, its temples, which may be counted by the hundred, are beautiful, and its silk factories have a wide reputation. The city of Tokei lies in latitude 35° 35' N., and longitude 139° 40' E., and in magnitude ranks next to Pekin in China. In 1861 it claimed to have about 1,500,000 inhabitants, but the population is now considerable less. While it has decreased in numbers, it has increased in commerce. Its gardens and open spaces are numerous, and give it an air of comfort and freedom which is unusual. It is intersected by many canals, and its bridges are numerous. As the present capital and residence of the Imperial court, it is the meeting-place of the national legislature, called a Parliament; it also has a well-endowed college, a governor and police force of three thousand, is supplied with hospitals and asylums for infants and paupers, and by means of railroads and telegraph-lines is daily facilitating its communication with the entire country. It became an open port in 1869. The second largest city in Japan is Osaca, on the island of Nipon. It is both an open port and the one through which Miako communicates with the ocean, from which it is distant thirty-three miles. Its canals and bridges are very numerous, the latter often very handsome. It has an extensive trade and is well fortified.

The next city in size is Yokohama, and is the successful rival of an older place in the immediate vicinity known as Kanagawa. It is on the Bay of Yedo, twenty miles from the capital, and within the last few years has become the most important seaport in the Empire. The harbor is spacious and secure, and is supplied with commodious piers, the accommodations being extensive, and the prevailing modes of living and of business giving to it the aspect of a port of the Western World. The next city of importance is Nagasaki, located on the island.

The Empire is partitioned into five kies, or departments, which surround the Imperial capital, and eight dōs or large divisions. The names of the former are Yamaciro, Yamato, Kawachi, Idume, and Settsu; while the latter, with the five kies, comprise eighty-four provinces, and the names of the dōs are Tokaido, with fifteen provinces; Tosando, with thirteen; Hokoorokdo, with seven; Sanindo, with eight; Sanyodo, with eight; Nankaido, with six; Saikaido, with nine; and Hokaido, with eleven provinces. In the vicinity of Saikaido are also two islands, each of which constitutes a province. The divisions which in this country are called counties, number one thousand three hundred and fifteen. In 1868 the Empire was divided into three political departments, the first of which embraced three foos, viz., Saikeo, or the western capital; Tokei or Yedo, the eastern capital, and Osaka; the second consisted of thirty-eight kens; and the third of three hundred and fifty hans.

Extending from one extremity of Japan to the other, across all its prominent islands, are mountains, many of them of volcanic origin and of great elevation. The highest of these, called Fusiyama, is about eighty miles from Yedo, about thirteen thousand feet high, and has a summit covered with perpetual snow. It is an extinct volcano, the last eruption having taken place in 1707. There are also thirteen other lofty peaks, bearing the names of Tookiyama, or "Moon Mountains;" Odaki; Nicquozan, or "Sunbeam Mountain;" Omine, or "Great Peak;" Sirayama, or "White Mountain;" Teteyama, or "Standing Mountain;" Kirisima, or "Fog Island;" Asozan; Tsukoobayama; Onsendaki, or

"Hot Spring;" Asawayama; Tourimiyama: and Iwakeyama. The most extensive range, known as the Hakoni, attains an elevation of six thousand feet, and traverses the island of Nipon from east to west. There are many volcanoes, and earthquakes are of frequent occurrence, but chiefly in the northeastern parts. The mountains of Yesso rise to a height of eight thousand feet, and a large part of the country is unexplored and covered with forests. The rivers of Japan are numerous, but short, on account of the mountains which send the waters in different directions. They are generally shallow, subject to great freshets during the rainy season, and their mouths are frequently obstructed by sand-bars. The three largest are Torregawa, Sinanogawa, and Kisogawa; and next to these come Oyeegawa, Fouzigawa, Sakagawa, and Okumagawa. The only fresh-water lake in the Empire of any size or importance is near the city of Miako. It is ten geographical miles wide and thirty-five miles long, and is called Biwako or Lake Omi. Small lakes or ponds abound, and hot springs are to be found in various parts of Kiusiu. Its harbor is very large and perfectly secure. This was the first port ever opened to foreigners in Japan, and a large trade has been carried on there by the merchants of China and of Holland, where they have for a long time been permitted to locate factories. The other principal cities of Japan are Neigata, an open port on the northeast coast of Nipon: Kobe, also an open port, near Osaca; Hokodaté, the open port of the island of Yesso; and Saki, formerly a place of importance and open to foreigners, but now holding no commercial intercourse with the outside world.

The climate of Japan is unequal, but as a general

rule the central and most densely populated portion is mild and agreeable. In the extreme south, however, the heat is often oppressive, while in the island of Yesso the mercury occasionally sinks far below zero, and snow falls to a great depth on the mountains and in the valleys. The sun during the hottest days is much less debilitating than on the coast of China or in India, and as to the general conditions of salubrity, the Empire is highly favored. The autumn is a kind of second summer, the months of October and November being the most pleasant and genial of the entire year, and amply compensating for the heat and frequent rains of May and June. A marked difference is said to exist between the climates of the eastern and western coasts of Nipon, the latter being much colder, and receiving a greater fall of snow, than the former; and this is attributed to the fact that on the east there is a broad belt of warm water flowing constantly to the northeast, while the Japan sea has a cold current constantly setting toward the southwest from the Sea of Okhotsk. The month of September usually brings with it rough weather, and those fearful hurricanes called typhoons, which do the greatest damage along the eastern coast of the Empire: and, as Japan is a land of earthquakes, it is said that they have had a palpable influence on the climate of the Empire.

The most ancient name by which the Empire was known was Yamato Zima, meaning "east of the mountains." Its present name is a corruption of Jipunquo, which is of Chinese origin, and means, as we have already stated, the "Country at the Root of the Sun," or the "Land of the Rising Sun," because, when so named, it was the most eastern in the known world; and Nipon, now used in Oriental countries, is the Chinese pronunciation of the same name. Another name which is sometimes used is that of "The Country of Many Islands." The true origin of its people is lost in tradition or fable — it is claimed that prior to the first Emperor it had existed 2479 years — but it dates its chronological history back to the year 667 before the Christian era. The first man of note connected with the Empire of whom any thing is actually known was Zinmu or Jimmu, who, after a career of conquest, established himself at the foot of the volcanic mountain called Keresemi, in the province of Fuga. From that point he extended his explorations and sway through the entire length of the Japanese territory, and is represented as civilizing the nation and reforming the existing laws and government. The credit is also awarded to him of having divided time into months and years, and in his person was vested the office of high priest, representative of Heaven, and Emperor or Mikado. He established his capital at Kasiwabara in Yamato, but the location of the capital was frequently changed by the succeeding Emperors to the various provinces of Yamato, Omi, Setten, Nagato, and Kawadi, and after 1464 years from the time of Zinmu it was fixed at Saikio, or Miako, in the province of Yamaciro; but after the revolution of 1867 it was located at Tokei or Yedo.

The total number of Emperors, Empresses and Shiogoons who have reigned over Japan in an unbroken line is one hundred and twenty-six. From the earliest times down to the present day they were called Mikados, although for about six hundred years the men who actually administered the Government were called Shiogoons or Tycoons; and it was in the year 1867 that the Mikado or Tenno resumed his ancient privileges. To give a minute account of all the rulers of Japan, and of the deeds which characterized their several reigns, is quite impossible; all that can be done in these pages is to pesent a summary of the most distinguished persons of the Empire, together with a passing notice of the more important events with which their names are associated. One fact which the reader should bear in mind is this, that the position of Emperor of Japan has always been hereditary and his person venerated; and while many sovereigns may have been comparatively powerless, the line of descent has been unbroken. In the person of the Mikado Zinmu, the founder of the line, vested the office of high priest, representative of Heaven and Emperor, and hence the modern idea of calling him the spiritual head of the nation. Another important fact to be remembered has reference to the title of Shiogoon or Tycoon. The possessors of this dignity were merely military chieftains who by intrigue or personal prowess acquired sway over the people. They belonged to various families, and the rivalries which naturally existed among them were the cause of the bitter wars which prevailed in Japan for hundreds of years. They never failed, with the people, to respect the office or position of the hereditary monarch, but while they wielded power they inspired fear rather than veneration. From the earliest period in the history of the Empire mention is made of three things which necessarily appertained to the person who sat upon the throne; viz., a sword, a mirror, and a ball of crystal. These are known by the name of Sanjioo no jinji, and considered as symbols of the Imperial power. The Emperor Su-jin-tenno, who lived in B. C. 97, was the last ruler of Japan prior to the commencement of the Christian era. He built a Sintu temple there, established an army over which he placed four generalissimos, ordered the first census of Nipon and Kiusiu, levied taxes for the purpose of building large ships, ordered the draining of lakes for irrigation, and was the first ruler to open intercourse with Corea. His successor was Sui-nin-tenno, who ascended the throne in A. D. 6. He acquired distinction by abolishing the barbarous custom which acquired, that on the death of the Emperor the Empress and all her court should commit suicide by hara-kiri. Although the Empress of Sui-nin came to a natural death, the highest of her lady attendants killed themselves by cutting their throats, and then the Emperor decreed that this custom should also be abolished. This ruler devoted his attention to agriculture, and during his reign eight hundred canals and ponds were built in different parts of Japan for irrigation.

The next man of note was Keko-tenno, who reigned between the years 71 and 130 A. D. After quelling obstinate rebellions in Kiusiu and the northern part of Nipon, he caused the arable lands of the Empire to be surveyed, and with a view of guarding against famine, caused the establishment of granaries in all the larger town of the Empire. The Emperor Senmu-tenno reigned from A. D. 131 to 190, creating the office of daijin, the second position of honor and power in the realm; and the first dignitary of that rank who ever left Japan as an embassador was Tomomi Iwakura, who visited America and Europe in the year 1872.

Among the men who distinguished themselves during the reign of Senmu was Yamato Daki; he held the office of commander-in-chief of the army, and was called the "Prince of warriors." His conquests extended as far as the island of Yesso; and because his wife Adzuma threw herself into the sea to appease a terrible storm, her name was given to the region of country which her husband had subdued. Chinai-tenno, who was the son of Yamato Daki, reigned for eight years, from A. D. 191 to 200, and the principal fact recorded of him was that he died from disappointment caused by being defeated in an expedition conducted by himself in person against the rebellion of a tributary prince of the Empire, named Kumaoso of Kiusiu.

The next ruler of Japan was an Empress, Jingu Kogu, the wife of Chinai-tenno. She accompanied her husband in his unsuccessful expedition, and after his death assumed the reins of power. She distinguished herself by leading an invading army against the kingdom of Corea, compelling the inhabitants to give up their treasures and to promise an annual tribute to Japan. She had several children, one of whom became a very distinguished Emperor. Her various conquests gave her a fame which surpassed all her predecessors, and her life and deeds of heroism are widely commemorated by the painters of Japan and in the popular literature of the country. Osin-tenno, the son of Jingu Kogu, ascended the throne in A. D. 270, and reigned about forty-three years. Although not born when his mother conquered Corea, the honor of that conquest has been given to him. In the second year of his reign the islands of Yesso and Saghalien voluntarily submitted to his rule, and three of the kingdoms of Corea continued to pay him an annual tribute. In 283 he brought a woman from Corea to teach his people the art of working in silk; in 284 an improved breed of horses was also introduced from the same country; in 285 a philosopher from China, named Wonin, introduced Chinese letters into Japan, from which time the works of Confucius became generally known; and in 300, from the wood of an old warvessel, a musical instrument called the *koto* was made and has been in use down to the present time. In 306, Osin sent an embassy to China for the purpose of obtaining further information in regard to the production and the manufacture of silk. It is related of this Emperor that, having been advised by the brother of his prime minister that the latter was conspiring against the throne, he caused them both to plunge their arms into boiling water, when, the ordeal proving favorable to the minister, the informer was executed. After his death the largest temples were erected to his memory, and he received the title of *hatchimang*, or the "god of war," and his reign has always been looked upon with national pride by the Japanese.

The next man of note was Jintoku-tenno. During his reign (313-399) extensive inundations led to the construction of dikes along the rivers, and rice-houses and mills for cleaning rice were for the first time built. He also sent an expedition to put down a rebellion in the island of Yesso. Lichu-tenno came to the throne in 400, and was the first to provide for the writing of a history of the Empire, for which duty he appointed two scholars; and under the patronage of Yuriyaku-tenno (479) mulberry-trees were planted throughout the Empire, and special attention was first given to the manufacture of silk. About this time also skilful carpenters were induced to emigrate from Corea, and an embassy was sent to that country to make certain collections of Chinese literature.

The first event of importance connected with the era beginning with the year 500, was the introduction of the Buddhist religion into Japan, which was destined to take the place, to a great extent, of the Sintu religion and the moral instructions of Confucius. This occurred in 552, when an embassy was sent over from Corea, and presented to the Japanese Emperor a collection of books, accompanied by an image of Buddha Sakya, the leading idea of the books being that a pure life was desirable, and that it could only be secured through self-denial.

One of the most active converts to the new religion was Moumaya-do-no-wosi, son of the Emperor Nakatomi; he was a gentle character and devoted to the new faith, and at the time of his death there were forty-six Buddhist temples, eight hundred and sixteen priests, and five hundred and sixty-nine *religieuses* in the Empire. The introduction of Buddhism through China and Corea brought with it some of the customs of those countries — the use of the *nengo*, or year-name, for marking events and dates, and also abdication by the Emperors after very short reigns, which was followed by the elevation of mere children, whereby the sovereignty was for a time reduced to a name, and the power of the nation given into the hands of the ministers. Among these child-rulers were the Empress Seiwa, who began her reign at the age of nine; the Emperors Yozei, at eight; Daigo, at thirteen; Reizan, at eighteen; Yenwou, at eleven; Goitsi, at nine; Konye, at three; and Rokusio, at two years of age. About this time a man named Nakatomi-Kamatari-ko obtained great influence, and is still remembered as the founder of the laws of Japan. In the middle of the seventh century Ten-si, a real emperor, ascended the throne, and distinguished himself in warlike exploits against Corea and Tartary, and then it was that Yesso was subjugated. In 794, the general government having been divided into eight boards after the manner of the Chinese, the central power of the Empire was fixed at Miako; and about this time was published the *Rits Rio*, a code of laws which are partly in force at the present time. Another notable event of this period was the introduction of an alphabet, called the Hira Kana, to facilitate the reading of Chinese, the name of the scholar and venerated man who brought about this change being Kobo-dai-si. It now became a custom with the Emperors on abdicating the throne to adopt the garb and religious life of the Buddhist priests, which did much to perpetuate the prevailing religion. During the reign of the Emperor Itsisio (987-1012) two terrible plagues visited the Empire. His successor, Go-ri-sen, became famous for his heroism in putting down a rebellion in the northern part of Nipon.

The 500 years which followed A. D. 1000, and now come under consideration, are of greater importance than the preceding era, and may be written in the successive rise to power of individuals connected with the peerage of the realm, and especially the families of Fusiwara, Sungawara, Minnamoto, Tatchibanna, and other names regarded as illustrious and held in veneration to the present day. Among these may be mentioned Ten-mang, the greatest literary character of his country and an able man, who through a rival was banished to the island of Kiusiu, where he was starved to death, and to whose memory many splendid temples were subsequently erected in Miako and Yedo. Another famous personage was Yoshi-iyé, who, as commander-in-chief, subdued the rebellious provinces of Mootz and Kwanto, and because of his bravery and other qualifications, was called "the eldest son of the god of war;" and still another celebrity was Kio Mori, descended from the Emperor Kwan-mu, who was a prominent actor in the affairs of the nation, and is remembered as the ablest and most unscrupulous minister of his time, when the whole Empire was devastated by war, but who at the age of fifty-one shaved his head and nominally became a priest. One of his daughters became an empress, and a grandson an emperor.

The opening of the twelfth century was marked by many deeds of rare valor and of cruelty, and the conflicts between rival families were continuous and desperate. In 1164 the ex-Emperor Sho-toku was banished to the province of Sanuki, where he wrote a letter to the reigning Emperor on a piece of his shirt with his blood, and then died of starvation. In 1170 Tame-tomo became famous for his power in drawing the bow and as a rover on the South seas, and because he was the original occupier of the Liookioo or Loochoo islands, came to be considered as a sacred personage. The most famous Emperor who reigned during this exciting period was Gozira-kawa, who died in 1192, at the age of sixty-seven. He had taken an active part in the working of the Government for forty years, and after abdicating the throne witnessed a part of the reigns of five emperors, his sons and grandsons, and finally died in tranquility. Two men who are generally regarded as among the greatest of their era were Yoritomo and Yoshitzuné. They were brothers, both attained the position of Shiogoon, and were desperate in their rivalry to each other. The first is generally regarded as the greatest hero in Japanese history, and the first Shiogoon of the dynasty which ended in 1867. He died in 1199, at the age of fifty-three, from the effects of a fall from his horse. The second man just named is looked upon as the mirror of chivalry, and his conduct is held up for the imitation of the youth of his country. The former conspired to take the life of the latter, and when reduced to an extremity destroyed himself after killing his wife and children. During the twelfth and thirteenth centuries the Empire of Japan was almost continually engaged in intestine wars; severe contests occurred between the Shiogoons of the north and south; and among the families which now rose to power were Hojio, Ashikanga, Nitta, Hossokawa, and others who occupied prominent positions, and it was during the period in which they lived that the following events occurred: In 1260 the Nitsiren sect of Buddhists was introduced, and it was one of the saints connected with this order, named Sayshogosama, who subsequently became famous as a persecutor of Christians. In 1276 Corea became tributary to Japan, and an embassy was sent from China to obtain tribute money from the Chinese. In 1281 the Chinese despatched a naval expedition, with embassadors, to Japan, when thirty thousand of the invaders were taken prisoners and killed, and one of the ambassadors was beheaded. In 1321 the office known as the Kirokusho, or "recorder of facts," was established at Miako, and twenty years afterwards an influential minister published a work called *The Red Book of the Court of Miako*. About the year 1367 there was an extensive war on the island of Kiusiu, when the Satsuma family largely increased its power at the expense of Kikootchi. In that year also Ashikanga, when ten years of age, was appointed Shiogoon; he died in 1408. He was a man of great ability and influence, was styled by the Chinese Nippon-wo, or king of Japan, and from the reigning Emperor received the title of Kubosama, having been the first person thus honored. The office of Shiogoon became hereditary in his family, and the seat of their power was Kamakura. In 1415 an arbitrary law was passed by which all mercantile engagements were at once ended and all debts cancelled, which was the cause of much trouble and anxiety among the people. In 1466 commenced the war known in history as the "Onin," which lasted more than ten years, and was followed by a famine in 1472, and an earthquake in 1475 destroyed a large part of the city of Osaka. A severe drought occurred in 1496, which was succeeded by another famine and a destructive disease among the forest trees.

From this time forward the leading events in Japanese history multiplied with increased rapidity, and hence, for the sake of convenience, we shall divide the remainder of our chronological record into centuries. The sixteenth century brought no cessation from intestine war and assassination. The year 1510 was signalized by the fact that Nango, a servant and relative of the minister at Kamakura, Ooyay Soongi, rebelled against his master, and took possession of his castle and territory in the province of Etsingo, and became a man of great power. In 1521, for the first time in many years, the Emperor made his appearance in public, and his court became impoverished. This condition of affairs lasted for at least fifteen years, when the Emperor Go Tsutchi died in such poverty that his body lay unburied for several days for want of money. Two years afterwards an attempt was made to trade with China, but it was unsuccessful, because the Chinese coasts were infested with Japanese pirates. In November, 1533, there was observed an extraordinary number of falling stars, and in the following year the country was visited by a fatal epidemic. Three years afterwards there was a bitter quarrel between different sects of the Buddhist priests, one of the results of which was the burning of one half of the city of Miako. In 1541, according to the best authorities, Antony Mora, Francis Zaimor, and Anthony Pexot, three Portuguese merchants, in their voyage from Siam to China, were wrecked upon the coast of Kiusiu, and the firearms which they had with them caused a profound sensation throughout the Empire, and the fact was noted in the national calendars. In 1543 the Portuguese merchants came back again, bringing with them Jesuit missionaries, and from that time the history of the Empire was chronicled in the literature of Europe. Francis Xavier visited the country in 1549, and after remaining there two years left it, disheartened with the realities of missionary work.

About 1557 the military chieftain named Nobu Nanga made his appearance on the stage of public affairs, and for more than twenty years was the master-spirit of the Empire, wielding the power of a Shiogoon. He was descended from Kio-Mori, and his rule was quite as grasping and severe as that of any of his predecessors. In 1557 he put to death, for private reasons, his youngest brother, and seven years afterwards he killed his father-in-law, the lord of Mino. and took all his possessions. He began in 1569 a crusade against the Buddhists, and in a few years succeeded in destroying a large number of their temples and massacred many of their priests ; at the same time, for selfish purposes, he encouraged the Jesuits. In 1572 he had a difficulty with the Shiogoon, Yoshi-aki, whom he arrested and put in prison, thus bringing to an end the real power of the Ashikanga family. He had many able generals in league with him, the three most famous of whom were Hideyoshi, Akitchi-mitsu-hide, and Iyeyas. Under his encouragement the Jesuits rose to favor and power at court, and in 1581 they claimed to have in Japan two hundred churches and not less than one hundred and fiffty thousand Christians. He was reputed a brave, ambitious, and able man, and not without many moral virtues, and he laughed at the worship of the gods and considered the bonzes as impostors. In 1582 he was gradually overrunning all Japan, and was liberal in giving to his kindred the property he had acquired by conquest. He built a temple in which he collected idols of all the gods of Japan, and placing in the midst of it a statue of himself called Xanthi, or "supreme ruler," he issued an edict commanding all men to worship that image and no other. The first to obey this order was his eldest son, and the example was followed by the gentry and people in their course. His end was in keeping with his life; after being surrounded in his castle at Miako, he was wounded with an arrow, and then consumed in the building where he was sheltered, in the forty-ninth year of his age. When he died the tide of prosperity turned and ebbed until it gradually swept the whole Jesuit priesthood from the shores of Japan. The immense treasures which he had accumulated in the course of many years in the city of Azutchi-yama were given away and squandered in three days by his late confederate, Akitchi-mitsu-hide. After the death of Nobu Nanga, the man who had once been his servant, and afterwards his chief military assistant, and who had acquired a great reputation as a leader, became the military ruler or Shiogoon. His name, which was originally Hideyoshi, was changed a number of times until he became known as Taikosama. He was of low origin and insignificant in appearance. His chief castle was at Osaka, which he did much to improve by digging canals and perfecting its fortifications. He had six wives. In 1583, with his permission, the Jesuit fathers induced four young noblemen to visit the Pope in Rome, which expedition lasted for eight years. In 1585 he received from the Emperor the family name of Toyotomi. About that time he became an earnest supporter of the Jesuits, although he would not accept their religion for himself; but when his plans had ripened, and the Jesuits were confident of increasing success, he suddenly gave them notice to quit the country within twenty days, forbidding them to preach their religion on pain of death. In 1586 he took forcible possession of Nagasaki, and made it a Government port and property, declaring it to be the only place where foreign trade should be permitted. The threat made by Taikosama was not carried out, and the Jesuits continued in the country, and he was charged with changing his policy because he desired to use their ships in a project to invade Corea. He led an army of three hundred thousand men against that country, one half of whom were destroyed, when embassadors were sent to Japan and the following demands were made: (1) That eight provinces of Corea be handed over to Japan; (2) that the Emperor of China give one of his daughters to Taikosama; (3) that there should be free trade between the two countries; and (4) that China and Corea should pay Japan a yearly tribute. In 1592 and the following year two envoys from Manila and the Philippines, were received by Taikosama, the first of which brought with them four recollets of St. Francis to enter the missionary service. Among their presents was a Spanish horse, whose blood has probably affected the breed now known in Japan. About this time events occurred which led Taiko to believe that his nephew intended to usurp his place, whereupon, after many intrigues, he caused him to be put to death, as well as thirty-one women and children, all members of his family. In 1596 a comet was visible in the Empire, and on its disappearance a terrible earthquake occurred, which seemed to prognosticate the death of the Shiogoon. While winking at the stealthy operations of the Jesuits, he caused twenty-five of them to be punished by the death of the cross. This act, as if in self-defence, he followed up with an order that all the Roman Catholics residing in Nagasaki should be at once sent home in their ships. But notwhitstanding this hostility, when he became sick in 1598, he admitted a Romish priest to his bedside, and then died, all his nobility, according to the Fathers, "being much better pleased to see him on the list of dead gods than in the land of living men." In the annals of Japan in the year 1599 is given as that in which the English and Dutch ships visited the country, and they are said to have come to the town of Saccai, near Osaka. Dutch pilots had already for several years been navigating the surrounding seas, and William Adams, the English pilot of the Dutch fleet of five sail which left Texel in June, 1598, did not reach Boongo until April, 1600, when his crew was found to be reduced to nine or ten men.

The great event which characterized the beginning of the seventeenth century was the accession to power of Iyeyas Mikawa-no-kami. He was born of a good family, but had succeeded as a military man by depending upon himself. At this period the Emperor was a mere boy, and although the grandson by marriage of Iyeyas, that man claimed and for a long time wielded, the sceptre of power. As the friend of the regent-Emperor quite a number of the provincial governors formed a league against him; and in October, 1600, near Lake Owomi, a battle was fought which has ever been considered one of the most important and decisive connected with Japanese history, and Iyeyas was the victor. His opponents were scattered, and he became at once master of public affairs. The most important of his many captives in the late battle was a noted chieftain named Konishi Setsu, who had been viceroy of Kiusiu and commander-in-chief both of the naval and military forces in the Corean war, who was beheaded. But, notwithstanding this act of severity, Iyeyas treated his late enemies with kindness and granted a general amnesty. He acquired great power, one secret of which seems to have been that when he once made a promise he never broke it, the most perfect reliance being therefore placed upon his word.

The portion of Japan which held out the longest against the new conqueror was the island of Kiusiu, but its principal ruler, Satsuma, was obliged to yield. Prior to the crowning military achievement of Iyeyas the Imperial, ecclesiastical and commercial capitals of the Empire had been Miako, Narra, and Osaka; but he removed the Government to Yedo, which at that time was an insignificant place with only one street, known then and now as Koji Matchi. He was reputed a true lover of his country, and was never accused of being personally ambitious. He was a friend to all kinds of internal improvements, ruled with wisdom and discretion, and was honored with the title of *Se-i-dai-Shiogoon*, or "tranquillizer of barbarians and commander-in-chief." The most important event of his reign was the promulgation of a code of laws, one hundred in number, which he bequeathed to his descendants in power as a guide to them in the office he hoped would be hereditary in his family. These laws have had a paramount influence with the rulers of Japan ever since the death of Iyeyas, and to a very great extent his ambitious hopes have been realized by the subsequent fame and power of his immediate family. Between these laws and the writings of Confucius and Mencius the similarity is manifest. Whatever their intrinsic merits, it is certain that their effect upon the nation was most salutary, for it was blessed with an uninterrupted peace for more than two hundred years after the death of Iyeyas. So impressed with this fact were the nobles and the people of Japan at a later day, that in 1806 they inaugurated a national festival for the sole puposc of commemorating this unprecedented fact.

For about twenty years prior to the year 1614, the Jesuits had obtained such a footing in Japan that they claimed to have visited the whole Empire, and to have made more than one hundred thousand converts. Although they entered the country as missionaries, they were subsequently denounced as preachers of sedition and organizers of rebellion. The opposition which they called forth soon became so bitter that in 1636 the Government issued an order that the image of the Saviour as it appeared on the copper medals should be periodically desecrated by being trampled under foot; and those orders remained in force until the conclusion of treaties with Christian nations in recent times. After such demonstrations it cannot be thought strange that when the time came for driving the Jesuits out of the country the expulsion should have been attended with many acts of cruelty.

The first decree of banishment was issued by Iyeyas in 1614, but some fifteen years elapsed before the movement was in any degree successful. A new edict against the Roman Catholic Church was issued in 1666, and two years afterwards an order was promulgated prohibiting the erection of Buddhist temples, which has remained in force to the present time.

In 1720 the Buddhist priesthood held a festival throughout the Empire, by which they commemorated the eleventh centenary of the establishment of their religion.

In 1839 the Portuguese and Spanish were finally expelled, but a single Dutch factory was permitted to remain at the island of Hirado. In 1709 another attempt was made to regain Japan to the Church of Rome, but it was unsuccessful. Various attempts at long intervals, were made by different foreign nations to re-open a trade with the country. The Dutch, as well as the Japanese, bitterly opposed all such measures — the former from cupidity, and the latter from a motive of self-defence. According to the native annals, the coast of Japan was visited by foreign vessels in 1637, 1673, 1768, 1791, 1793, 1796, 1803, 1808, 1813, and 1829. American ships first arrived at Nagasaki in 1846 under Com. Biddle, and Com. M. E. Perry made his visit in 1853, made memorable by resulting in a treaty with the United States. In 1854, Sir James Stirling, an English admiral, visited Nagasaki, and also concluded a treaty with Japan; and in 1858 it was proclaimed by the Japanese that they had concluded treaties with the

American, English, Dutch, Russian, and Portuguese nations. The last of the Shiogoons who really held the reins of power was Iyaymutchi; he reigned from 1859 to 1866, when he died, having been the leading figure in the late Rebellion which resulted in dissolving the dual government which had existed for six hundred years, and in restoring to his proper position the true Emperor of Japan. In 1867 an effort was made by Yoshi-hisa to be recognized as the legitimate successor of Shiogoon Iyaymutchi, but it was unsuccessful; and before the close of that year the spiritual Emperor, who had just found himself received as the true and only ruler of the Empire, died in the thirty-eighth year of his age, and left upon the throne his son, a boy of fifteen years, who is the present Emperor of Japan.

As to the events which have taken place in that Empire during the last twenty years, they resemble the stories of romance, and are among the marvels of the age. Into that subject we cannot fully enter at present, but the following particulars may be mentioned for purposes of reference, and those who may desire more elaborate information will find it admirably set forth in a volume entitled *New Japan*, from the pen of an English diplomat, Samuel Mossman. The treaty with Com. Perry was ratified in 1854, at Kanagawa, and the ports of Hakodadi and Simoda were opened to foreign commerce; in 1855 the Russian Government, through Admiral Poutiatine, visited Simoda and secured the ratification of a treaty, which fact was strangely commemorated by the destruction of Simoda by an earthquake; in 1858 treaties were also concluded by England and France, and the ports opened to them were Kanagawa, Nagasaki, Hakodadi, Hiogo, Osaka, and Neigata; in 1859,

British and American legations were established at Yedo; in 1860, Dutch and Prussian treaties were signed at Yedo, and several assassinations occurred in that year, as well as in the preceding and succeeding years; in 1862 a diplomatic mission of about thirty-five members was sent to Europe by way of America, having sailed in an English frigate called the *Odin*, and the envoy was Takeno Votschie Shemodze; in 1863 the British and American legation buildings were destroyed at Yedo, and a retrograde policy was inaugurated by the Japanese officials, one of the results of whose hostile action was the payment of an indemnity to America and the leading powers of Europe; in 1865 the allied envoys received the consent of the Mikado to the treaties; in 1866 and 1867, as already intimated, the Imperial Government was changed from the old to the new form; in 1868 was commenced the civil war in Japan, and the Mikado became the sole monarch; in 1870 the Japanese Government resumed with great ardor its work of reform, the prominent ideas being the education of Japanese students in foreign countries, and the establishment of diplomatic relations with America, England, Russia, Germany, Austria, and France; and in 1872 the great embassy, headed by Tomomi Iwakura, visited the United States and Europe, the calendar of the western nations was substituted for that of old Japan, and the Empire found itself rapidly becoming an important member of the family of nations.

And now for a few remarks respecting the people of Japan as they existed just prior to their new birth. They are divided into eight classes, as follows: the Koongays, or Mikado nobility; the Daimios, or Yedo nobility; the Hattamotos, or lower Daimios; the Hiakshos, or farmers without rank or title; the Shokonoris, who are artisans; the Akindos, or merchants; the Kiveiamonos, or actors and beggars; and the Yaytas, who are turners, shoemakers, and manufacturers or dealers in leather. In the Island of Yesso are to be found a people called Ainos, who closely resemble the Indians of North America. The religions of the Empire are two; Sintuism and Buddhism, while the higher classes seem to be partial to the moral teachings of Confucius. The Japanese language is one of letters, and not of characters, like the Chinese; but because of the very frequent use of the latter by people in every sphere, a great many difficulties arise both in speaking and writing. The literature of the country is quite extensive, cheap books and instructive art-productions are always in great demand, and a very large proportion of the people are able to read and write, and a love of drawing and painting is very common. The food upon which they subsist is rice, the chief production fish and a great variety of vegetables; and among their leading productions may be mentioned silk, tea, cotton, hemp, salt, gold, silver, iron, copper, coal, and lead. Opium, which is the bane of China, they do not use, but they substitute for it a good quality of tobacco, which they grow and manufacture in large quantities. Their fruits are numerous, and their knowledge of horticulture and the secrets of the soil is so extensive that many of the Japanese in this country have looked upon the agricultural mission of Mr. Horace Capron, who was invited to teach them the science of agriculture, as a most useless enterprise. Their skill in manufacturing is of the highest order, and when they shall have learned the importance of increasing the number of useful articles in every department of labor under the influence of modern improvements, it is likely they will hardly be equalled by any of the nations of the world. It has already passed into history that their display at the great Vienna Exposition was wonderful, and superior to that of any of the Asiatic nations. One of the most striking illustrations of intellectual activity among the Japanese is found in the use they are making of the press; books and newspapers, both in the Japanese and English languages, are multiplying every day, and are universally becoming modelled upon the literary plans of the Western nations. In speaking of the press of Japan, one of the Yokohama papers lately made this remark: "It is now but three or four years since the press sprang into existence in Japan, yet it is already being used for the serious discussion of weighty questions, and certainly by its vigor and earnestness, its candor, fearlessness and courtesy, puts to shame a large section of the local European press, which seems only to exist to prove how little salt is worth which has lost its savor." In literature and religion, in commerce and education, very great changes have taken place within the last four years; and from a chart of Japan, recently published by authority, we gather the following items of information:

"The total number of temples in the Empire devoted to the Sintu religion was ninety-seven, of which thirty-five were supported by the general Government, and the rest by the provincial authorities; the Buddhists temples numbered two hundred and ninety-six thousand nine hundred, to which were attached 268,654 priests, divided into eleven sects; but all this religious machinery has since been abolished by Imperial decree; the population of the metropolis of Yedo had been reduced to 1,194,390; the two colleges in that city contained five hundred and sixty-three pupils, but have greatly increased since 1872; there were also thirteen hospitals and almshouses; the Imperial army consisted of seven battalions of infantry, four of artillery, and two companies of cavalry; regular army, twenty battalions of infantry: cadets in military schools, seven hundred and twenty-six; ships of war sixteen, including one iron-clad, officered by one thousand three hundred and seven men; steamships, sixty-nine, including twenty-two iron ships, and the large sailing vessels numbered eighteen; lighthouses, sixteen; dockyards, two, at Yokohama and Nagasaki; mines worked by Government, three; it was also stated that manufacturing establishments were on the increase in Yedo, Yokohama, and Hiogo, and two railroads between Yedo and Yokohama, and between Osaka and Kobi, were both in partial operation. The working Government of Japan, as now organized under the supreme control of the Emperor, is divided into ten departments: executive, with two hundred and thirty-seven officials; public works, three hundred and seventy-five; department of religion, one hundred and thirty-eight; judicial department, one hundred and sixty-nine; foreign affairs, one hundred and sixteen; treasury department, five hundred and thirty-nine; agricultural department, one hundred and ninety-two; war and navy departments, eight hundred and ninety-one; educational department, two hundred and twenty-one; and the Imperial court consists of two hundred and forty officials. The name of the reigning Emperor or Mikado is Mutsuhito, born in 1852, and recognized as heir in 1860, and he came to the throne in 1867. He is married, the Empress being his senior by two years. His six uncles and great-uncles (one of whom was recently in Prussia and another in England), and sister in Yedo, also three brothers (one of whom has been a student at Annapolis), with an aunt in Yedo, constitute the royal family of Japan.

The thinking men of Japan now claim — and the facts support them in their views — that the revolution of progress now going on is needed, stands upon a firm foundation, and will be triumphant. All the officials and the higher classes, and a large proportion of the masses, are anxious to throw aside every impediment calculated to retard their progress in the career upon which they have entered. They would be loyal to the Mikado and the Empire, but they want more civil if not religious liberty than they have hitherto enjoyed, protection in their commercial interests and all the advantages resulting from a high order of education. That they are thoroughly in earnest is proven most conclusively by the truly wonderful changes that they themselves have carried out during the last twenty years.

The barriers of exclusiveness have been removed, and many seaports, as already stated, opened to the trade of foreign countries; the Imperial ruler has thrown aside all the mystery and seclusion which have been held sacred for a thousand years, and with his dynasty has entered the comity of nations; the feudal system has given place to a Government allied in character to the enlightened nations of the earth, and the Daimios have given up their estates for the benefit of the whole country; foreigners who were treated as enemies, are now welcomed as friends; customs like those of wearing two swords and committing enforced suicide have been abolished; money has been liberally expended by the central Government in sending its youth to be educated in foreign lands; schools, seminaries of learning, scientific and benevolent institutions, all founded upon the models of the Western nations, have been established, and are daily becoming grounded in the elements of prosperity; a free press, as we have seen, has been established and is respected ; also a new postal system ; the sea and land forces have been re-organized, and placed upon a basis of such stability as to make Japan the most invulnerable nation in the Orient ; all the modern helps to a safe navigation of the extensive coasts of the Empire have been introduced ; the old Japanese calendar has been superseded by that of the Western nations excepting Russia ; talented men in literature and science and diplomacy have been invited to take office in the Empire for the benefit of their experience ; a gold and silver currency similar to that of the United States has been established ; a system of railroads has been organized and partly completed, which has already added wonderful facilities to travel and commerce ; and by a line of telegraph news may now be transmitted from Yedo to London in less than fifty hours.

Such are some of the marvels that have actually been accomplished, and they surely prove that the Japanese are not only in earnest in all that they are doing, but that their genius for going ahead is allied to that of the "universal Yankee nation." What they have accomplished in less than one generation has not in any part of Europe been secured in less than a century.

But there is another wonder connected with this great Japanese revolution; which is, that the nation is marching upward and onward without casting a thought upon what the great empires of India and China may think or desire. The nation, like the individuals who have come to the front, is fearless, proud, delicately strung, and independent.

Where can be found a better illustration of lofty courage than was presented by Japan in her recent difficulty with China about Formosa? She felt that she had justice on her side, and looking upon the thirty-five million of her united and loyal people with perfect confidence, she said, "The five hundred million of China shall not frighten us from the path of duty and right." China did the proper thing in submitting, and ought to be applauded for her course; but when the subject of indemnity came up, Japan (unlike certain so-called civilized nations), true to her lofty instincts, asked only that the necessary expenses should be paid, and scorned to manifest a grasping love of gain.

The only great questions connected with the prosperity of Japan which are not yet settled, are those having reference to taxation and revenue, and the opening of the entire country to foreigners and to religion. The difficulties attending each of them cannot be fully understood by people in other countries; and yet there is nothing singular about them, if we remember that even in the United States we have never been free from some sort of excitement growing out of these identical questions. Good men and true are to-day working hard in Japan to perfect a system of taxation and revenue which will help the public purse and make the financial resources of the Empire equal to its natural progress; when the European powers, headed by England, shall stop their domineering demands to have the Empire thrown open at all hazards, then perhaps the Imperial Government may listen to reasonable appeals; and when the Japanese are convinced that religious fanaticism is a blessing, even in such countries as England and America, and that by giving the largest liberty they will not be made wretched by the intrigues of the Romish Church, then they may consider the policy of opening wide the gates to all denominations of Christians.

With regard to the question of allowing foreigners to trade in all parts of the interior of Japan, a leading Japanese newspaper of Yedo recently made this remark: "The chief reasons why this measure cannot be carried out to-day are — firstly, that we cannot make foreigners submit to our laws; secondly, that the Japanese Government is unable to alter the tariff by its sole authority; and, thirdly, that we cannot make them obey the regulations agreed to by the localities."

Of the signboards proscribing Christianity which were formerly seen in Yedo, there is not one remaining at this day. But the fact is, that in Yedo and other large towns there are ministers of the gospel representing a number of sects who hold religious meetings regularly, and whose teachings are thankfully received by many of the native inhabitants. The prevailing sentiment towards the missionaries seems to be — "We have no objection to your instructing those who come to you for information, but we must not have any compulsory appeals;" and so we perceive that the hostility to the Christian religion is not by any means as active as it was in former years. Indeed, there is much talk among the Japanese about organizing a "new religion," which would of course be a long step towards recognizing Christianity in all its borders.

And now for a few words upon the prominent characteristics of the Japanese. They do not bestow the same honor upon women that is theoretically shown by the Western nations, but in that particular they are in advance of the other Asiatic nations. As already stated, several of their rulers have been females — nine out of one hundred and twenty-six, and one of them was the conqueror of Corea — and to-day, let any woman manifest a superior mind and she will command the highest respect of her associates. Much has already been done to emancipate woman from her former degraded condition, and the last two ministers accredited to this country had the manliness and good sense to bring their wives with them. The Japanese, like human beings generally, may be fond of indulging their appetites, but drunkenness is not so common as it is in this country, and against the use of opium the most rigid regulations have been established. Although wedded to all kinds of aristocratic notions, they admire and foster intellect wherever found, and in their public offices always endeavor to find the best man for every position to be filled. They are also remarkable for their unsordid ideas of life and duty. They are an intellectual race, and their native education is wellnigh universal; the commonest people, we repeat, can read and write the Japanese language, and all who make any pretension to culture are well founded in the Chinese language, which to them is like Latin to the English scholar. All the writers who have associated with the Japanese in their own country, or while sojourning in America or Europe, coincide in the opinion that they are remarkable for their amiable and agreeable manners; and in this respect the great Iwakura embassy was most conspicuous — to such an extent, indeed, as to have been frequently commented upon both in this country and England. The porcelain, lacquer-work, paper and silk, and the bronzes of Japan have never been surpassed, and in some particulars not equalled, in any other part of the world; and with regard to their pictorial art, their genius has been misapprehended. Contrary to the common opinion, they understand and practise the rules of perspective, and foreigners have made a mistake in judging of their skill as artists by the pictures which in Yedo are sold by the millions for the tenth part of a penny. A large proportion of the books are regularly illustrated, and the writer of this paper has in his possession many pictures which display abilities of the highest order for correctness and freedom of handling.

The relations existing between Japan and the United States have been, and are now, of the most friendly character. There is not a bone of contention between them, but there is one great fact on the side of the latter which is humiliating to our national honor and pride. We allude to what is called the indemnity fund. In 1864 a noted Daimio, who hated the new order of things in Japan, fired upon a foreign vessel in the employ of another Daimio. The allied powers thought themselves insulted, and brought the matter to the attention of the Imperial Government, which disclaimed all intention of doing wrong, and confessed that it could not control the rebel Daimio. The powers in question, the British, Dutch, French, and Americans, then formed a little fleet, and inflicted severe punishment on the offending Daimio. That done, a convention was called, and Japan was made to promise that she would pay an indemnity of three million dollars. The sum-total of that indemnity payable to the United States is nearly one million, two hundred thousand dollars. When more than one half of the amount due the United States had been paid, and which our Government was ashamed to put in the treasury, Professor Joseph Henry took the lead and suggested to Congress that it should be appropriated to educational purposes in Japan. The President was in favor of the proposition, but Congress did not act ; and so the question rested for a while. In the meantime, the interested European powers were trying to force the Mikado to open his Empire to the trade of all nations. His Majesty objected. "Then," said the powers, "you must pay us the money you owe." The Japanese Government paid the balance of their debt to the three European powers, and there was another pause. It was soon found, however, not to be diplomatic for the United States to refuse the unpaid balance due our Government. The arguments were successful, and the American minister had to go up and present his bill, which was instantly paid. For a moment the friendly feelings of the Japanese towards America were slightly abated, but when they saw the diplomatic necessity, and thought of what Professor Henry and the President had tried to do, the former kindly feelings were restored. And now there is a great, and in some particulars a disgraceful, squabble going on in the United States over this ill-gotten gain. One of two things on this subject is true ; either that it was right for the United States to take that money from a country like Japan when in a state of revolution, or that it was not. If the United States have no right to the money in question, then every dollar of it should be returned without any conditions. If, however, there is a bill for actual expenses, that amount, (perhaps less than twenty thousand dollars) ought to be paid, and the very large balance should be returned. But what do we see now going on in the way of schemes for handling this money ? (1) The very proper and most wise idea of Professor Henry, to appropriate the money for educational purposes in Japan under the auspices of the Japanese themselves; (2) a proposition to divide the money among the American officers and sailors who on one steamer did such wonderful work at Simonoseki; (3) the founding of a college in Japan, to be wholly officered and controlled by Americans; (4) to build an American legation in Yedo; and (5) to educate a few dozen boys in the Japanese language for service at the American consulates in that country. Indeed, the preposterous propositions may be counted by the dozen, and the public will be surprised to learn that there was once a scheme suggested for taking this Japanese money to build a new State Department in Washington. What will finally be done is doubtful, and we cannot but earnestly hope that the reputation of the United States for liberality and fair play will not be tarnished by the selfishness and cupidity of educational leaders or Congressional demagogues.

And now, with a few remarks on the literature and language of Japan we will conclude this article. The Japanese possess a copious literature, have a fondness for reading, and indulge themselves in study to a remarkable degree. Their catalogues of published works are numerous and voluminous, and the native books are divided into three general classes, as follows: Kangaku, or Chinese classical literature and works on the subject. In this class may be included works on Buddhism, written in Chinese, as well as the commentaries on these, and the form of verse known as Shi by native authors; Wa-gaku, or native books upon exclusively Japanese subjects, such as history, geography, books upon subjects of local interest, art, and ancient legends written in verse; and Kesaku, or novels, tales, and historical events worked up into romances. Of this class they possess an immense variety, and many of the circulating libraries are chiefly composed of these productions. Among the more noted of the older writers may be mentioned Kiosan, Kioden, Sekku, Samba, and Hokuba, whose productions range from romantic history to very romantic fiction. Some of the more popular writers of later times are Bakkin, whose tales embodied real names and descriptions; Tanehiko, who described his own times, just before the advent of Europeans; Tamenaga, a very popular novelist; Rei Sanyow, noted for his histories; Seigan, a poet writing in Chinese; Motoori, a writer on language; Atstane, an essayist; Oguni Takamasa, a poet; and Nakamura and Fukugawa, both of whom are English scholars, but stand at the head of the more useful writers of the present day, and who have translated into their language selections from the writings of very many of the modern writers of America and Europe. The writers of legends, travels, and romantic tales swell the list of modern Japanese authors to a large number. Unhappily, many of the books of Japan do but little to edify or improve the morals of the people.

With regard to poetry the Japanese are by no means deficient in the true sentiment, but their ideas of metre and melody are peculiar. What is called long poetry is formed of sentences of seven and five syllables alternately. Short poetry consists of thirty-one syllables only, the first sentence comprising five, the second seven, the third five, and the fourth and fifth seven syllables each. These poems are generally written on long and narrow strips of ornamented cardboard, measuring fourteen by about three inches, which are called Tanzaku. In the Honka poetry the syllables follow in the same order, but are read differently. The Zootoka has the same number of syllables, but so formed as to demand a poetical reply of the same order. Seidooka possesses a similar syllabic order and formation, but the beginning and ending consist of words or characters of like meaning. The Kioka is the ordinary poem of thirty syllables in the same order. The Omugayashi is similar to the Zootoka, with the exception that the two verses, question and reply, have only one of the thirty-one syllables different. In the change of this the merit of the performance consists. The Oriku is an acrostic of thirty-one syllables, divided into lines of five and seven syllables, twice alternating in one of seven syllables. The first syllable or character of each line is given arbitrarily. The Haikaiku is of the same number and order of syllables, but is simply a poetical play on words or a proverb. The Renga is the Raminoku or verse of five, seven, and five syllables, answered by the Shimonoku, of seven and seven syllables, the whole forming a poem of thirty-one. The Haikai is similar to the Renga, though commonly employed upon more trivial subjects. Both are called Tzukeai or "joining." The Hokku is the five, seven, and five, or poem of seventeen syllables. The Senriu has five, seven and five syllables, and is a jeu-de-mots. It only remains to be added that a people who have such a variety of styles in expressing their thoughts cannot but be gifted in the utterance of the most noble and beautiful and inspiring of sentiments and poetical reflections.

Without going into a learned disquisition on the language of Japan, the subjoined general statements may be accepted as correct. Prior to the period, nearly one thousand two hundred years ago, when the Japanese imbibed certain ideas from the Chinese in regard to language, their own tongue does not appear to have been reduced to writing. In the earliest known writings, in prose as well as poetry, the square and unabbreviated form of the Chinese characters is used phonetically to represent the sounds of the Japanese syllables. These characters were called Karina, or borrowed names, and subsequently contracted into what is now called the Kana, which is syllabary, and consists of forty-eight letters; and when more or less abbreviated and simplified in form these characters are called Hirakana, or plain letters, and are at the present time the common symbols used in writing the native Japanese. Another class of characters are called Kata-kana, or side letters, which are also derived from the Chinese, but in which only a part of the character is used. These are more ancient than the Hira-kana, and are commonly only used by scholars or in dictionaries. Another form of the Kana was invented by a Buddhist priest about one thousand years ago, for the purpose of assimilating it to the letters used in the sacred books of the Buddhists throughout the great countries of Asia. The syllables of the Japanese language number seventy-two, and the fact that the greatest care has to be taken not to write them indiscriminately, and thereby infringe upon ancient usage, the difficulties of uttering and writing them are very great and not often fully surmounted by English speaking people. In its sound the Japanese language is soft and allied to the Italian. The books that have latterly been published upon it are not numerous, but by far the most important and valuable is the *Japanese and English Dictionary*, prepared in 1867 by J. C. Hepburn, and in which that indefatigable scholar has defined not less than twenty thousand words. The only works of this character, and of special value, which preceded that of Dr. Hepburn, were published by W. H. Medhurst, in Batavia, in 1830, and by the Jesuit missionaries to Japan in 1603. In writing, the Japanese begin on the right side of the page, and proceed in vertical columns, and make free use of diacritic and punctuating signs.

As no adequate idea of the sound of Japanese words can be obtained without first understanding the alphabet, we submit it to the reader, as follows: i-, ro-, ha-, ni-, ho-, he-, to-, chi-, ri-, nu-, ru-, wo-, wa-, ka-, yo-, ta-, re-, so-, tsz-, ne-, na-, ra-, mu-, u-, i-, no-, o-, ku-, ya-, ma-, ke-, fu-, ko-, ye-, te-, a-, sa-, ki-, yu-, me-, mi-, shi-, ye-, hi-, mo-, se-, sz-, and n-; in all, forty-eight syllabary letters. The characters represented by the above are written in two ways, and occasionally an extra meaning is given by the addition of marks and signs. In expressing the sound of the Japanese vowels the continental pronunciation has been followed, because of its being more definite than the English; the Japanese have been accustomed to it for two or more centuries, and in all the books written by Europeans it has been regularly adopted.

Dialectic variations are numerous and depend chiefly on modifications of sound. In the Japanese grammar there is no gender, the male sex being indicated by *wo*, and the female by *me*; substantives are nearly allied to adjectives; there is no proper article; cases are indicated by suffixes; the plural is formed by suffixes, which signify all, much, many; the genitive precedes; the numerals are various; of figures there are three sets of numbers; of pronouns, those of the first and second have been lost in the words of etiquette; demonstratives are numerous; relatives are wanting; verbs are perfect; certain particles denote the moods; the participles are of extensive application; adverbs are similar to adjectives; the syntax adheres to a strict order; compounds and derivatives are easy and frequent; and many simple words have significations which are discriminated by sinograms.

By way of giving the reader an idea of Japanese when spoken, we submit the following specimens from a standard vocabulary: God, *Kami, Shin, Kotoke;* man, *h'to, nin, ningen otoko;* woman, *ouna, fujio, jo;* husband, *otto teishu, muko, tszma, tonogo;* wife, *tszma, kanai, niyōbō, naigi kamisan, okusama, sai;* world, *sekai, chikiu, tenchi tenka, seken, yo scjō, seji;* country, *kuni, koku, tochi, inaka, saigō, koka;* rice, *momi;* silk, *kinu, ito;* porcelain, *setomono;* enemy, *teki, kataki ada;* friend, *tomodachi, hōyu, hōbai, mkiata, yorube tayori,* and religion *oshiye, michi hō dō.* It will thus be seen that there are often many ways of expressing the same idea, and that it is not to be wondered at that the natives of one province of the Japanese Empire are often unable to understand their fellow-countrymen residing in another province.

# THE ISLANDS OF OKINAWA.

THESE islands have recently become a regular province or ken of the Japanese Empire, but are still a subject of serious controversy between Japan and China. Their ancient name was Liu Kiu, which has been corrupted by modern navigators into Loo-Choo, Lew-Chew, Licou Kicou, Riou Kiou, Loung Khicou, and by the present natives into Doo-Choo; but the more musical name of Okinawa was given to them by the inhabitants themselves centuries ago, and the meaning of it is "the cord lying upon the sea." The entire group consists of thirty-seven islands, the largest of which is eighty-five miles long, by from three to twenty-three in width, and has a circumference of one hundred and fourteen *ri*, or about two hundred and seventy-eight miles. Upon this is the seat of Government, called Shuri, and the principal port, Napha. It is the largest as well as the most central of the group, and has for centuries been called Okinawa. At one time when this largest island with two others of the group had three rulers, the one who occupied the central portion called himself the "king of the Middle Mountain Region," while the other two had jurisdiction respectively over a northern and a southern portion, independent of each other. The islands which rank as the second group of Okinawa are Miakoshime, and number nine islands; the third group consisting of ten are called the Ishigaki Islands; and the fourth group numbering seven are called the Oshima Islands, but these were subjugated in 1610 and became a portion of the province of the Prince of Satsuma, in Japan. Taken as a whole, the islands of Okinawa lie within 24° and 28° 40' north latitude, and 122° 50' and 132° 10' east longitude, and about midway between Formosa and Japan.

According to the latest census the population of the Okinawa Islands is 167,067, including 27,164 families, one of which is of the nobility, 5,370 of the Samurai, and 21,793 of the common class; while the numerical equality of the sexes is almost complete.

The surface of the largest island is hilly if not mountainous; and while the high lands are covered with forests of soft-wood trees, the lower hill-sides and level country are highly cultivated and noted for their sylvan attractions. The people are chiefly occupied in agricultural pursuits, and many of the women weave a kind of cloth which finds a ready market in the neighboring province of Satsuma. But before fully describing the country and people, it will be better to submit an outline of the history of Okinawa.

The first man and woman associated with the islands, whose names are preserved by tradition, were Shinireque and Amamiko; their son Tenson, or "offspring of Heaven," was the first ruler of the kingdom, and his dynasty continued for twenty-five generations from the time of his accession, of which period, however, there are no recorded dates existing. In 607 a Chinese vessel made its appearance at the island with an embassy; but although permitted to land, they could not hold any intercourse with the natives, and therefore accomplished nothing. In 610 another Chinese embassy arrived.

These envoys brought an interpreter with them, and politely invited the islanders to become tributary to China; and, upon receiving a positive refusal of their civil request, they burned the king's palace, took a number of men as prisoners, and returned to their country. In 616 a small colony of thirty men arrived in Japan from Yaku, one of the so-called "Southern Islands" of Liu Kiu, for the purpose of living in that country; and they not only acknowledged the jurisdiction of Japan, but brought a tribute with them, which was the first time such a manifestation of allegiance had been given by them to any nation. In 753, while a Japanese embassy was returning home from China, they were forced by stress of weather to make a harbor among these islands; and then it was that they became known as Okinawa. In 853 another Chinese vessel visited the islands, but those on board were not permitted to land. In 1168 a Japanese general named Minamotono-Tametomo, uncle of Yoritomo, who had been defeated in battle, was exiled to one of the islands south of Yokohama; from that place he escaped with certain followers to one of the islands of Okinawa, and having reached the main island subdued it, and settled there.

He married the sister of a feudal lord, by whom he had a son named Soujin, who in 1187 became the king of Okinawa, bearing the title of Shunten-no. From that period began the regular Japanese dynasty. He was the man who introduced the Japanese alphabet into the country. It was at this period, also, that the Prince of Satsuma became identified with the islands as a kind of overseer or governor, his family name being Shimadzu, which has been duly transmitted to all his successors. It is stated that in 1168, the time of the first Shiogoon-Yoritomo, three generals of the Taira family, who had been defeated by him in battle near the Straits of Shimonoseki, fled to Oshima with their followers, and having subdued the island divided it among themselves. In 1238 the son of Soujin was proclaimed ruler of Okinawa, and was succeeded also by his son, who, however, abdicated, and so brought to an end the rule of Japan.

In 1253 Yeiso, said to have been a descendant of Tenson, was proclaimed the ruler; and by him were first built the tombs and Buddhist temples. In 1290 Kublai Khan, Emperor of China, sent a letter to Okinawa, inviting its people to become tributary to his Empire; but there was again some trouble on account of the diverse languages, and after a little fighting the envoys returned home unsuccessful. In 1297 still another Chinese mission arrived and was equally unfortunate. In 1314 the dynasty of Yeiso came to an end, and then it was that for a time the country had three rulers. In 1350 one Satsdo, whose pedigree is unknown, became the ruler; and in answer to another appeal from China in 1372 he consented to pay tribute to that Empire, and sent his brother in 1373 as an envoy to the Flowery Land; he also sent several students to that country, and was the first one to introduce a Chinese court uniform into Okinawa.

The other two rulers followed his example and continued to pay tribute. In 1451 tribute was paid to the Shogün of Japan, and the first Shintü temple was erected; in 1465 a calendar was established; two years afterwards a mission was sent to Corea; in 1471 a decree was issued by Japan against the practise of smuggling between that Empire and Okinawa;

and in the two following years missions were sent to Satsuma, and trade regulations were established. In 1480 the Shogūn ordered the Prince of Satsuma to demand an annual tribute from the King of Okinawa; and this was not only complied with, but the king soon afterwards sent his congratulations to the succeeding prince. In 1503 an expedition was sent to Malacca for commercial purposes; but the vessels were wrecked, while the men found their way to Canton, and were duly returned to their own country by the Chinese authorities.

It was also about this period that the men of Okinawa adopted the curious custom of wearing hair-pins, which marked different distinctions, and were made of gold, silver, and copper, thereby imitating the women of Japan, who alone wear such ornaments in that Empire. In 1516 a considerable number of restless Japanese fitted out twelve junks for the purpose of invading Okinawa, when the Prince of Satsuma became indignant at this interference with the islands which had long been his tributaries, and having obtained the Shogun's permission he encountered the proposed invaders, destroyed them, and took their vessels. In the year 1591 the Shogun Taiko, better known as Taiko Sama, conceived the idea of sending an expedition to Corea; and having called upon the Prince of Satsuma and his tributary of Okinawa for the necessary soldiers, he suggested that Okinawa should be called upon to furnish supplies instead of men.

In due time the news of this expedition was sent to China by the islanders, which greatly incensed the Shogun; whereupon he repeated his demand, and the supplies were furnished. After the lapse of some eighteen years the King of Okinawa neglected to send his regular tribute to Japan, whereupon the Prince of Satsuma collected a fleet of one hundred war junks, and putting into them about three thousand soldiers, made sail for the rebellious island, subjugated it, and carried its ruler as a prisoner to Japan, all within the space of forty days.

As a result of this expedition Oshima, with four other islands, was ceded directly to the Prince of Satsuma, who was made Governor of Okinawa. An agreement was soon afterwards made, which contained among others the following provisions: That Okinawa should have no intercourse with China, excepting by the permission of Japan; that no men should be enslaved, and no servants should be bought or sold for purposes of gain; that there should not be a surplus of temples; that no trade should be carried on with any foreign nation without the consent of Japan; that the people should not be over-taxed; that a stop should be put to all gambling; and that the weights and measures of the islands should be made to accord with Japanese standards. After the conclusion of this agreement the exiled king was permitted to wait upon the Shogün, and afterwards to return to his own people.

During the prolonged tranquility which followed, the inhabitants of Okinawa began to turn their attention to new sources of national wealth. From certain prisoners who had been brought to Satsuma from Corea they obtained the art of manufacturing porcelain; they also sent to China for sugar-cane, and a limited trade was opened with that Empire. In 1644 an official delegation was sent to Tokio for the purpose of congratulating the new Shogun on his accession to power; and all the rulers of Japan have from that date to the present time been honored in the same manner, while each successive king of Okinawa has received his investiture from Japan.

The first regular history of Okinawa was prepared in 1650, under the general supervision of a prince named Kimbu, assisted by one Dairi Oya Kata, and was in the Japanese language. About this time the idea was conceived by the Sing dynasty of conferring a kind of investiture upon the King of Okinawa. The compliment was reciprocated by sending a tribute to China, and this romantic diplomacy was continued for many years. In the meantime the doctrines of Confucius were becoming popular, and in 1672 the first temple was erected and dedicated to that philosopher. It was at this period also that a vessel bearing the annual tribute to China was overtaken and seized by the chief of Formosa, who was apparently a kind of corsair, and who had fled to that island after the fall of the Ming dynasty of China. The king of Okinawa was helpless to avenge this wrong, and he appealed to the Prince of Satsuma for his assistance, which was duly promised. Not long afterwards a well-freighted vessel from Formosa arrived at Nagasaki, and an indemnity for the outrage was demanded from the captain, which was turned over to Okinawa by the Shogun's government. In a remonstrance which the Formosan authority sent to Japan, he said he had proven his friendship for the Shogun by sending back certain shipwrecked men; that he had attacked the Okinawa vessel because no one could tell whether a vessel carrying tribute to the "Barbarians of China" (alluding to the Manchu rule which succeeded the Ming dynasty) belonged to Okinawa or not; that Okinawa had no communication with Formosa, and that this trouble had endangered the friendship between Formosa and Japan.

During the whole of the eighteenth century the islands of Okinawa would seem to have remained in a state of perfect tranquility. They continued to pay a double tribute to Japan and China, and having faithfully done so they felt that they had a right to bring in from abroad any new ideas that they might fancy. Hence they imported the paper mulberry from Japan, and began to manufacture paper; and from China they obtained the secret of making India ink, and also as an article of food when young, and for the beauty of its wood, they imported and cultivated the famous *moso* bamboo. They also adopted a code of criminal laws and of laws for reward, and not only established a national school, but many local schools in the various districts. Nor was the reign of Arcadian simplicity disturbed until towards the middle of the present century.

In 1844 a French vessel made its appearance in the harbor of Napha, but when its captain proposed to do a little trading, he was told that Okinawa was a small country and the people had nothing to sell; wherefore he took his departure, leaving on the island a missionary with a Chinaman who had accompanied him on the voyage. Two years afterwards a second French vessel arrived, but no trade was accomplished; it however also brought another missionary, who was left behind, while the former one was taken away. An English merchantman having arrived, the refusal to commence trade was still insisted upon. Then in 1853 came Commodore Perry, who succeeded in making a compact with them, and the story of whose visit was pleasantly recorded by his *attaché* Bayard Taylor, while various graphic pictures of the men and things at Okinawa were drawn and published by William Hine, the regular artist of the expedition.

The year following Perry's departure the islands were visited by a mission from France, when another compact was made; and three years afterwards the Netherlands made still a third agreement or treaty. At some of the official interviews which occurred at this time there were two men who were uniformly present, and, while they appeared to be natives of Okinawa were in reality secret emissaries from Satsuma, Japan. In 1871, when the Daimio system was abolished in Japan, the islands of Okinawa were attached to the ken of Kagoshima; and in the following year the late king, Shotai, sent one of his leading officials and a prince to Tokio to congratulate the Emperor of Japan on the restoration of the Imperial Government. Then it was that Okinawa was established as a han, the king invested with the title of Han-no — a rank resembling that of viceroy — created a member of the Kazoku nobility, and placed in the rank of first class officials, and an official residence assigned to the han authorities in the city of Tokio.

In 1874 the affairs of Okinawa were transferred from the department of Foreign Affairs to that of the Interior Department. About that time also a kind of mission arrived at Tokio from Okinawa, for the purpose of looking after the interests of those islands; and about six months ago they expressed a wish that their ruler might be permitted to continue his old custom of paying tribute to China. For the several reasons that China has never claimed Okinawa as a dependency, that these islands are geographically connected with Japan, and belong to that Empire by the right of conquest and of possession, the appeal of the embassy was rejected; nor indeed was there any other course for Japan to pursue consistently with her honor, her dignity, and the welfare of the Empire as well as of Okinawa. The reply of Japan to this appeal, as it is understood, was followed by the despatch of Matsuda Michiyuki on a special mission to inform the ruler of Okinawa of the Imperial decision. On April 5, 1879, an official notification appeared abolishing the Liu Kiu Han, establishing the Okinawa Ken, and placing the seat of government at Shuri.

The peculiarities of the inhabitants of Okinawa may be summed up as follows: They are noted for their natural intelligence, though the majority have few opportunities for acquiring the knowledge contained in books; their language is closely allied to that of the Japanese; their occupations are chiefly agricultural, the leading productions being rice, wheat, sugar, millet, sweet potatoes, beans, peas, radishes, turnips, tobacco, cotton, indigo, and flax; their manufactures are limited to cloths made from cotton and grass, to porcelain and lacquered goods, and such other things as are needed for a simple rural population; the men are generally stout, well-formed, and fond of wearing beards; the women are small, and kept in a low social position; all classes are industrious and neat in their persons and habitations; their style of dressing is Oriental, and suited to the climate; the homes are comfortable and picturesque; the table and household customs are similar to those of the Japanese; in religion they are generally Buddhists, although some of their rites are peculiar to these islands; they pay special attention to the dead, placing their remains in stone tombs, and, when reduced to bones or dust, in vases, which they keep in suitable vaults, or hide away in the clefts of the rocks; their commerce is limited, and they are dependent chiefly upon Japan for their currency.

They know not what it is to have an army, nor any

such offspring of civilization as a political demagogue; their policy is to carry on their public affairs in a spirit of courtesy and kindness. When they have deemed it necessary to carry guns on their little vessels, they have borrowed them from Satsuma. They use the Japanese alphabet, and write after the manner of their neighbors and protectors; and in speaking of their language they claim that six tenths of the words are Japanese, three tenths a local dialect, and one tenth Chinese. When any public business is to be transacted, the people are called together in their several districts, and the men in authority accomplish the purposes of the Government by kindly admonitions.

The cultivated portions of Okinawa bear but a small proportion to the total area, and the stranger who is permitted to journey through the principal island will find much to interest him in the way of picturesque scenery. While the mountains attain an elevation of only about one thousand feet, they are covered with forests of pine, banyan, box-wood and bamboo, and fantastic formations of coral rock abound; the sides of the lower hills are often terraced and highly cultivated; the small streams of the main island are spanned by many quaint, ancient, and beautiful bridges; mills for crushing sugar-cane and grinding the various other grains are frequently seen by the road-side, with horses or bulls for motive power. The villages are numerous, and often present an appearance of great antiquity, the granaries being a leading feature of each village; and there is one ancient castle upon the island, the walls of which are fifty feet high and twenty feet in thickness, giving evidence in its construction of unusual skill.

As the custom of paying tribute to two countries

seems peculiar to Okinawa, an additional remark on the subject may be made. The payment has been made to Japan from the seventh century to the present time, with the exception of about one hundred and sixty years. It has generally consisted of various articles of produce, and the amount has been estimated by kokus of rice, the value of one koku ranging from five to seven *yens*, or dollars. The largest tribute or tax paid to Japan was 8600 kokus, and on one occasion, when the object was to send 3680 kokus of rice, brown sugar was substituted to the amount of 970,000 pounds. The tribute to China has sometimes been paid with sulphur, copper, and tin; and this intercourse with China has been carried on by two vessels, having each about two hundred men.

With regard to the climate of these islands, it may be stated that the summer heat averages 93° and the winter temperature 57°. If the irrigation were more complete, it would be easy to raise two crops of rice per annum; and five crops of sweet potatoes are easily produced in two years. The foliage of the country is always fresh and green, and there is no such season as autumn. By way of giving an idea of the material wealth of the islands, it may be stated that the chief productions in a recent year were of rice, 32,000 kokus; barley and wheat, 5000; peas, 2800; goma, 1300; salt, 15,000; and of sugar, 5,000,000 pounds, and of sweet potatoes, 135,000,000 pounds, one Japanese pound being equal to one and one third English pounds. The leading exports to Japan are sugar, linen goods, mats, porcelain, spirits, pork, and lacquered ware; and the imports, all from Japan, are rice, peas, sack, oil, tea, wax, tobacco, seaweed, dried fish, macaroni, raw cotton, stationery, copper, iron, tin, lumber, as well as cooking utensils.

On March 27, 1879, an official of the Japanese Government arrived at Okinawa with the Imperial order, transforming the islands from what was formerly a *han* into a *ken*, or province. The deposed king was at the time quite ill, and his son, Prince Shohitsu, acted for him during the mournful ceremony. The officers of the new ken examined the documents of the han, and placed them under a seal. Policemen were then stationed at all the gates of the castle, and the people, who were assembled for that purpose, were advised of the intentions of the Japanese Government, and received the regulations which were in future to be observed by them. This caused some excitement and a remonstrance, but no open opposition was manifested. On the night of the twenty-ninth, the ex-king retired from his palace, and it was immediately occupied by a detachment of Japanese troops. By this evacuation was signified the determination of the people to obey the orders of the Japanese Government, and on the second of April, the ex-king proclaimed the abolishment of the han. According to a subsequent notification from officials of the Imperial Government, the leading officers of the old han were to be superseded, while the local officers of the three departments and of the wards and villages were to be retained. In commenting upon this important change in the condition of Okinawa, the Japanese press has manifested much sympathy for the people of the new province, and has urged the Government to treat the dethroned Han-no and his family with the uttermost kindness and consideration. Until some time in the month of May, the Han-no was still too seriously indisposed to visit Japan, as he had been ordered, but he sent his son, a boy of fourteen, who was kindly received by the Emperor, and was entertained at several banquets; after which ceremonies the sensible youth asked permission to be received as a student in the Imperial College for the education of noblemen.

On June 9, 1879, the Han-no of Okinawa, following in the wake of his son, arrived at Tokio, accompanied by a retinue of one hundred personal attendants. He was comfortably lodged, and handsomely provided for, but no special attentions were shown, as it was considered necessary for the Japanese Government to emphasize the fact that the ex-king is now a subject of the Empire, although one of a high rank.

With regard to the controversy between China and Japan, the following particulars are the latest which have been received in this country. During ex-President Grant's late visit to China, a leading official of that Empire requested him, on his arrival in Japan, to act as a peace-maker between the two countries in regard to the controversy about the islands of Loo-Choo, or Okinawa, and he promised to do what he could with propriety as a private individual. When the General came to Tokio, the Chinese minister resident there waited upon him and informed him that the Chinese Government claimed Okinawa as a vassal, giving various historical reasons for the claim, and speaking in severe terms of the "violent and coercive conduct of Japan." The diplomatic correspondence which had taken place between China and Japan, and which was noted for its Oriental ability and sharpness, was first submitted to the General; and by a special appointment he also had an interview with the Japanese ministers for the Interior and War Departments and the Japanese minister to the United

States (at home on leave of absence), when the Japanese side of the controversy was submitted. The historical evidence brought forward was in keeping with what has already appeared in this paper, the principal points of which were that Okinawa had been ruled by Japan for many centuries; that there was a geographical as well as family alliance between them; and that the allegiance of Okinawa was proven by the famous "oath of Shonei," a noted chieftain of Okinawa, which oath in terms recited that the islands had been subject to Satsuma for many centuries. After fully considering all the questions submitted to him, General Grant said in substance that he had mentioned the matter only at the earnest solicitation of the Chinese Government; that it would be safe in the hands of the American minister to Japan, to whom he would refer it; and that he must be excused from giving any opinion as to the merits of the question in dispute. He of course deprecated any thing like serious hostility between the two Governments, but added that the army and navy of Japan were stronger than those of China; that the latter country was really defenceless, although possessed of immense resources; and that, because of her position, Japan could afford to consider the whole question from an elevated and magnanimous point of view. In the course of his remarks on this subject it is understood that General Grant alluded in pointed terms to the arbitrary and selfish schemes of certain European powers, in connection with the nations of the Orient, and his words were but an echo of the sentiment existing throughout the United States.

# THE OGASAWARA ISLANDS.

THESE islands, generally known by the name of Bonin, lie about five hundred miles from the coast of Japan, in a southerly direction; they are divided into three groups, bearing the names of Parry, Peel and Bailey; and their total area is about one hundred and twenty square miles. The distance between the two extreme islands is about eighty miles, and the largest, which is near the centre, measures seven and a half miles; and the only one that is inhabited, is four and a half miles long and called Peel Island. They were discovered by the Japanese in the latter part of the sixteenth century, and until 1624 were held as a fief by the Daimio Ogasawara Sadayori. From that date until 1728, their history is an entire blank, but in that year they were again visited by the Japanese. In the year 1823, Captain Coffin, of the American whaling ship *Transit*, landed there, established the position, and bestowed his name upon the locality. In 1827, Captain Beechey, in the English surveying ship *Blossom*, touched at the same spot, and, though fully aware of the prior discovery by Coffin, which he acknowledged, claimed possession of the whole group for Great Britain, and re-named the several islands. This, it is remarked in the narrative of Commodore Perry's expedition, was done "with the proverbial modesty and justice of English surveyors, as if they had been then first observed." The act of appropriation was commemorated by an inscription upon a copper plate, which was nailed to a tree. One year later a Russian captain named Lutke, also landed, and left upon record a claim of ownership in behalf of his sovereign. This was written upon a board likewise fastened to a tree. During all this period the islands were never regularly inhabited, unless, perhaps, at some early and forgotten date, by Japanese; but in 1830, a party of colonists consisting of two Americans, one Englishman, one Dane, one Genoese, and some twenty-five or thirty natives of the Sandwich Islands, arrived and established themselves upon Peel Island, the largest of the central group, with a view to permanent residence. The Genoese was the first leader of this party. In the course of a few years, the five whites either died or withdrew, with the exception of Nathaniel Savory, a Massachusetts man, who thenceforward, throughout his life, was recognized as the head of the community, which was from time to time enlarged by stragglers from whaling vessels. While his influence lasted, it appears that a fair system of order and propriety prevailed; and, in 1853, a very respectable constitution was drawn up for the organization of the settlement, Savory being elected chief magistrate over the eight inhabitants of American or European birth. In addition to the reputable whalers who sometimes looked in upon them, piratical adventurers made occasional descents, one body of whom, in 1849, ransacked the village, plundered all the available property, and forcibly abducted some of the women.

In June, 1853, Commodore Perry, with a part of his squadron, arrived at Port Lloyd, the harbor of Peel Island, in fulfilment of part of his general purpose of exploration in this vicinity. He found the inhabitants indisposed to acknowledge the authority of England, or indeed of any government, and was unable to discover any trace of the copper plate upon which Captain Beechey had left his record in 1827. This may perhaps have then been purposely concealed, for it has since come to light, and is now in the hands of the British authorities in Japan. It was a significant circumstance that the nomenclature of several of the islands, as arranged by the British navigator, was totally disregarded by the occupants. Peel Island (as we may call it for the sake of convenience) was the only one then settled; and of its whole area, only one hundred and fifty acres were under cultivation. The soil, however, was very prolific, and amply supplied the wants of the little colony. But to add to their comforts, a number of cattle and sheep were landed, the latter of which, it may be observed, have since increased to enormous numbers, considering the limited space to which they are confined. Garden seeds of every kind were also distributed, of which, for a while, good use was made. Commodore Perry was much struck by the importance of the geographical position of these islands, and, in order to secure a coaling station for ships of the United States, he purchased a title to a suitable piece of land in the excellent harbor of Port Lloyd. This transaction led him, not long after, into a brief controversy with the British superintendent of Trade at Hong Kong, Sir J. G. Bonham. That official communicated to the Commodore the fact that he had been instructed by Lord Clarendon, Minister of Foreign Affairs, to ask for information as to the object in view. He furthermore advanced a formal claim to the islands, based upon Captain Beechey's proceedings; upon an alleged original discovery by an English whaling ship in 1825, and the colonization in 1830, which, it was assumed, was undertaken by Englishmen. In reply, it was pointed out that the first visit, by a Western mariner, was that of the American, Coffin, and that, of the earliest settlers, the larger number were Americans, while the leader was a Genoese. Commodore Perry therefore declined to acquiesce in the position taken by Sir George Bonham. He had a short time previously sent Commander Kelly, in one of his ships, to take possession of the southern group — that upon which Coffin landed — in the name of the United States. This was done in October, 1853, and a new chart was laid out, in which the name given by Beechey, "Bailey's Islands," was set aside, and that of "Coffin's Islands" substituted. The usual formality of affixing a metal plate to a tree was here repeated. Another and final visit by one of Perry's squadron was made in April, 1854, when the settlers expressed a desire to place themselves under the American colors, and a flag was left with them to be displayed as occasion might arise.

For several years thereafter, nothing of interest occurred in connection with the Bonins. Savory died, and the creditable attempt at self-government which was commenced in 1853, was not sustained. Peel Island gradually became a resort for extremely questionable characters, and reports of disorders grew to be so frequent, that in 1861 an inquiry was made — by Sir Rutherford Alcock, the British Minister — as to whether the Japanese Government was prepared to undertake control and jurisdiction there. An affirmative reply was given, and a competent officer was despatched to assume the direction of affairs. Sixty families were transported thither, to form the nucleus of a colony. A form of local administration was established, and, for a brief term, maintained. But this was just at the time when the internal troubles of Japan were beginning, and it was soon found impracticable to continue the arrangement. The effort toward regular occupation was given up within a year. After that, until the end of 1863, periodical visits of inspection were made by officials duly appointed for the purpose. At last these ceased; the emigrants were brought back to their old homes, and the Japanese thenceforward neglected to pay any attention to this comparatively unimportant station. They left behind them, instead of the customary metal sheet, a stone monument, with an inscription proclaiming the proprietorship of their nation. Four years later the Government of the Taikuns fell, and the Imperial party on resuming the executive functions after a lapse of six hundred years, had no leisure, in its pressure of urgent business, to consider a detail so trifling as the management of the Bonin Islands then appeared. The subject was next brought into prominence in April, 1873, when a certain Captain Benjamin Pease, an American, called upon Mr. De Long, the United States Minister to Japan, to make inquiries on his own account as to the sovereignty of the group. This Pease appears to have been little better than a freebooter. He owned a small schooner, and was engaged in all sorts of dubious traffic among the islands of the Pacific, the kidnapping and selling of human beings occupying his chief attention. This was probably not known at the moment, inasmuch as Mr. De Long undertook to investigate the subject for him. It appeared, according to the information which he brought, that there were then upon Peel Island twenty-five Americans, seventeen Englishmen, four Frenchmen and a considerable number of Hawaiians and others — all living in a state of lawless irregularity. His ostensible, and possibly his genuine, motive for inquiry was to discover if any means of preserving order could be supplied. Mr. De Long wrote to Secretary Fish, and received an answer dated May 21, 1873, disavowing all responsibility for any Americans that might be on the islands, and declaring that the United States Government would not undertake to protect them. Captain Pease had previously disappeared from view, carrying with him two Japanese women, whom he decoyed away from Yokohama. At the close of 1873 intelligence arrived that he had been murdered by some of his fellow-islanders. As he has not since been seen, the report is believed to have been correct.

It was towards the end of 1874 that the latest phase of the subject came into view. Whether it was then revived by foreign agents or by the Japanese, it is difficult to say. It is certain, however, that from the outset, several of the diplomatic corps were extremely active in it. As soon as it was discovered that the Government were about taking steps to re-assert their authority, they were confronted by a declaration that, as they had abandoned the islands twelve years ago, they could not now reclaim them. In response to this, it was stated that though the exercise of jurisdiction there had been "neglected," the rights of Japan had never been "abandoned," and that the acts in contemplation were not in the nature of "reclamation," but simply a resumption of powers temporarily laid aside. The obstacles, however, were overcome without serious inconvenience. In November, 1874, a commission consisting of attachés of the Interior and Foreign Departments, and under the direction of an officer who had before been sent from the capital in 1861, sailed for Peel Island. They paid little attention to the northern group — Parry's Islands, according to Captain Beechey — or to the insignificant cluster just below them, these being uninhabited. They landed upon Peel, which is and always has been called by the Japanese Chichi Sima (Father Island). Here they found some seventy persons of various nationalities, corresponding pretty nearly to the description given by Pease to Mr. De Long. Next visiting Coffin's group, which they call Haha Sima (Mother Island), they discovered that the only residents were one couple and a child. These were all living in a state of indigence and ignorance. There was no pretence of social law, to the re-establishment of which a stolid indifference seemed to be shown. They appeared, however, somewhat gratified at the prospect of a renewal of the Japanese rule, for the reason that the chances of violent misdeeds would thereby be lessened. The reports brought back by this commission respecting the physical aspect of the islands, were almost identical with that of Bayard Taylor, written in 1853. The productions, as may be supposed, had somewhat increased, although no endeavor had been made to raise more than would be necessary for the support of life. In the way of vegetables there were found sweet potatoes, wheat, corn, pumpkins, onions, taro, sugar, tomatoes and tobacco. Of fruits there were melons, bananas, lemons, oranges, and a few varieties of berries. Of animal food the supply of mutton was abundant, but there were also oxen, hogs, goats and poultry upon the island.

A photographer who accompanied the commission

brought back conclusive proofs of the romantic and picturesque character of the scenery, and thereby confirmed the impressions originally made upon the public mind by William Heine and Bayard Taylor, through their pencil and pen contributions to the history of Perry's Expdition, of which they were both most useful members.

The latest, and perhaps the best account yet given to the public of the Bonin Islands, was written by Mr. Russell Robertson, of Yokohama, in 1876, of which the foregoing is a partial summary, printed in the *Tokio Times*, and we conclude this compilation with his own final observations :

"Popular rumour had ascribed to the Bonins a colony of semi-savages, murdering one another, and altogether leading a barbarous existence. I found a small colony of settlers, living to all outward appearances in decency and order, cleanly in their attire, civil in their address and comfortable in their homes. Such is the bright side.

"The dark picture is the utter apathy of the settlers; their indifference to any thing outside of what goes to satisfy their immediate wants; their suspicion in some cases of one another. No religion, no education, old men and women hastening to their graves without the one, children growing up without the other—and there is a darker picture than this. This paper records the fact of two men Gilley and Bob (so called) having fallen by the hand of their neighbours. On the ninth of October, 1874, Benjamin Pease, a resident at Port Lloyd, disappeared, and, it is believed, met with a violent death, while on the eleventh of June, 1875, a negro, Spenser by name, strongly suspected of having been Pease's assassin, also disappeared, receiving his death blow, it is said, at the hands of one of the residents. I was informed by a settler that during his stay on the Bonins, now extending over twenty-five years, no less than eleven men had met with violent deaths. I would not have it assumed, however, that these tragedies are to be ascribed altogether to the bona fide resident population, if, indeed, the word population can be ascribed to such a little band.

"It must be remembered that the component parts of the population are a few old residents, a few comparatively new, some born on the Islands and now getting on in years, runaways from whalers, and men perhaps purposely left behind, and these latter, we may be sure, not the most orderly of the crew.

"I trust that if communication comes to be established with these islands with anything like regularity, that the claims of the settlers on the sympathies of the foreign communities of Yokohama and Yedo will not be overlooked, and that an attempt at ameliorating their condition will be made from one or both these settlements, if not indeed generally from the open ports in Japan. I can vouch for it that kindly sympathy expressed either in word or deed will not be inappreciated there, and that in spite of many drawbacks, there are as warm hearts on the Bonins as any that beat amongst ourselves."

# COREA.

IN 1877 intelligence reached this country that both England and Russia had expressed their intention, without being invited to do so, to participate with Japan in the advantages of opening commercial intercourse with Corea. The question is one of considerable interest, and as the public generally know very little about the actual condition of that isolated kingdom of the East, we submit the subjoined particulars, obtained chiefly from Japanese authorities.

Prior to the year 1876, the kingdom of Corea, formerly called Kaoli, but now Chôseu, or Morning Calm, was virtually the only country on the globe which was disconnected from the great family of nations. It is true that it paid an annual tribute to China, and had a little trading intercourse with the frontiers of Russia, but it was in reality an isolated and unknown land. In the year just mentioned, however, the Empire of Japan succeeded in obtaining or regaining the friendship of its obdurate neighbor, and in negotiating a treaty of commerce, public relations, navigation and friendship. On several occasions during the eight preceding years efforts had been made by Japan to induce her nearest neighbor to be a little more sociable, but unkindness and insults were the only results, and at one time there was danger of war. But Japan was magnanimous, and only repeated her friendly offices. The excuse given by the Corean

Court in 1875, for refusing to receive the Japanese Ambassadors, was decidedly Orientalish: "You come to us," said they, "in clothes of the West, which smell of a region which is hateful to us. Come in the costume worn by your fathers and we will receive you as we have done before." And again, when the Japanese envoys presented a watch and a gun to the Corean king, in 1876, he refused at first to accept them because they were inscribed with Roman letters; but he was finally induced to reconsider his decision, and took the presents, and for a Gatling gun he returned sixty skins of the tiger. The head of the Japanese Embassy here mentioned was a noted man named Kuroda Kiyotaka, the Governor of Yesso, and a successful general, having distinguished himself in the late Japanese rebellion. He took with him in his retinue an experienced photographer, and the collection of portraits and landscape scenes thus taken is not only unique, but of a very great interest.

Corea is a vast peninsula, lying between the Yellow Sea and the Sea of Japan; and although its exact area has never been decided, it is estimated in round numbers to be about six hundred miles long and one hundred and thirty miles in width, excepting on the extreme north, beyond the peninsula proper, where it measures about two hundred and fifty miles. It has a rock-bound coast, is highly picturesque, and is bounded on the west and south by many small islands, with one that is nearly fifty miles long, and famous as the scene of many shipwrecks. It lies on the south, and is called *Quelpart;* while two other important islands are *Kang-wha* on the west, and *Ollong-to* on the east, and they are all thickly inhabited. The whole surface of the Corean peninsula is mountainous, some of the higher elevations reaching nine thousand feet and always covered with snow ; and while the northern portion abounds in forests of pine and fir, and is sparsely populated, the southern part has but few trees and is to a great extent cultivated, but often sterile, and it is watered by the following large rivers, namely : the Kiang, Kokwa, Yaloo, Piengang, Dungang, Tsin, Tumen and the Kangko, as well as many smaller streams. The population is estimated to be about eight millions, almost universally poor, and, from famine and pestilence, is said to be on the decrease. The towns and villages numbering three hundred and fifty, are chiefly located in the south, and the houses are not only small and rude, but very much scattered. The national capital is Kingkiato, or Saoul, and is located near the centre of the kingdom on the river Kiang, and is surrounded with a low wall of masonry five miles in extent ; and it contains about one hundred and fifty thousand inhabitants. The only buildings in it honored with tiled roofs, excepting the King's residence, are a single temple and one Government Department. The fortified portion of the city, which holds the King's castle, is quite imposing. There is a high wall, built with cut stone, but without a moat, and open spaces are left for guns, or for archers who do the principal fighting in times of war. The houses outside the castle gates are all thatched and built after one general pattern, and the rural homes are about as desolate as many of the inhabitants are shiftless and improvident.

Their mode of paying taxes is to work for the Government three months in every year. The people are barbarous and indolent, know a little of the Chinese language, and consider Russia the greatest power in the world. The country is divided into eight provinces, each one having a governor, and its ruler is a king whose despotism is unlimited, and who claims that his kingdom has existed for four hundred and eighty-six years. The names of the provinces are Kingki, Pingan, Hoanghi, Tchusin, Tsulo, Kinhan, Kiang and Hienkin. The officers of the Government are exceedingly numerous — all Government orders issuing from a Council of State, assisted by six ministers — and the annual expenses out of all proportion to the revenue, which is limited and uncertain. The country was once subjugated by the Tartars, then passed under the control of China, was conquered by Japan in A. D. 200, under the leadership of an Empress, and, as already stated, now pays a voluntary tribute to China, and is bound to Japan by the only treaty it has made in modern times.

The prevailing language, of which little is known, is allied to the Chinese, though claimed to be a strict idiom, and is only written by the higher classes. The people have a few books, which are printed from wooden blocks; they produce pictures on screens, which are generally in India ink, but sometimes highly colored; and their printed poetry is very limited. They boast of their civilization, calling America and other western countries, "cross-lettered countries," and they claim that the only regions where the people are as advanced as themselves, are Japan, China, and Loochoo, or Okinawa. On the other hand, one of the foreign officers who lately visited Corea, summed up his opinion of the kingdom in these words: The upper classes crush the lower classes by their cruelty; the lower classes deceive their official superiors by calumny and flattery; and because both classes are hypocrites, discord and disorder are the order of the day.

Hitherto the Corean calendar has been that of

China, but this was abandoned at the signing of the treaty of 1876, the Japanese envoy having insisted that the country must henceforth be recognized as entirely independent. When the aforesaid treaty was signed, the Japanese officers were entertained with a repast, at which an unearthly music was performed, and the following dishes were served, viz.: Confectionery made of sugar, flour and oil; boiled eggs, goma, honey, chestnuts, dried persimmons, pine seeds, rice cooked in red gravy, macaroni soup, with fowl and boiled pork, all of them washed down with a native wine made of rice, but inferior to the Japanese sake. The dishes were of earthen ware, the tables covered with oiled paper, and the wine was offered in cups made of copper. With regard to the merits of the treaty in question, we may say that its most important provisions are that three ports, including Soris in Fusan, which had previously been visited by Japanese, shall be opened to the commerce of Japan, and the time fixed for going into complete operation was about the middle of the year 1877, when an envoy might be sent from Japan, as one had already been sent to that country from Corea; and that all offenders against the treaty belonging to Corea or Japan shall be punished according to the laws of their respective Governments. Another provision was that, as the coasts of Corea were dangerous for navigation, the Japanese might, if they should desire to do so, survey these coasts, and it is a rare evidence of enterprise that the best map of the whole of Corea now extant was prepared and published by the Japanese authorities in 1876, under the direction of the War Department.

The commerce of Corea is limited, although its

capabilities are great, and its chief productions are rice, silk of an inferior quality, good cotton and linen cloths, skins, millet, paper which is of superior quality, pottery, and an inferior porcelain, various kinds of drugs, including ginseng, a black variety of tobacco, the oil of goma, fish of various kinds, and, what is rather uncommon in the far East, an abundance of good beef and pork. Minerals are said to exist in abundance. Many of the hills are without any vegetation, which fact gives color to the opinion that there is much mineral wealth. But the iron mines are all that are now worked; copper, gold and silver, if they exist, are yet untouched, with the exception of a little gold dust, which has been annually sent to China, and some black lead. Indeed, the people have a kind of superstition against the precious metals, and, unlike the civilized Americans, have a contempt for jewelry and ornaments. The copper and tin used in the country came from Japan, and out of the former are made the only two coins used in the realm. There is undoubtedly much coal in the country, as well as gold, silver and copper, and although wood, in some parts, is very scarce, coal does not seem to be appreciated.

The Coreans, in their persons, are a stalwart race, claim to be warlike, and although they have a number of well-mounted fortresses, their army is small. The prevailing religion is Buddhism, but the temples are comparatively few, and none of them are noted for their beauty, as in Japan and China. In imitation of the Japanese they once did a large business in the way of slaughtering certain Jesuit missionaries who had invaded their country, and made many converts. Like the Chinese, they keep their women secluded from the gaze of strangers; they are often untidy in their personal appearance, and afraid of water for purposes of ablution; as to their clothing, their upper and under garments are white and without ornamental work; some of the officials wear silk, the common people cotton; the hats worn by the men are black, tall and stiff, made of braided horsehair and also bamboo, and, like the Quakers, they greet their friends with their hats on their heads; the men wear long hair; the women dress somewhat like the poorer classes among the Western nations; marriages are prohibited between relations within the fifth degree, but take place at an early age; men of distinction who have died are kept unburied for one or two years, when imposing monuments are erected to their memory; and it was because some of these were desecrated by the men of a foreign vessel a few years ago, that the hatred of outside barbarians was greatly enhanced. Their houses are universally one-story high, warmed by a fire lighted underneath their floors of mortar, and are without chairs or beds, or any of the comforts which prevail in most other countries. Nor are they any better off on the sea than on the land. Their largest vessels are not over fifty feet long. They are built without the use of nails, and the prow and stern are precisely alike. For masts they use the stems of trees in their natural state, and the sails are made of straw, one to each boat, and that very near the stern, and although uncouth to foreign eyes they are managed with dexterity and accomplish good speed. In religion they are chiefly Buddhists, and it is said that in their monasteries, there are many thousand priests. The people allege that in ancient times they did not lock their doors and that few crimes were committed, but that the introduction of modern luxuries has caused a great change, and much wickedness prevails. The three leading modes of punishment are decapitation, imprisonment and whipping — the latter being very frequent and performed with a kind of paddle. To such an extent is this kind of punishment practised that strangers might be led to believe that it is a leading occupation of the people; and it is said that when a punishing officer happens to neglect his duty, he is himself ordered to lie down, when he is also *paddled* by a superior official.

In its natural history Corea is undoubtedly an interesting country. The bear, the deer and the wolf abound in the northern forests; an animal resembling the tiger is found in the middle regions, and birds of many varieties are numerous. The domestic animals are horses, which are small; horned cattle and hogs, which are abundant; dogs and a great variety of fowls. The yak is also found in the northern parts, and, according to Commodore Ammen, is an animal that should be domesticated in the country. Sharks of immense size are found all around the coasts, and the seal and other fisheries are susceptible of being made a source of wealth if they could only be managed according to modern ideas. That the opening of Corea to the commerce of the world would be of advantage to all the parties concerned cannot be doubted, and this thought carries us back to what Japan has accomplished in that direction. Before she negotiated the late memorable treaty, her ambassadors were told that they must not hope to gain a brain victory over such a barbarous people as the Coreans, that France, England and America would have to do the work of opening their country to the world, and that Japan must be ready to fight before succeeding; but the result has proven the prophecy to be at fault. As Japan had recently become a convert to the spirit of modern progress, she was anxious to give some evidence of her own faith, and not only determined to become, but has succeeded in becoming, a missionary of progress; and the very men in Japan who ridiculed her aspirations have been compelled to applaud her for her wisdom and enterprise.

With regard to the present government of Corea we have but little to communicate. In 1864 the widow of a former king, bearing the title of Queen Cho, took forcible possession of the great seal of the kingdom, and proclaimed herself Regent; soon afterward another "connection of the family," named Ni Kung, went to work and did the same thing; and then followed a bitter quarrel which resulted in this curious feast. It was given by Queen Cho, and the only participants beside herself were the opposition Regent, Ni Kung, and a nephew of the former, and son of the latter, named Cho Sung, whom she had intended to make king. When they were all seated she announced that the chief ingredient of the principal dish was poison. She lamented the family feuds, deplored their effect upon the country, and, as the only way out of the difficulty, she suggested a joint suicide. But the guests objected, and, out of the feuds which followed came the death of Queen Cho, the retirement of Ni Kung and the enthronement of Cho Sung, the present ruler of Corea.

Not less romantic is the character of the intercourse existing between China and Corea, as obtained from a Japanese authority. In order to secure as complete an isolation as possible, Corea has always decreed that a broad belt of land upon her northwestern border should be a perpetual desert, and notwithstanding the richness of its soil, this, until recently, has been agreed to by China. If cultivated at all by the Chinese, it has been done by stealth. Upon the Chinese line of this forbidden space, and forty miles from the Corean boundary, stands a little village called the "Border Gate," from the fact that it contains the real and only opening through which communication has hitherto been permitted between the two nations. This opening is in the central compartment of a small house, which is occupied by the customs officials of both nationalities, the Coreans residing at one end and the Chinese at the other, with an eastern and a western door. These are opened only four times a year, when they remain unclosed, for traffic, for a total period of ten weeks, the keeper of these doors being a Chinaman, who receives a salary of four hundred taels from the Corean Government. It is through this gate that the annual embassy from Corea to Peking is obliged to pass. But about two years ago many depredations occurred on this neutral ground, committed by Coreans, whereupon the Chinese authorities became exasperated and proceeded to take such steps as would result in the cultivation of the disputed territory, so that the abandonment of the Border Gate and the opening of the country to Japan are likely to be remembered as the representative facts of the recent history of Corea. Another of the curious customs of this people is that of "Fire Signals," which are used to announce a foreign invasion. They extend from the Capital to the sea coasts, and consist of fires which are built on the tops of the hills and mountains, — one fire meaning *peace* and two fires *danger ahead.* These beacons are lighted every night, and this system of telegraphing has existed for centuries.

But during the year 1877, Japan succeeded in making a second treaty with Corea, whereby it is assured that all the crews of foreign vessels wrecked upon the coast of that country shall be treated with kindness, and be assisted in pursuing their voyages. And more wonderful than that is the fact that the Government of Corea, for the first time in its history, has actually sanctioned the getting up of a national exhibition, which will be international only so far as respects the admission of Japanese exhibitors. The arrangements were assigned to an influential mercantile firm in that country, and invitations were sent to all the provinces of the kingdom. The exhibition was to begin in October of the current year, and is supposed to be in full blast at the present time. These first steps of Corea out of darkness into the light of civilization are an agreeable evidence of the beneficial influence of Japan upon her Oriental neighbors.

Among the Corean islands, to which reference has already been made, is one lying south of the peninsula, and known as Quelpart. It is about fifty miles long by twenty-five wide, and contains perhaps ten thousand inhabitants. It is traversed by a range of mountains, one of which is six thousand feet high, and its eastern extremity consists of a lofty and picturesque headland, and all around its shores are to be rude stone towers, which resemble lighthouses, but are really nothing but watch towers. Its principal town is called Chlegiufu, and surrounded by a stone wall; and while its chief officials are Coreans, the majority of the people are natives of the island. Extensive forests encircle the mountains; a large proportion of the country is cultivated; the principal farm productions are wheat, barley, buckwheat and turnips; the more common animals are small horses, cattle, deer and wild hogs; and the habits of the people are allied to those which prevail on the neighboring peninsula.*

And now in further elucidation of the character of Corea, we append the following from the *Ogura Company* residing in that country, which was published in 1877, in the *Chôya Shinbun*, of Tokio.

"Fusankai is the place where Japanese subjects reside, and though the place is small and confined, it has pretty well assumed the appearance of a commercial town. There are two streets called Bentenchô and Honchô respectively. On the seashore are numerous godowns, with a line of houses behind them. The office of the Japanese Consul is at the top of Honchô, and looks on the sea; right and left are fine pine woods, while in front lies spread out the island called Bokutô (?), presenting thus a splendid prospect. At this office are transacted diplomatic, domestic, judicial and police affairs, but there is no appearance of a great pressure of work.

"Since last spring the stream which runs through the settlement has been cleaned out and the streets cleared of dirt. Great attention has been bestowed on the wells, and arrangements made for clearing away all kinds of filth in times of pestilence, and in all matters great improvements have been effected by the efforts of the Consul, Mr. Kondô. There is a small hill on the seashore, called 'Dragon's-tail Hill,' from which the view is very fine, but the Coreans who

---

* As the commercial world has long felt a special if not a covetous interest in Corea, the following particulars bearing on its exports to Japan in 1879, are not without interest: rice, $179,209; white beans, 89,995; bull skins, 56,802; gold dust, 36,936; irico, or sea weed, 16,047; silk goods, 14,325; bones of horses and bulls, 11,863; iron, 2,275; funori, or sea weed starch, 9,358; raw silk, 4,920; ogon, 800; ogon powder, 3,454; sardines, 1,463; old bronze, 2,620; sharks' fins, 1,768; kantengusa, 945; hooks, 945; awabi shells, 629; oil cake, 565; ginseng, 904; and wheat, 1,429; or a total of exports of $450,039; while the imports, all from Japan, amounted to $395,632.

come ashore use it for various purposes, the consequence being that it is filthy to the last degree, and the stink is so strong as to be injurious to health. The Consul, taking this to heart, has cleared away the filth, and has begun to convert it into a public promenade for the residents.

"About seventy-five miles to the north of Fusankai lies a place called Têkeup, where every year a large fair is held during the space of thirty days in the second and tenth months according to the old calendar. They call these the Têkeup fairs. Merchants assemble from all the eight provinces of Corea at these fairs, and Japanese goods are principally exposed for sale; they say that the number of spectators and purchasers is enormous. It is also said that a great fair for the exchange of merchandise with Chinese subjects is held twice a year at Ichiu and Chanshiêng, in the province of Piêngan-tô.

"The commerce of the Coreans passes for the most part through the hands of the officials, who trade under the name of agent of the governor of such-and-such a city. Most of the men who deal in gold dust are such agents.

"PRODUCE: The best gold dust comes from Tanchion and Shontayasan, in Hankiêng-tô, Niyonwon, in Piêngan-tô, Honchion, in Kangan-tô, and Hanan, in Kiêngsan-tô and a little is also said to be produced in Chênla-tô. Quantities of cotton, fans and bullocks' hides are produced in Chênla-tô. The best ginseng comes from Kaiwhon and Rionshon, in Kiêngki-tô, while the best bullock hides are considered to be those which are produced in ———

"Coal is said to exist at Kirchiu, in Hankiêng-tô, and at Urusan and Changki in Kiêngsan-tô. Tiger skins come chiefly from Fwanha-tô. There are silver mines in Chênla-tô.

"Great strictness is observed in Corea with regard to questions of religion. Some ten years ago French missionaries came into the neighborhood of Kanghwa and began to teach their doctrine, but on account of a disposition in the people to band together and obstruct the Government, the officials drove away some (missionaries) and slew others. There are at the present time about thirty or forty Buddhist priests, chiefly of the Zen sect, in the neighborhood of Fusankai. At Chindzu, in Kiêngsandô, there is a large monastery containing about three thousand monks. If they are all like this it must be something wonderful.

"Inside the settlement is a building which was formerly a Buddhist monastery, called Tôkôji. Previously to the Restoration of the Mikado it was an agency of the monastery of Saisanji, in the island of Tsushima, and a new abbot was sent thence every three years. It is said, however, that the monastery had very little work to do, beyond examining the composition and interpreting the meaning of the letters sent by the Coreans and by the Government, and at present there is no such work at all. This ex-monastery is under the jurisdiction of our Consulate, and is said to be used now and then as temporary quarters for our naval forces. Up to the present moment no Japanese monastery has been provided.

"About three hundred and sixty yards north of this ex-monastery is the Japanese cemetery. In former days the prince of Tsushima had the Japanese settlement enclosed, and protected by a guard, and the Coreans gave the name of Poppei (a corruption of *bampei*, guards) to the cemetery, from the circumstance of its being situated alongside.

"The oppressive character of the Corean Government in its dealings with the people is such that they seem most like mutual foes, nor have the people the slightest idea of such a thing as a 'right.' Being ensnared by an oppressive system, they habitually resign themselves to their poverty, and take their hard circumstances quietly. If, which seldom happens, there be a wealthy man, the Government urgently commands him to make them a present of money, and to such as obey the command they grant a patent of rank. But if he refuses, the district officials put pressure upon him, and in some cases go so far as to inflict punishment. For this reason the people preferring rather to lie down in poverty than to be punished for being rich, make idleness their chief occupation. The whole nation is stupid and ignorant, and the only matter in which they excel is cunning. In commerce they make a practise of fraud and treachery, nor do they feel any shame when reproached therefor.

"The heartlessness of the Government is indescribable. Although crowds of people were dying of hunger by the roadside during the famine of last year, they took not the slightest heed of their sufferings. And because the spiritless and powerless people never took it into their heads to brandish bamboo-spears and wear mat-banners (figurative expression for an insurrection of a pauper population), and to reproach the Government for not giving them help and succor, the Government were perfectly at ease in their own minds, and pretended to be glad that the people were enjoying the blessings of peace, and patting well-filled bellies. It is impossible to describe in language the unfortunate condition of the people who are born under such a Government. It suggests a doubt whether the Creator is not sometimes unjust.

"The Coreans as a general rule are very particular about forms of salutation, and they will spend the whole day talking with pen and paper (*i. e.* writing down what they want to say in Chinese, which is understood by the Japanese). Our people are very much annoyed with their long visits. Although they are very polite in their pen and paper talk, their manners are extremely bad, for some of them sit cross-legged, and others converse standing. Servant and master sit down together in the same company, and no distinction seems to be observed between noble and mean.

"It is probably owing to the famine of last year that there are so many thieves. Cases of shoplifting are extremely frequent, and they surpass even the ' Little-boy Rat ' (nickname of a famous thief) in the practise of that art. They will take a pen in the right hand, and put down the language of the most honored sages, while with the left they are practising the style of the ' Little-boy Rat. ' One has to keep a sharp lookout.

"All the men are lazy, and the women work to support the men. In Occidental countries men and women have equal authority; in Japan the men are absolute, while in Corea the women exercise all the power, so wonderful are the species of rights. Every man has a wife and a concubine; rich men from three to five of the latter, while many noble officials have six, seven, or even ten.

"If, as seldom happens, a benevolent person among the population builds a house called a depot, and distributes food to the poor in seasons of scarcity, they coolly devour what is given them, without the slightest expression of gratitude.

"According to Corean law no woman may enter the Japanese settlement, but since the famine of last year many women have come in secretly at night to beg for food. * * * *. In consequence of the crews of our vessels, and our residents taking pity on them, and giving them food, it is difficult to get rid of them, and an institution is growing up like that of the "sheep" at Yokohama. This state of things having been discovered by the Corean officials, policemen have come in from Tongkua, and arrested five women. It is said that according to Corean law they will be decapitated, a dreadful thing indeed.

"There is a hospital in the Japanese settlement under the charge of Mr. Yano, a naval surgeon. Japanese and Coreans are equally attended to, and great success has been obtained in the treatment of epidemic disease, such as that which has been prevalent this year. The Coreans are much astonished, and think that there must be something supernatural in the treatment

"There was a Corean patient who had a paralyzed arm from the effects of rheumatism during a long period of years. This man applied to the hospital for treatment. The chief of the hospital passed a current through his arms by means of an electrical machine, and the limb which had been useless for so many years, recovered its powers again. The patient was astounded and said: "This man is Shinnêng (Chinese god of medicine) come to life again;" and in the excess of his joy he became as one mad.

"As to the dress of the Coreans, the men look like Shintô priests dressed in *hitatare*, the women being dressed like servant girls in Europe. They wear tight sleeves and wide plaited trousers.

"A great many Corean beggars come into the settlement to ask for food. Some die by the roadside. The Japanese have agreed together to give them raw and boiled rice; the Ogura Company gave a quantity of corn (wheat or barley). The Coreans say 'The merchant of the Eastern capital is good.' "

The Corean wild animals are the tiger, leopard and wild cat, which has hair like the tiger and is shaped like the *tanuki* (a species of wild dog). There is also a tree-mouse and an animal like the kangaroo of Australia. Its forelegs are short, its hind legs long, with a sack in its belly, into which it puts its young. The Corean name of this is unknown to us.

---

In view of the fact that Corea is to-day the only country on the globe which refuses to have any intercourse with the world at large, the interest generally felt in its history is something quite unusual; and as Japan is the only nation which has any official relations with this "sealed Empire," the subjoined additional facts obtained from a reliable Japanese authority, cannot but be acceptable to the Western public.

The first instance of formal intercourse between the two countries authentically recorded, occurred in the reign of the Mikado Suijin, the tenth of the dynasty which still holds the throne of Japan, thirty-three years before Christ. At this time a messenger from Amana, one of the kingdoms into which Corea was then subdivided, visited Japan bearing presents, and expressing a desire for the interchange of such evidences of mutual good will as were then recognized. This is believed to have been the first occasion of a political visitation from any nation, and may perhaps have been prompted by the wide-spread reputation of Suijin for warlike enterprise. He was the originator of the office and title of "Siogun," which he conferred, not upon one person alone, as was the custom in later years, but upon no less than four military commanders, all of whom were members of his own family. The route taken by this earliest of Corean embassadors, brought him to the place now known as Tsuruga, in the province of Echizen. The envoy remained three years, and, according to the ancient chronicles, was looked upon as the representative of a country that acknowledged itself to be tributary. In the reign of the following Mikado, Suinin, a messenger from the more powerful nation of Sinra appeared, bringing tokens of amity in the shape of mirrors, jade-stones, and various richly decorated weapons. These friendly advances do not appear to have long retarded the aggressive disposition of the Japanese rulers. It is related that a son of the twelfth sovereign, Keiko, led an army through various kingdoms of Corea, in the first century of our era, and reduced them all to submission — but this is less clearly established than other events of the period. The expedition of the Empress Jingo, in the third century, however, is universally accepted as an historical fact. This Amazonian ruler overran the whole of the peninsula, and brought it to such a state of subjection that, for ages after, no thought of omitting the regular tributary embassies was ever entertained. They were continued without interruption until toward the end of the sixteenth century, when the Coreans manifested a preference for China. The military chieftain of that date, Hideyoshi, sent formidable armies to chastise them, and, notwithstanding a stubborn resistance, in which forces from China were joined to those of Corea, he not only secured a renewal of the periodical tribute-bearing messengers, but held, for several years, a large part of territory as well. The war which ended in his triumph was, by the accounts of both Japanese and Chinese historians, one of the most sanguinary upon record.

One of its memorials may be seen to this day, at Kioto, in the extraordinary mound wherein the ears of a vast number of slaughtered Coreans — sixty thousand, it is said — were buried.

During the greater part of the rule of the Tokugawa family in Japan, the regular transmission of costly presents was continued. Some of these, which were sent to Iyeyasu in the beginning of the seventeenth century, are to this day visible in and around the great temples of Nikwo. Again, for many scores of years, the messengers of conciliation brought their offerings, and the practise was not understood to be set aside until after the overthrow of the Siogun, in 1868. But even before that time, it had been suffered to lose much of its form and stateliness, and had altogether ceased to be a direct visitation to the true sovereigns of the Empire, none of whom were approached by the representatives of Corea. It is doubtful, indeed, if the court at Kioto ever even heard of the time of their coming for a couple of centuries or more. The Tokugawas, in their might, ordained that journeys of congratulation should be made, not upon occasions of the Imperial succession, but upon the assumption of power by each of the hereditary chieftains of their house. All tenders of courtesy were proffered, therefore, to the heads of the clan whose seat was Yedo. The visitors were brought, by nearly the same route as the Dutch travellers, to this city, until nearly half a century ago, when their reception was found to involve such heavy and increasing expenses, all of which fell upon Japan, that the plan of cutting short the journey at the outskirts of the Empire was proposed and adopted. The envoys, with their attendants, sometimes formed a body of between three and four hundred men.

At last, in 1837, when the Siogun Iyeyosi succeeded to office, the voyage was so far shortened that the Coreans were required to come only as far as the Island of Tsu, which lies midway between the two nations. After that, no official visits were made during the Siogunate. The rulers of the neighboring kingdom had little disposition to repeat them, and when the next regular occasions returned, the authorities of Yedo were too busily occupied with complications in which Western nations were concerned to attempt to exercise compulsion. After the Restoration of 1868, when the Emperor was firmly re-seated in the Eastern capital, Corea was invited to revive the old methods of intercourse. This appeal, however, was not responded to with cordiality. The Japanese settlement upon the territory of Corea had, indeed, never been surrendered, and was still occupied for purposes of traffic; but, while no desire to break up this connection was manifested, the proposition to renew the periodical embassies was virtually rejected.

For several years prior to 1877, the controlling power of the Kingdom of Corea had been in the hands of individuals whose connection with public affairs began in 1864. Chul Chong, the predecessor of the sovereign now reigning, died in that year, leaving no descendants. It is the custom of the country for the monarch to nominate a successor from among his children, if there be any, and if not, from among his surrounding relations. In this case, however, the death was sudden, and no appointment was made in the usual and expected way.

Certain insignia are associated with the possession of Corean sovereignty, especially a Great Seal, which, in the event of direct succession, is delivered to the acceding king, if he be of age, or to one of the wives of the king who has just died, if the new comer be an infant. This is not understood to be an unalterable rule, but long usage has given it a traditional force which makes it equivalent to established law. The control of the vacant throne became, in 1864, a subject of desperate intrigue, in which many prominent nobles took part, and which threatened, for a while, to throw the country into a state of anarchy. Of the leaders in the dispute, three queens were the most conspicuous. These were the widows of Chul Chong, just deceased, and the two preceding rulers. The matter was at last summarily determined by the eldest of the dowagers, Queen Cho, who laid forcible hands upon the Great Seal, and, armed with this indisputable emblem of authority, proclaimed herself Regent. Precedents and formulas go a great way in lands like Corea, but it is not to be supposed that the contest which was raging, would have been so easily terminated by a *coup de main* if the ambitious woman had not been strongly supported. She had certainly the advantage of age and experience, and no person who has examined the processes by which government control is secured on the Asiatic continent, is unaware of the power which these afford.

The recent resumption of Imperial sway in China by two dowagers, when the young Empress was permitted to die before her consort was cold in his grave, is a case in point. Queen Cho had been more or less familiar with public business for a third of a century. She was the widow of Ik Chong, whose reign terminated in 1830, and the mother of Hen Chong, who acceded in 1834. From this date until 1848, her influence was always indirectly manifest, but in that year, when Chul Chong was appointed, she became less prominent, and gradually appeared to have abandoned all thoughts of supremacy. Chul Chong was not a near relation of hers, having been selected out of the direct line, as his predecessor left no issue. He was therefore placed in a position where he could resist or evade her manœuvres, in case she had attempted to guide him according to her will. But it does not appear that she made any serious effort of the kind. It was not until the energetic act above described after the death of Chul Chong, that she gave evidence of an unchanged spirit and a determination to establish herself, at once and finally, as the dominant power in the nation. Having seized the Seal she first rid herself of the inconvenient rivalry of the two other queens — one of whom, at least, the young widow, was a woman of acknowledged ability — by placing them in confinement, and then looked about her for a suitable occupant of the throne, to reign under her management and dictation. Her preference was for one of her nephews named Cho Sung, a youth of some attainments and considerable promise, who, in more recent times, has gained notoriety in a way that will be described hereafter. But Cho Sung was not sufficiently near to the hereditary line of sovereigns to make the experiment a safe one. He was not, in fact, a member of the one eminent family, which alone is supposed to be eligible. After consultation with her advisers, the Queen concluded to waive her inclinations, and to nominate a child twelve years old, too young to have a voice of his own in the administration of affairs. This was the son of a royal prince named Ni Kung, who, like the renascent Queen, had long been looked upon as indifferent to the sources of supreme authority, so long as his individual comfort and dignity were well assured. Thus the sway of the dowager Cho appeared to be substantially settled. She had not ventured to defy the opinions of the higher classes by making her favorite nephew king, but she kept him within her court, and allowed him to share the privileges of her exalted station. It would be years before the real sovereign would be able to assume control on his own account, and no interference was to be apprehended from his father, who was outside the pale of politics.

This was Queen Cho's dream, but it was too bright to last. The King's father, watching his opportunity, got possession of the Seal, and then commenced a series of pitiless descents upon all those who presumed to array themselves in opposition to his new claims. The onslaught was as triumphant as it was abrupt and unlooked for. Ni Kung at once obtained control of the kingdom, which he continued to hold without effective molestation until the autumn of 1873. He governed with extreme severity, and it is said that the harshest administration previously known, was mild in comparison with his despotic rule. All classes were speedily embittered against him, but the dexterity and ingenuity by which he surrounded himself with impenetrable methods of self-protection were sufficient to baffle all their schemes of retaliation. Circumstances of external contact combined, moreover, to add to his prestige and augment the power he had invested himself with. The French and American visitations were made during his régime, and these, being resisted with what passed for magnificent success among the people, were employed by him as new elements of personal glorification. These repulses of foreigners, as the events were represented to have been, were achievements all in keeping with the national sentiment, and they added to his fame and strength, in spite of the hatred he had incurred. In the same spirit, though not with violence, he caused the several endeavors of the Japanese towards renewed intercourse, to be repelled. It appears that he spared no effort to preserve the conservative traditions of the kingdom in an unbroken perfection. At home he tyrannized, oppressed, extorted and persecuted without limit. Abroad, he recognized no possible contiguity except that of China; and even with that country the relations were so jealously guarded that they could only be considered as strictly formal, and not in any just sense friendly.

To explain the temper of the Coreans respecting the outside world, even as regards their "most favored" nation, it may be interesting to state briefly the manner in which the connection with China was maintained. In order to secure as complete an isolation as possible, Corea has always decreed that a broad belt of land upon the further side of her border shall be a perpetual desert, and this has been agreed to until a very recent period, by China, notwithstanding the fact that the soil of the vacant territory is extermely fertile. A few Chinese risk their lives by cultivating small patches of this neutral ground, but they do not venture to live there, and only plant and gather their produce by stealth.

Upon the Chinese or Manchurian line of the forbidden space, forty or fifty miles distant from the Corean boundary, stands a little village known as "Border Gate," from the circumstance that it contains the real and only opening through which communication is permitted between the two nations. This is described as being in the central compartment of a small house, which is occupied by the customs' officials of both nationalities. At one extremity the Coreans reside; at the other, the Chinese. An apartment in the middle is devoted to the actual business of collecting taxes.

The term "Border Gate" has probably a wider significance than the precise meaning of the words would convey, but, in point of fact, there are two doorways, one at each end of this interior room, respectively under control of the representatives from east and west. These are opened only four times a year: — in the third month of the Chinese calendar, when they remain unclosed for traffic during about ten weeks; in the eighth month, for three weeks; in the ninth month, for six weeks, and in the twelfth month, for twenty-five days. The first and third of these occasions are considered of superior importance, and the gates are unlocked by the principal magistrate of Fung Wang Cheng, the nearest Manchu town, who receives a present of four hundred taels from the Corean official who leads his deputation. The second and fourth are of less moment, and the duty is performed by a subordinate, to whom two hundred taels are presented.

It is obvious from this, that the Coreans look upon the periodical opportunities for trade as privileges worth paying for, although their Government binds them within such narrow limits. At these periods, only, is the interchange of commodities allowed, and it may be mentioned that these commodities are very few in number; skins, hair, ginseng and gold on the Corean side, and the simplest articles of produce on the other. Western cottons are greatly desired by the former, but the Government restrictions upon the admission of European manufactures are so severe, that little can be done in this way. Political communications are regulated with the same caution and reserve.

The chief annual embassy to Peking passes through the Gate when it is opened in the ninth month. Other visitations are said to take place each year, but they are merely journeys of routine, and no importance is attached to them.

Such being the rigorous seclusion in which these people entrench themselves in distrust, if not defiance, of the neighbor for which they profess a certain degree of regard, it may be imagined what their feeling is toward other and remoter nations. The system of seclusion has not been materially changed for centuries; but it will not be inappropriate to mention that events have lately occurred which threaten its overthrow by the usually inert hands of the Chinese themselves.

A long continued series of depredations by bands of Manchu marauders aroused the indignation of Li Hung Chang, the celebrated Chinese general and viceroy of Chihli, to such an extent that he resolved upon the almost unprecedented step of taking measures to suppress them. He sent forces to the borders of Corea, and a gun-boat to coöperate upon the Yalu River, which formed the northern boundary of the kingdom. When it was proved by practical experience that ships could thus penetrate and command the territory of the peninsular kingdom, the necessity for respecting the belt of neutral ground began to be doubted, and preparations were made for occupying it without delay. It is said that a considerable portion has already been measured and laid out by the Chinese surveyors.

This last mentioned incident did not occur during

the term of power of the Regent Ni Kung. Recurring to the career of this arbitrary potentate, it is to be stated that his long course of aggravated misrule came to an end — at least for a series of years — in 1873. The circumstances leading to his deposition are variously narrated, but the following appear to be the best authenticated, and the occasional touches of what might seem a romantic exaggeration to readers far removed from the scene have no unnatural aspect to those who are acquainted with the usages of a people whose intellects have been trained upon a system of Chinese ethics. The old Queen Cho, whose power had been wrested from her a dozen years before, and who had never forgotten nor forgiven the offence, was always unrelenting in her thirst for revenge, and her residence became the rallying place for all the influential disaffected. The leader of this party, which for a long time shrouded its movements in the profoundest secrecy, was her nephew, Cho Sung, who has been spoken of as her first, though impracticable choice for the succession to the throne in 1864. He was now a man of about thirty, and apparently full of activity and vigor. His efforts at concealment were not, however, successful, and at the moment when he was about to put into execution a plot of some magnitude, an order was issued for his arrest. He fled for protection to his aunt, whose arm was still sufficiently strong to give him shelter while he remained within reach. The dowager's fertile invention now conceived a new scheme. Even in retirement, her great age and force of character gave her a pre-eminence which the Regent could not afford to despise. She issued invitations for a private feast, a sort of *déjeuner à trois*, in which the participants were to be herself, her nephew, and the obnoxious Ni

Kung. When they were all seated she announced that the chief ingredient of the principal dish was poison. She lamented the family feuds, deplored the effect they had had upon the country, and said that the only way out of the difficulty was a joint suicide, unless the Regent would accept reasonable terms of reconciliation. To refuse a proposition for self-immolation, under such grave circumstances, would not comport with high Corean dignity ; but as an alternative was offered, and as the lofty functionary did not particularly care to die, he consented to every thing. A truce was patched up, which, however, having no elements of endurance about it, was written in short order. New intrigues were set on foot, and after much difficulty, a petition exhibiting the grievances of the nobles and the people was placed directly in the hands of the young king, who had reached the age of twenty-one. This exploit was a service of no little danger, for if the messengers had been detected in their errand, or if the king had revealed their action prematurely, they would have suffered instant death. He said nothing, but presently began to institute a series of investigations in disguise, in order to discover for himself what amount of truth resided in the complaints addressed to him. He was doubly bound not to accept them blindly, inasmuch as, in addition to the changes of public policy toward which they pointed, they involved accusations of grave crimes on the part of his father. His cause of inquiry soon satisfied him as to the general correctness of the charges, but still he hesitated to act. Although a totally different sort of man from his immediate predecessors, who were semi-idiotic imbeciles, he was not quite prepared to reverse the rôle of Brutus and execute justice on his own sire. Finally, Queen Cho determined upon her last resort. She shut herself up within her own walls, and gave out that she was starving herself to death. Whether she did or did not introduce alterations in her diet is matter for speculation; probably she continued to eat quite as much as was good for her; but at any rate the report spread abroad, until it reached the ears of the king, perhaps during some of his erratic ramblings, whereupon he hastened to visit her, and, with many signs of respect, due to her years and former station, asked an explanation. This was the opportunity she had longed for. She poured out all her troubles, and, it is to be presumed, did not spare her ancient enemy, although she was speaking to his son. The result of the conversation was the announcement, on the part of the king, that for the future he would take the government under his own direction, and that the aged queen need be apprehensive of no more abuses. In the course of a few days he really made his words good. He relieved his father from active duty, and requested him to remain tranquil for a while within the precincts of the palace. This done, he proceeded to throw himself into the arms of the opposition — whether recklessly or with due caution, wisely or unwisely, events have still to prove. Acting by their advice, he abruptly dismissed the great ministers nearest the throne, of which there are three, as in Japan, and replaced them by friends and partisans of the notable Cho Sung. Upon this dignitary, however, the real and welcome weight of power and authority was now thrown, although the king had renounced the regency of his father, who presently withdrew to retirement at some distance from the capital. The monarch reigned, but Cho Sung was the power behind him. And, so far as can be now discovered, he continued to hold that sway until the approach of the Japanese complications.

During the year 1872, attempts at negotiation were continually repeated by various deputies, the most urgent and impressive of which were conducted by an attaché of the Foreign Department, named Moriyama, an officer of skill and address, though not of elevated rank. He did what he could to modify the stubborn temper of the Coreans with whom he came in contact, and, in 1874, succeeded so far as to secure a promise from the magistrates of Torai Fu, the chief town in the neighborhood of Fusan, that letters explanatory of the Japanese views and intentions should be received and properly considered. This pledge, however, was disavowed by the central authorities. The documents were duly prepared and presented, but were rejected without a reason being offered for the breach of faith. By this time it was clear that the obstinacy of Corea could be overcome only by a demonstration — pacific or otherwise — sufficiently imposing to teach them that they were trifling with their own destiny in an extremely hazardous manner.

As to the feelings by which the Corean Court was animated at that time, it is impossible to speak with equal certainty, although we are not wholly without information upon the point. It was first awakened to the possibility of a rupture by a false alarm communicated by the Chinese Government at the time when the Japanese Commissioner, Okubo, was driving the Tsung li Yamen to the wall with his irresistible arguments upon the Formosan question. The Chinese thought it a fine stroke of diplomacy to kindle a spirit of active enmity against Japan among the people of Corea. This was their idea of a strategetic diversion. They sent several successive messengers, in the summer of 1874, bearing the fictitious intelligence that an alliance had been concluded between Japan, France and the United States, for the purpose of subjugating the little kingdom. An immense excitement spread through that land in consequence.

At this period no great fear appeared to be entertained respecting France or America, for the reason that expeditions from these countries, which were looked upon as invasions, had been met with forcible resistance, and, according to the self-satisfied theory of Corea, had been victoriously repelled. But in regard to Japan the feeling was different. Tradition had preserved a lively recollection of the horrors of Taiko's conquest at the end of the sixteenth century, in which parts of the country had been utterly devastated, and whole provinces depopulated. Taiko's war was virtually one of extermination, and the ferocity with which he waged it may be understood from the circumstance of his decree, before alluded to, that the whole population of the fortified city of Kishin — the last Corean stronghold — should be destroyed, and that the ears of the dead should be sent to fill a mound at Kioto. The Coreans of 1874 were apprehensive of a renewal of these cruelties. While they instantly applied themselves to preparations upon the largest scale of which they were capable, they despatched extraordinary embassies to Peking in quest of further information and advice. These messengers were told that when the combined attack should be made, or beforehand, if occasion served, the most judicious course would be to make treaties with America and France, based upon those which China had concluded, but to oppose and defy Japan to the last. So far as has since been learned, a good part of this counsel — that is, the pacific part — commended itself favorably to the young king, who forthwith declared his resolution to discontinue the excessive preparation for war, and to maintain only the usual armament of the country. His nearest advisers, Cho Sung and the three great ministers, fell in with his ideas, but the ex-Regent, his father, sent strong protests, and was vehement in urging unconditional resistance to all invaders, or even visitors, on friendly grounds. About this time a new element of influence began to appear at Court, in the person of the legitimate queen, a young woman to whom great intelligence and force of character are attributed, and who, it is said, seized upon this crisis as the first convenient opportunity for asserting herself.

The chosen favorite of 1873, Cho Sung, had not long exercised his functions of familiar councillor to the king, before he was accused of practises almost as nefarious as those which had blackened the reputation of Ni Kung. Corruption of all kinds was ascribed to him and his associates, and the question began to be agitated whether the country had gained a particle by the radical change of administration. But the king clung to him for a long time, and, in fact, does not appear to have ever wholly abandoned him. It is open to doubt whether the sovereign is capable, in a country like Corea, of carrying out any extensive plans of reform. His intentions may be excellent, yet he may have no power to enforce them. It is possible that in taking up with the Cho party he merely made the best of a choice of evils. In one or two important crises since 1873, he undoubtedly displayed a disposition to assert himself with considerable firmness in the management of affairs. Precisely what his qualities are, nobody can presume to say with confidence. It is clear enough, however, that, in 1874, the influence of the young queen Min became paramount, and her voice was strong in advocacy of an amicable attitude towards Japan. An absolute change of policy could not, however, be suddenly agreed to. The opinion of the highest authorities gradually settled itself upon the retention of the old forms of refusal to recognize foreigners, to the extent of repulsing them by force up to a certain point, and then yielding, slowly and reluctantly, such concessions as should seem unavoidable. In one matter the Coreans were indisposed to listen to China. They did not feel inclined to exclude Japan from participation in the privileges they might find it expedient to grant. In fact, partly from fear of consequences, and partly from the influences of old association, they were a trifle better affected towards the Japanese than to the others.

Such, with few changes, the condition of affairs remained up to the autumn of 1875, when the assault upon the Japanese ship *Unyo K'wan*, and the immediate destruction of a Corean fort in retribution, gave a new color to the transactions. The operations of this vessel of war previous to the memorable engagement in which she was concerned, are not without interest in connection with the general subject. Her two cruises in 1875 were distinguished by many incidents which gave rise to much discussion.

In May of that year she paid a visit to Fusan, where the captain entertained a number of native officials on board, regaling them with, among other things, a sham fight between his own ship and another that happened to be in harbor, at the tumult and explosive uproar of which the timorous guests were terrified almost out of their wits. Sailing northward, she touched at a port named Hamikian, where her crew went ashore for the purpose of extinguishing a conflagration which had broken out, and which the inhabitants could not master.

This having been accomplished, and the captain, compassionating the sufferers, having bestowed a sum of two thousand cash upon them, she again turned to the north and anchored in the bay of Unkotsuki. It has never appeared whether or not her officers considered the question of her right to enter these places. However, no opposition was offered, and the people appeared wholly taken by surprise.

There was a trifling difficulty with some minor officials in Unkotsuki, who behaved with a rudeness that indicated ignorance rather than evil intent, and a deputation went on shore to insist upon apologies. During an interview with the Chief Magistrate, attempts were made to intimidate them by the assumption of a somewhat offensive demeanor, and by the collection of a considerable force of soldiery, three hundred or four hundred in number. But the Japanese were firm, and at last a promise was given that the culprits should be severely punished. Here, however, having secured an acknowledgment of the error, they interposed, and only a simple reprimand was administered. After this, the *Unyo Kwan* returned to Japan in July, and in August again started for a cruise in the Yellow Sea, etc., her first destination being Niuchuang.

On the nineteenth of September, her supply of water falling short, she put into the Bay of Kokwa—in the waters of which the fight with the American ships had taken place—and attempted to land a boat's crew. The question of her right to make this adventure, under the existing conditions of intercourse between Japan and Corea, may have been an open one. The boat was immediately fired upon from the shore, and a smart exchange of shots from small arms ensued. Presently the large guns of a fortification upon the island of Kokwa (or Yeiso) were discharged, and the boat prudently withdrew. It was not in the captain's humor to receive an assault like this without inflicting retribution. The next day he opened fire from his ship, but without decisive effect, in consequence of his inability to get near the shore, and the difficulty of navigation in the strong currents produced by the outflow of the river of Seoul. On the morning of the twenty-first he despatched two boats with a force consisting of three officers, ten marines, and twenty-three sailors. More could not be spared, as the *Unyo Kwan* is a small ship — merely a gunboat — but these were enough.

They landed close to one of the gates of the fort, and advanced to the attack without delay. In the first onset, two Japanese were wounded. The little band of assailants was divided, the larger number engaging the attention of the besieged at the eastern extremity, while some half-a-dozen were sent to cut off a retreat in the opposite direction. An entrance was effected in a very few minutes, the Japanese climbing over the wall and driving the defenders before them with little difficulty. After one shock, the Corean soldiers fled in a panic, and endeavored to escape by a bridge to a neighboring island. Here they were intercepted by the little flanking party, and, forsaking the usual route, they took to the water and endeavored to swim across the channel. The greater number of them were either shot or drowned, and only five or six reached the opposite shore. About a dozen prisoners were seized, from whom was ascertained that the garrison had been composed of two hundred and fifty men. These captives were straightway employed in transporting the spoils of the victory to the ship. The fort was entirely dismantled, and all the buildings within it were burned. The trophies secured were thirty-six bronze cannon, some scores of matchlock muskets, numerous bows and arrows, spears and swords, together with several drums and trumpets. A Chinese translation of a French treatise on gunnery was also among the abandoned effects. Detachments of marines and sailors remained on the island during the day of the fight and that following, with the Japanese flag conspicuously displayed from their quarters, but no token of a disposition to renew the contest came from the defeated party. On the twenty-third the *Unyo Kwan* started for Nagasaki, setting aside the projected visit to Niuchuang. As soon as she reached Japan, the news of what had occurred was telegraphed to the capital. It does not appear to have been looked upon as an event necessarily leading to immediate war, for the envoy Moriyama, who had recently returned home, was immediately sent back with fresh instructions to his old post at Fusan. But it at once became the absorbing topic in ministerial circles, and the necessity for prompt action in the matter was recognized on all sides.

Early in the autumn of 1875, these complications had grown beyond the proportions which, under ordinary circumstances, would properly belong to them in consequence of domestic political dissensions. In Japan, as elsewhere, if differences arise within the Government, or if the opposing forces outside the Government succeed in making themselves formidable, any topic of public significance is sure to be seized by both parties and variously used to suit the necessities of the occasion. This matter of Corea was undoubtedly serious to some extent, standing by itself. The rulers of the continental kingdom had persistently shown a quarrelsome determination, and it had become an important problem whether they should continue to be dealt with by the gentle methods of argument and persuasion, or by summary force. For a considerable while the opponents of active hostility had the advantage. They carried the weight of intellect with them, although they were perhaps inferior in numbers, and so long as the Coreans abstained from acts of positive violence, no convincing reason for taking arms against them could be alleged. But the situation was materially changed by the affair of the *Unyo Kwan.* There were some who went so far as to say that the assault was purposely provoked, with the intention of strengthening the hands of the war party.

This accusation was not worthy of belief, but still the turbulent spirits did unquestionably gain power by the transaction. The peace men, however, were as firm as before. They insisted that, even in the new aspect of events, nothing appeared to warrant an organized invasion. They were supported by all the prominent public journals, and by the best instructed part of the community at large, and if nothing but the naked question of Corean relations had been allowed to mingle in the discussions, they would have carried their point. But just at this time other elements of discord in the administration began to declare themselves.

Topics of far greater importance, in many senses, than a foreign war—since they involved the entire re-adjustment of the management of public affairs — agitated the members of the Cabinet, and with these the business of Corea gradually became so interwoven that no separation was possible. One of the results, by no means so indirect as was then supposed, was the withdrawal from office of Shimadzu Hisamitsu, the second officer under the crown, and Itagaki Taisuke, of the Imperial Council. The radical changes which these leaders were struggling to introduce had no legitimate association with Corea, but the majority of the Government felt that they must be controverted at all hazards, and they consequently waived their disagreements on other points, in order to offer a combined resistance to the innovators. In this way the chief opposition to a demonstration of force disappeared. It was agreed that the contumacious little kingdom should be vigorously dealt with. The party of prudence and forethought took their last stand on the necessity of making proper provision in all directions, and the propriety of prefacing the actually hostile demand with a final urgent appeal to reason. For more than this they felt it would be useless to contend.

One of the most earnest advocates of this policy was Arinori Mori, the Shoyu, or third official, of the Foreign Department. He was appointed envoy to China, and, in December, 1875, went to Peking to discover the opinions held by the Chinese on the subject. It was not forgotten that, two and a half years before, when the embassador Soyezima visited that capital for a similar purpose, and secured an acknowledgment of acquiescence in Japanese movements, both as regards Corea and Formosa, he neglected to obtain this assurance in writing. Of course no oversight of this kind could be repeated. On every account it was essential to know with as definite a precision as possible, the view that China would take, and the action, if any, that she would pursue. Whatever Mori might procure, he was to get in a form that should leave no opportunity for subsequent evasion. It was hoped that China would be persuaded to remain passive, and this hope was fortunately realized; but if she had refused to define her position, or shown herself arrogant and obstructive, preparations would have been rapidly made to conduct operations on a broad and sweeping scale. The ultimate enterprise, however it might have been delayed, would never have been abandoned. In point of fact, there were not a few who ardently hoped that China would be unreasonable, and declare a determination to interfere in the dispute. Many Japanese of prominent station still smarted under the recollection of the behavior of the neighboring empire during the Formosa affair, and would have welcomed a chance to deal a sturdy blow in retaliation, no matter at what desperate hazard.

The conditions under which the direct expedition was organized immediately after Mr. Mori's departure, led both sides, the war extremists and the partisans of peace, to believe that their views were in the ascendant. It had been decided that the Coreans should have one more chance of averting hostilities, and that then, if they would not show themselves repentant for their acts of violence, and willing to open relations with Japan, they should be forced into submission. But it was not now believed that they would voluntarily yield, and a conflict was looked upon as a foregone conclusion. It was settled that an officer of the highest rank should be despatched, bearing the same credentials and titles as those of a minister to a friendly nation. If his overtures should be accepted, no occasion for a contest would arise. If rejected, the application of force would follow in due season. This plan having been adopted, all parties were contented. The advocates of "moral suasion" gained a concession, and the combative spirits were entirely satisfied for the reason that they felt sure that the Coreans would again resist, and thus strengthen their position more than ever.

On the thirteenth of December a decree was promulgated, giving notice of the appointment of Kuroda Kiyotaka, Lieutenant-General of the Army, Imperial Councillor and Chief of the Kai Taku Shi, or Colonization Department, as Envoy Extraordinary, Minister Plenipotentiary and Consul General to Corea. The selection of this officer for the post was looked upon as another point gained by the belligerently disposed. He was known to be essentially a man of war. His nomination, though probably not intended as such, was taken in the light of an offset to that of Mori, who was all for peace, if it could be maintained in any honorable way. And his position of head of the Kai Taku Shi was made to serve the same kind of argument; since, it was asked, if Corea was not to be subdued and annexed as well, why should it come within the scope of a Colonial Bureau? This, however, was going altogether too-far. General Kuroda's instructions were to sail to the Bay of Kokwa, to wait at a reasonable distance from the capital, Seoul, and to communicate with the shore in such manner as should seem most favorable for his purposes, without provoking hostilities. He was to request that a statement of the circumstances of his appointment, his rank and powers, and the general objects of his mission be transmitted to the highest authorities. If he succeeded in producing the required impression, he would advance to the nearest city and seek an interview with some dignitary empowered to represent the sovereign. He would then demand that certain ports be opened for trade, that regular diplomatic intercourse be established, and that all Japanese ships seeking shelter upon the coast should be properly protected. These were laid down as the principal stipulations. If they should be agreed to, "war thoughts would leave their places vacant." If rejected, the preparations that were to continue without interruption, in Japan, during the progress of the mission, would be hurried forward, and the campaign would begin as early as practicable in the spring or summer of 1876.

An assistant commissioner, Inouye Kaoru, was appointed to share the labors of General Kuroda. This well known politician had been a prominent agent of the Chosiu clan in former days, and had held various offices of responsibility under the new Government. At the outset of the difficulty, one of the Imperial Council, Kido Koin, from Chosiu, prepared a comprehensive memorial for the Government, suggesting methods of settlement, and it was for a time supposed that he sought the appointment of Commissioner. This, however, was evidently not his desire, for when the question of sending him was raised, he absented himself from public view, and refused to be seen or consulted. The general conviction was, that Inouye was chosen as an indication that the wishes of the Chosiu element should not be disregarded. And he undoubtedly had powerful personal friends, among whom the Minister of Public Works was most conspicuous. They were companions in European travel, and had ever since been close allies, and the Sangi Ito's voice was never silent when the interests of his old associate were concerned. In addition to this companion, Kuroda was attended by Moriyama, and a large staff of subordinates. One of these was a native Corean named Kin Rinshio, who, escaping from the persecutions of his Government a few years ago, first placed himself under the protection of the Russian authorities, and then came to Japan, apparently in the genuine belief that from the action of this country, whatever it might be, great benefits would flow to his countrymen. In his somewhat circuitous way, he considered himself a patriot, and in no sense a traitor to his own land. His hatred was all for the Government, which he declared was ruining the kingdom as well as destroying the populace, and he was ready to assist in any work that should promise the overthrow of the present system of misrule. For the time being he regarded himself as a Japanese, and his sincerity was unquestioned.

The expedition sailed in January, 1876, and proceeded to its appointed destination. For about a fortnight, its progress was communicated with regularity to the Government at Tokio, after which a long hiatus ensued, during which no official intelligence of any kind was transmitted. The fleet, passing through the Strait of Simonoseki, touched at the Island of Tsu, the connecting geographical link between the two countries, and reached the Japanese settlement of Fusan on the fifteenth of the month. On the twenty-third it started northward for the point fixed upon for debarkation. But from this date, until the positive settlement of the subsequent negotiations, no despatches from the Commissioners were received. It was known, informally, that they had reached Kokwa, and effected a landing, but all details were withheld. The omission gave rise to no anxiety, though possibly to some slight dissatisfaction.

It was argued by the Japanese authorities, that no important event, either of an amicable or a hostile character, could have occurred. If the embassy had gained a diplomatic success, or if, on the other hand, it had been menaced by the Coreans, there would probably have been no such delay. While Government, as a body, was perhaps not pleased with this protracted reticence, the individuals composing it appeared ready enough to make excuses on the ground that Kuroda had a right to withhold communications until he had done something worth telling about. Messages were more than once sent to him — not in complaint, as was alleged by a few newspapers, but to acquaint him with the progress of affairs at home, and to impart the information received from Minister Mori, which was to the effect that China disavowed all responsibility for the action of Corea, and admitted the propriety of Japan's taking measures to secure redress for the various injuries inflicted. Mr. Mori had now been in Peking for a month, and from the time of his arrival there he had found that such a disavowal was to be expected. If the Chinese had put forward any claim of authority over Corea, in this case, they would have rendered themselves liable not only to the Japanese demands for compensation, but also to those of the French and United States Governments, both of which had similar accounts to be settled. Their declarations of neutrality were not so informal as in the matter of Formosa, when, as has been mentioned, they gave only a verbal pledge of non-interference, and broke it at the first opportunity. The one mistake of Japan's representative, on that earlier occasion, was the failure to secure a written promise on this point. That error was not again committed, and the Chinese authorities were firmly bound, so far as the seals of the Tsung li Yamen could bind them, to abstain from participation in the impending events, whether the contact should be friendly or hostile. A special mission had been sent from Peking to Corea since the arrival of Mori in the Chinese capital, and to this circumstance a great deal of importance was attached by many observers; but in fact these messengers had been appointed and charged with their specific duty a long time before the trouble with Japan came to a crisis, and it was only through accidental delay that they failed to start before Mori reached his post. They went to carry an Imperial patent of investiture for the son of the Corean king, as heir apparent to the throne, which patent had been petitioned for nearly two years previously. It is likely enough that advantage was taken of the opportunity to convey the opinions, desires and purposes of China upon the Japanese question, but that was a very different proceeding from the express despatch of an embassy to discuss this point alone.

During the interval of uncertainty, namely, from the twenty-third of January until the end of February, the Japanese preparations were continued without any abatement. Arms, ammunition and supplies of all kinds were forwarded in great quantities to Simonoseki and the Island of Tsu. Artisans and mechanics of various craft were also in readiness near the scene, to be transferred to the continent at short notice. Numbers of ships were fitted up for the transportation of troops and horses. Maps and charts were printed by the War Department, supplying complete guidance to every part of the kingdom, and exhibiting a truly extraordinary degree of research, considering the impenetrability of the territory and the obstinate determination of the Coreans to keep their land unknown. The naval charts contained all the verified soundings of the coast that had been obtained by Western visitors, with the additional results of Japanese observations, and, in particular, a detailed and elaborate statement as to the accessible harbors, the extent to which the rivers were navigable, the force and direction of the currents, etc. The land maps were accompanied by books describing the ports that might be safely entered, the distance from each one to the capital, the character of the routes, the rivers and chains of mountains that would have to be crossed, and the capacity of the several regions to contribute to the support of an invading army. It now came to be understood that, in the event of strife, Lieutenant General Yamagata, Minister of the War Department, would take the chief control of army operations. For the command of the navy, Admiral Yenomoto, was to be recalled from his post of Envoy to Russia.

While the Japanese Government at home remained in a somewhat protracted ignorance of the movements in Corea, events of great interest were in fact progressing there. General Kuroda and his associates had sailed from Fusan, as has been mentioned, on the twenty-third of January, the objective point being the mouth of the river upon which the Corean capital, Seoul, is situated. The progress was necessarily moderate, it being considered of importance that the ships should all keep together, and the rate of advance being thus determined by the slowest. They met in rendezvous on the twenty-fifth, at the Island of Kualio, and on the twenty-ninth, at the Island of Taifu. From this point the walls of the capital were plainly visible, and here a delay of several days took place, for the arrangement of the final preparations. One other island (Chosan) was visited before the place of debarkation was reached.

On the tenth of February the envoys and their suite landed without opposition upon Kokwa, near the scene of the skirmish between the Corean soldiers and the crew of the *Unyo Kwan*, and at once proceeded to a distance of about two miles toward the centre of the island, where they established themselves in the chief town of the neighborhood, occupying the premises usually in the possession of the military ruler of that district. The entrance was made as effective as possible by the aid of detachments of marines and sailors from the various ships, who acted as escort, and whose movements appeared to excite the greatest astonishment on the part of all who saw them. The members of the commission, dressed in full uniform, reached their quarters in the middle of the afternoon. With very little delay they were visited by two officers appointed to receive them and their attendants.

These delegates, named Ji Shin-Ken and Inji Shio, aged respectively about sixty-five and fifty years, represented themselves as having full power to treat with the visitors upon all subjects. The former was announced as holding the highest rank in Corea, the equivalent of "Ip-pon" in Japan, a fact of which it was thought desirable to obtain evidence before entering upon discussions. Formal salutations were exchanged, and the remainder of the day was occupied in ceremonies of courtesy, and such offerings of hospitality as the Corean dignitaries were able to supply. A simple feast was prepared, the entertainment being enlivened by the performance of specimens of ancient Chinese music. During the evening the Japanese despatched a messenger requesting that the work in hand be entered upon the next day. Accordingly, on the eleventh, the subject of a treaty for the maintenance of friendly relations was taken up, not without manifest reluctance on the side of the Coreans. It was earnestly debated for three days, at the end of which an interval of ten days was requested, in order that the matter be referred for consideration to the court of Seoul.

This appeal was urgently combated by Kuroda and Inouye, who argued that as the capital was only twenty-five miles distant, the demand was unreasonable. They proposed that the answer should be returned within five days, but as the Coreans expressed great anxiety to secure a longer time, it was firmly agreed that the ten should be conceded, but only upon condition that there should then be no further conferences, and that at the expiration of the term allowed the treaty should be returned, signed and approved by the King. With this understanding the native officials took leave and departed for the seat of Government.

During their absence opportunity was taken to examine the locality with some minuteness. Many sketches were made, and voluminous descriptions prepared by attachés who appeared, from the quality of their work, to be adapted to the duties of quick and comprehensive reporting. Their narratives were not found on subsequent examination to be of a character to inspire much admiration for the social condition of Corea. The town of Kokwa is looked upon as a place of considerable importance, and may be at times a residence of the sovereign; but it consists of only some two thousand houses, few of which are more than twelve feet high, and all, with the exception of half a dozen official dwellings, being meanly built of mud and coarse straw. The people appeared to be in a state of abject degradation.

At the expiration of the ten days agreed upon the native officials presented themselves, but only to announce their inability to fulfil the conditions to which they had pledged themselves. The envoys at once adopted a very short method of dealing with them. They declared they could now listen to no arguments or remonstrances, and that nothing but a positive promise to produce the treaty, signed and ratified, within a specified time, should induce them to remain a day longer on shore. This having been met.with an apparent attempt at evasion, the entire Japanese party abandoned their quarters, and went on board the ships, excepting only two subordinate officers who remained to collect baggage, etc.

The Coreans thus fully persuaded that their visitors were not to be trifled with, besought these two attachés to carry to the Chief Commissioner their entreaties that he would return, and their assurances that no further cause of reasonable complaint should be given. Upon the strength of these protestations the communications were renewed, but in a spirit, on the Japanese side, that plainly demonstrated the inexpediency of further efforts to protract the settlement. It was timidly intimated by the Coreans that the main obstacle to a prompt conclusion was the requirement by Kuroda and Inouye, that the actual signature of the King should be affixed to the document as a guarantee of fidelity in its execution. This was a matter which had previously been argued at some length, but chiefly by members of the embassy representing the Japanese Foreign Office, and not by the leader.

The native commissioners now represented with

great earnestness the difficulty, which they pronounced insurmountable, of yielding this point. It was explained to them, however, that it was deemed indispensable, for the reason that the Corean Government might hereafter repudiate the whole transaction, and claim that the arrangement had been made by irresponsible agents, without the knowledge or sanction of the highest authority, unless this proof of royal acquiescence were obtained. Then came a flood of asseverations that such a thing had never been done or even heard of in Corea; that the monarch never attached his name to any thing; that to ask him to append it with his own hand would be an act of temerity they could never venture upon, and much more of the same sort. All this was cut short by the curt announcement of a new departure, from which there would be no recall. Messrs. Ji Shin-Ken and Inji Shio then surrendered without further struggle, and asked only for sufficient time to go to Seoul for the ratification and return.

After this all went smoothly. The two additional days required were passed in amicable intercourse, exchanges of presents and consultations respecting the probable course of future relations between the two countries. The gifts offered by the Japanese were in some instances looked upon with grave suspicion. Several of them were of European or American manufacture, and the inscriptions or trade marks upon them were recognized and regarded as carrying with them some direful influence of Western blight and destruction. In regard to the methods of conducting a diplomatic connection they seemed greatly at a loss, and no doubt they sincerely felt so. The treaty arranged for the visit of a Corean ambassador to Japan at an early date. They frankly admitted that they knew nothing about such usages, and that they had no means of sending a representative, being without suitable ships, or the means of buying them. The Japanese set aside this obstacle by undertaking to supply transportation for all that might be appointed to come. A partial understanding followed, to the effect that much good might be accomplished by selecting young men from Corean families known to be the most hostile to the idea of foreign associations and sending them to Japan for education in the national schools. Ample apologies were offered for the discourteous responses given in late years to messages from the Court of Tokio, and also for the attack upon the gunboat *Unyo Kwan*, the nationality of which vessel, it was protested, was entirely unknown to the assailants. The objections of the Coreans to other outside nations, excepting Japan, presented themselves in a very strong light. They pleaded that the Japanese should do all that they could to prevent strangers from a distance attempting to visit them, and, above all, they wanted Christians to be kept away.

But to appeals of this kind no response was given, although an erroneous impression gained currency at the time among foreigners in Japan to the effect that stipulations were made subjecting Europeans and Americans to Japanese rule in case they should go to the newly opened land, and requiring Japan to be responsible for their behavior. No such thing was done or even remotely thought of. The Japanese negotiations had reference only to what concerned this Empire and its people. In regard to commercial operations, a disposition was shown to obtain a promise that certain objectionable articles, like opium, should never be introduced; but details of that kind were all postponed for consideration at a much later period.

On the twenty-seventh of February, the Treaty was brought to Kokwa, duly signed and attested, and affirmed by the King's autograph, all as required. Early on the twenty-eighth, the embassy started homeward, arriving on the first of March at Simonoseki, whence an outline of the proceedings was telegraphed to the capital. On the fifth Kuroda and his companions landed at Sinagawa, near Tokio, finishing their journey by railroad. They were received with great distinction in the hall of the Dai Jo Kuwan, by the Emperor and the highest officials of the state. The effect produced by the intelligence they brought was not confined to the governing and the noble classes. All Japan seemed to be presently in a glow of excitement over the peaceful and successful result of the expedition. The satisfaction was not so clamorously expressed as that which followed the settlement of the Formosa affair, a year before, but it appeared to be quite as general and profound.

There is no doubt that the vast majority of the Japanese at last accepted the view that a triumph thus obtained was the best possible event that could have happened for the country. Even those who had been most resolutely bent upon a conflict were silenced, if not wholly convinced. The Government gained a strength with the masses that it never before possessed. Foreign observers, including many of the envoys, were almost enthusiastic in declaring their surprise and admiration. Now and again it was whispered that it came a little hard upon some of the official representatives from abroad to have to acknowledge that Japan had once more carried through a work which Western powers had undertaken in vain.

Two or three of the most prominent among them had withheld their encouragement from the beginning, and prognosticated nothing but humiliation and defeat for the enterprise; but now, the difficulties having been overcome, even they joined, though somewhat faintly, in the general congratulations. On all sides it was received as a happy conclusion that, in spite of the almost universal expectation of one period not long past, and the avowed desire of an influential party in Japan, peace would be maintained, and the vast preparations for hostilities turned to no immediate use. These preparations were nevertheless admitted to have had great weight and many indirect advantages. It was the knowledge of the readiness of Japan to enter upon a conflict, in case of need, that most deeply impressed Corea with the necessity of abandoning her pretentions. Exactly the same result had come from the Japanese demonstrations in respect to China a year and a half previous. It seemed to have been adopted as a principle by the Government, to engage in no dispute the result of which was doubtful, without simultaneously providing for the worst emergencies that might arise. The American and French expeditions to Corea were feeble affairs, and were known to be unsupported by a determination to push them to an extremity. For this reason they were repulsed. At least one half the secret of Japan's success was the character she had acquired, and which she seemed resolved to maintain, of proving herself in earnest by straining every energy to meet the possible necessity of an appeal to arms long before that necessity became inevitable.

The Treaty which followed on the part of Japan was signed by Kuroda Kiyotaka and Inouye Kaoru, and for Corea by Shin-Ken and Inji Shio. It was considered only as a preliminary paper, upon which a more permanent Convention should subsequently be based. Conditions of trade were especially to be arranged, and these were subsequently agreed upon in the Corean capital, by officers especially assigned to that work. But to give complete validity to the whole transactions of February, 1876, it was thought necessary that the provisions of the second article should be expressly carried out. Corea was urged with some earnestness to avail herself of "the right to send an Envoy to Tokio" at the earliest practicable moment. On this occasion, no disposition to interpose obstacles was manifested. An embassy was appointed in April, and on the third of May a steamship was despatched to Fusan, to bring over these bearers of reciprocal messages. They embarked with little delay, and arrived in Yokohama Bay on the evening of May twenty-eighth, having stopped briefly on the way at Tsu Island, Simonoseki and Hiogo. They finally landed on the morning of the twenty-ninth, and their appearance on shore was signalized by the gathering of a crowd whose eagerness to view them may be estimated by the fact that while the name of Corea has always been familiar in the mouths of the Japanese, no inhabitant of that nation had before been seen in this locality by any now alive.

It has been mentioned that the relations between the two countries were virtually discontinued two generations ago, but more than forty years had passed since Corean travellers had come as far eastward as Yokohama or Tokio. In very early days, the formal visits were paid to the ancient Mikados or their direct representatives, in Kioto or thereabout, but this practise was set aside nearly three centuries ago, and was now resumed for the first time. These visits were not altogether interrupted, but they were subject to peculiar regulations, in consequence of which, as has been explained, it is probable that the Mikados never even heard of them.

The new ambassador was more moderate in respect to the number of his retainers than his ancient predecessors, who were sometimes attended by four hundred followers. But even he was surrounded by a somewhat formidable party, when it is considered that the entire expenditure for the journey and maintenance of the guests was to be sustained, as in other days, by the Japanese Government. The number was about eighty. There was but one envoy, properly speaking, by name Kin-ki-shiu. The rank of this official was high in his own land. He was of course a nobleman, or he could not hold any position whatever, Corea being in this respect unlike Japan, where men of extremely humble origin may now rise to the highest political grades. In the line of his functions of state, at home, he was understood to be equal to the Sangi, or Imperial Councillors, in Japan. The question of his exact station appeared, however, to be complicated by an effort to classify him in some way as an officer for foreign affairs. The Coreans, of course, have no Foreign Department, and, in their lack of general acquaintance with the subject, invested him with powers equivalent only to those of the person holding the third position in the Foreign Office of Japan. But his movements were not hampered by considerations of this sort. It was determined, from the first, to allow him the fullest privileges of an ambassador, as they are understood in common diplomatic usage. This was partly out of goodwill, and partly from motives of sound policy. On the one hand, it was desired to make him as comfortable and free from restraint as possible; on the other, it was not considered judicious to give his Government the opportunity of denying claims that might in future be made by Japanese envoys on the ground that none such were put forward by the representative of Corea.

The effect of the procession formed by the visitors after landing, on the morning of May twenty-ninth, was curious and amusing, though not impressive, estimating it by a Western standard. Two soldiers led the way. They were followed by a band of about twenty, who played upon instruments which, having been accepted as musical when they were invented, some thousands of years ago, are so regarded to this day — in the East. They consisted of tubes of reed and wood, in various forms, the tones of all of which were harsh and dissonant to foreign ears, and numerous objects of percussion in skin and brass. The performance was not agreeable to American or European listeners, though why the Japanese derided it, as they persistently did, it is difficult to understand.

Following the band, marched two young men, who were then and afterwards generally mistaken for girls, in consequence of their hair being parted in the middle and braided in long tails. They belonged to a class to whom the care of important documents of state is confided. Next came a body of military attachés, bearing spears and flags. Then the envoy, seated high in air, upon a tiger-skin covered bench or stool fitted into a platform some eight feet square, which was held aloft by the arms or shoulders of eight men. He was especially escorted by the four officers next below him — at a great distance — in rank, and was followed by a servant bearing a huge umbrella. The few remaining members of the suit rode in Japanese "jin riki sha," drawn by native laborers.

The costumes of the party, as a rule, were not striking. The hues were various enough, but were far from harmonious in their disposition, and the best of the silks were coarse and ill-wrought. In form, the garments were nearly all alike. Shoes of Chinese shape, tightly bound leggings after the Chinese pattern, trousers broad and loose, reaching a little below the knees, silken coats fitting with partial compactness and half hidden by a species of loose overshirt were worn by all. Hats were common, but apparently not indispensable. The best were constructed of horse hair cloth, semi-transparent, and stretched upon light frames. Others were of more solid fabrics, but all were similar in shape, conical and broad brimmed. Some were decorated with artificial plumes, some with natural feathers, and some with drooping chains of variously colored beads, which also served as fastenings. From the usual method of dressing the hair, fastening it in a heavy knot on the top of the head, there was no variation excepting in the cases of the two lads before mentioned. Most of them wore beards, though not in profusion. The majority of the party were tall, as compared with Japanese, and well-proportioned. The envoy himself was a man who would attract attention wherever he might travel : of good stature, dignified and manly bearing, and with a countenance which, when not half hidden by the unwieldy home-made spectacles he generally used, indicated intelligence.

After breakfasting at the Town Hall of Yokohama, the guests proceeded in the same order of march to the railway station, and were conveyed to Tokio in one of the regular trains, extra carriages being provided for their accommodation. Their arrival was witnessed by the largest crowd of spectators that had assembled upon any occasion within the memory of foreigners. It had, indeed, only recently come to the knowledge of the Japanese populace that they were permitted to gather in great numbers for any purpose.

From the terminus in the capital the envoy was conducted to the residence prepared for him and his followers — a distance of about two miles. The same stately precision was observed in the formation and movement of the procession, and the same music desolated the air as before. The immense body of spectators were profuse, in good humor, and by no means slow to demonstrations of mirth, but never rude or intrusive, which, in fact, Japanese throngs have not yet learned how to be. During the remainder of the day the strangers rested quietly; excepting that at nightfall their orchestra saluted the departing sun with a burst of clangor.

On the morning of the thirtieth, the envoy, attended by a portion of his retinue, including the band, visited the Foreign Office, to deliver the credentials from his Government. It was then discovered that he had been entrusted with no missive to the Emperor, and had not come prepared to claim an audience with any person higher than the Foreign Minister. He was, however, informed, according to the determination before spoken of, that all irregularities in his commission would be overlooked, and that he would be duly received at court. For a time it was doubted whether he would be gratified with this offer, but the fact of its being tendered placed the Japanese where they wished to stand in regard to the reception of their own ministers, in future, by the King of Corea. Thus the present messenger, who came only with the rank of Chargé as the diplomatic world generally understands it, was made an ambassador in spite of himself. No business of importance was transacted in this interview, and, after returning home to reflect upon the proposal of an audience, the envoy sent word later in the day, that he would gratefully accept it.

On the morning of the first of June he proceeded to the Imperial residence, where he was welcomed with more than the usual ceremonies, large numbers of high officials being present in their most resplendent uniforms, in order, probably, to produce as imposing an effect as possible upon the new-comers. For this occasion, the Corean leader was dressed entirely in white silk, with a few ornaments of polished silver in different parts of his attire. The contrast between the antique simplicity of this costume and the shining glitter of the Japanese, was very striking, and once again it was apparent that, whatever the public functionaries of this country may have gained, or think they have gained, by assimilating their dress to that of European courts, they have lost more than can be described in grace, elegance and picturesqueness.

The Corean envoy took advantage of the opportunity to present a number of packages containing specimens of the products of his country. These were found to be interesting in some respects as curiosities, but without substantial value. They were of the class of complimentary gifts which foreign writers have always designated as "tribute," although that word does not at all convey the sense of the Chinese character from which it is erroneously translated, nor properly represent the spirit in which the offering is made. The presents sent by the ruler of one nation to that of another, in the East, do not necessarily carry with them an acknowledgment of submission, as is generally supposed by distant commentators. After leaving the palace, the visitors were shown the gardens in the old castle, and were entertained in the guest-house of "Hama go ten." Here the dinner served for them was wholly in the European style, and although the table implements were awkward to manage, it was observed that the food itself appealed to their taste much more pleasantly than it did to that of the Japanese when they first endeavored to accustom themselves to it; from which it may be presumed that animal food is more in accord with the physical needs of inhabitants of a rigorous country like Corea, than with the requirements of the people of Japan.

After the day of the audience, the guests occupied themselves chiefly with the inspection of public departments, numerous industries and other matters of interest in which the working of the new Japanese system is illustrated. The post-office, fire extinguishing companies and paper factories especially attracted their notice. Daily journals were supplied to them regularly by order of the Government, and to these they were said to give much attention — possibly because their own movements were minutely chronicled by the Japanese reporters. On one day they witnessed a military review in the principal parade ground of the city, which did not fail to impress them deeply, as in this sort of display the Japanese have reached a point which few Western nations can surpass. On another, they were shown the practical operation of torpedo explosions, before which their accustomed affectation of stolidity gave way in an excitement that much resembled a panic. They received invitations to several Japanese private entertainments, most of which were readily accepted; but they exhibited the greatest objection to meeting, or coming in contact with, persons of any other nationality. It is said that more than one attempt was made by influential foreigners to obtain interviews with the ambassador, which efforts were always resisted with unvarying firmness. On the eighteenth of June, the visit having lasted about three weeks, the party started homeward, reaching their own land again at the end of ten days.

While reading the proofs of this volume, the author stumbled upon an article published in the *Pall Mall Gazette*, on the affairs of Corea, which is so truthful and interesting that he takes pleasure in reproducing it in this place:

"The conclusion of a treaty between the United States and Corea, adds another to the peaceful successes of American diplomacy in the far East. Nearly thirty years ago the American Commodore Perry, overcoming obstacles which had baffled almost every European nation, and without firing a shot or leaving ill-feeling behind, succeeded in opening Japan to foreign intercourse. Four years later Mr. Townsend Harris, the American envoy, from the seclusion of his legation at Shimoda, without the "moral" support of a single gunboat, negotiated the treaty with the Japanese which has been the model of all the treaties made up to the present moment with that people. Two years ago Commodore Shufeldt, in the course of a cruise round the world in the United States war-vessel *Ticonderoga*, called into one of the Corean harbors with a letter for the King, expressing the desire of the President for a treaty of amity and commerce.

"Leaving this document, he departed as peacefully as he had arrived. When the Coreans had had ample time to digest his request, and to consult their suzerain, the Emperor of China, the Commodore returned alone to the United States, to obtain the ratification of a treaty in which the King of Corea expresses 'his earnest desire to establish relations between the two countries on a permanent and friendly footing, and to facilitate commercial intercourse.'

"The history of European intercourse with the inhabitants of the little peninsula in northeastern China is brief and melancholy. The touching story of the crew of the Dutch vessel wrecked on the island of Quelpaert in the middle of the seventeenth century, who were detained among the Coreans for more than thirty years, as told by their 'secretary,' will be found in the pages of *Pinkerton*, and need not be further referred to here. It was not until the treaty of Tien-tsin had opened North China and Manchuria to the zeal of Roman Catholic missionaries, that Corea was again visited by Europeans.

"The Jesuit fathers seem to have made their way there about 1862-63. We have now only their own accounts of what took place. Their efforts to make converts were, they say, crowned with success for a few years. But in 1865 commenced a persecution unparalleled even in the frightful annals of religious persecution in the East. It is said that one hundred and fifty thousand Coreans, men, women and children, lost their lives on this occasion. Of the French priests four alone escaped in disguise, and assisted by some of the faithful of their flock. An attempt was made by the French fleet in the China seas to take vengeance for this slaughter, but it was unsuccessful.

"Until the history of modern Corea is studied by our scholars in the native works themselves, we cannot correctly ascertain the cause of this persecution. Meantime the student of the history of other Oriental nations who finds analogous events will probably look for analogous causes. The subsequent attempts of the Jesuits to cross the Corean frontier, and the success that attended them, will be found recorded in the *Missions Etrangères*.

" Monsignor Ridel, who evaded the frontier guards and entered the country in 1878, has left us an account of his adventures. He penetrated Corea, he tells us, in the hope of attaining the crown of martyrdom. In this he was disappointed, for he was promptly discovered and imprisoned, to be released a few months afterwards at the intercession of the Governments of China and Japan. But tens of thousands of wretched Coreans, who were supposed to be tainted with Christianity, suffered death, and many of them with the most horrible torture, because of this gentleman's ambition to become a martyr. An American naval expedition sent to punish an outrage on a ship which sailed up the Corean rivers, met with little more success than its French predecessors.

" In 1868, a steamer manned by American and European filibusters, set out from Shanghai to rob the tombs of Corean kings, either for the sake of the gold coffins in which Mendez Pinto says they were enclosed, or because the Jesuits reported that the body of a dead king could be held for almost any ransom.

" In 1860, Ignatieff, then Russian representative at Pekin, taking advantage of the Chinese difficulties with England and France, obtained the cession of a vast tract of Corean territory lying in the Amour region.

"These are a few of the salient points in the history of Corean intercourse with the civilized nations of the West; and it hardly seems a matter for great surprise that Corea should have preferred exclusion to more intercourse of this description. Nor is it difficult to believe the tales told by Japanese travellers of pillars erected over the whole country, calling down a curse on the head of him who should first propose friendship with the hated foreigner.

"Political considerations have ultimately prevailed. Chinese and Japanese statesmen have long been persuaded that the only chance of preserving Corea from absorption into Russia, and their own countries from a standing menace, was to open it to foreign intercourse. Following their counsels, Corea has now entered the comity of nations. Commercial advantages she has few to offer. Her total trade with Japan during 1881, at the three opened ports, hardly exceeded a quarter of a million sterling. There is said to be much mineral wealth, but this must be mere surmise at present."

The news has recently reached this country that Commodore Robert W. Shufeldt had succeeded in concluding a treaty between the United States and the King of Corea; and it is certain that, however this event may have been brought about, the credit will be chiefly given to the Japanese Government for indirectly paving the way to the successful negotiations.

While the preceding pages were passing through the press, intelligence was received from Corea that an insurrection had taken place at the capital; and that many members of the Government had been murdered, as well as certain Japanese merchants and others residing in the leading port of the country.

During the first week of September, 1882, additional information was received at Washington to the effect that the Chinese authorities had boldly interfered to restore peace in the kingdom, and that the ruling authorities of Corea had agreed to pay to Japan as compensation for the outrages committed the sum of two million, five hundred thousand dollars, and two hundred and fifty thousand dollars, to the relatives of the murdered Japanese subjects. We thus see that, as on other occasions, the honor of Japan has been vindicated; while the reputation of the United States and Great Britain, because of their disgraceful treatment of Japan, are both resting under a cloud of condemnation.

# ORIGIN OF THE AMERICAN EXPEDITION TO JAPAN.

THE subjoined correspondence on the above subject is submitted as the concluding chapter of this volume:

WASHINGTON, March 30th, 1879.

MY DEAR MR. L.:—I said to a friend that the inception of Commodore Perry's expedition to Japan was due to Mr. Webster. As Secretary of State from 1850 to the time of his death, he saw that the acquisition of California rendered necessary and most opportune the opening of communication with Japan, and that it should be done in the most friendly and conciliatory manner. According to my memory, I saw some official letters from Daniel Webster which influenced legislation (if any was needed) or executive action. But looking to the sketch of Webster by you in Johnson's Cyclopædia, you do not (as you should) claim this as the crowning work of his career — the great triumph of his official life as Secretary of State.

He spent his life mainly in the Senate, and mostly in opposition, so that any evidence of executive skill and statesmanship is the more highly prized.

Your connection with the Japanese Legation places you in a position to know so well the signal fruits of that inception, that I venture to write this note.

The lives of Commodore Perry throw no light on

the question.  My access to the proper authentication is so poor that I appeal to you.

Yours, cordially,<br>
BENJAMIN ALVORD.

Mr. CHARLES LANMAN.

GEORGETOWN, D. C., April 10th, 1879.

MY DEAR GENERAL : — In reply to your note of the 30th ultimo I beg to submit the following :

The Rev. Dr. Francis L. Hawks was a superb orator, but in giving Commodore M. C. Perry the credit of originating the expedition to Japan he committed an error. In all other particulars the record which he prepared of the expedition was eminently worthy of both the historian and the diplomatic Commodore.

As I have always understood, Commodore John H. Aulick was the first one who suggested the expediency of sending a kind of naval embassy to Japan, but Daniel Webster was the first member of the Government who took official action on the subject. In proof of this assertion it is only necessary that I should submit to your inspection the following letters, which are not generally known, both of which were dictated by Mr. Webster, although one of them bears the signature of President Millard Fillmore :

DEPARTMENT OF STATE,<br>
WASHINGTON, May 9th, 1851.

HON. WM. A. GRAHAM, SECRETARY OF THE NAVY.

SIR : — You will doubtless have seen in the public journals that a number of Japanese were some time since picked up at sea, six hundred miles from the Japanese Islands, by the barque *Auckland*, Captain Jennings, by whom they had been treated very kindly, brought into the port of San Francisco, and subsequently placed on board the revenue cutter *Polk* to await arrangements for their return to their native country.

Commodore Aulick has suggested to me, and I cheerfully concur in his opinion, that this incident may afford a favorable opportunity for opening commercial relations with the Empire of Japan, or at least of placing our intercourse with that island upon a more easy footing.

Under these circumstances I have the honor to inquire whether there is any small national vessel on the western coast of the United States that could, without inconvenience to the public service, be ordered to take these unfortunate men on board at San Francisco and proceed with them to Hong Kong? Commodore Aulick is charged with the delivery of a letter from the President of the United States to the Emperor of Japan. And if these Japanese mariners can be thus forwarded to Hong Kong, there to await the arrival of the Commodore, he could then take them on board of one of the vessels under his command and return them to their native land. Accompanied by an imposing naval force, as he probably would be on this service, and with the kindly disposition awakened in the bosom of the Emperor towards this Government by the act of restoring these unfortunates to their homes, the occasion, it is believed, would be most auspicious for the accomplishment of the more important objects of Commodore Aulick's mission. I am, sir, respectfully,

Your obedient servant,

DANIEL WEBSTER.

The Japanese sailors were in due time sent back to their country according to the suggestions of the foregoing letter, and the following letter was duly communicated to Commodore Aulick, but never delivered because of his subsequent recall:

MILLARD FILLMORE, PRESIDENT OF THE UNITED STATES OF AMERICA, TO HIS IMPERIAL MAJESTY, THE EMPEROR OF JAPAN:
GREAT AND GOOD FRIEND: — I send you this letter by an envoy of my own appointment, an officer of high rank in his country, who is no missionary of religion. He goes by my command, to bear to you my greeting and good wishes, and to promote friendship and commerce between the two countries.

You know that the United States of America now extends from sea to sea; that the great countries of Oregon and California are parts of the United States; and that from these countries, which are rich in gold and silver and precious stones, our steamers can reach the shores of your happy land in less than twenty days.

Many of our ships will now pass in every year, and some perhaps in every week, between California and China; these ships must pass along the coast of your Empire; storms and winds may cause them to be wrecked on your shores, and we ask and expect, from your friendship and your greatness, kindness for our men and protection for our property. We wish that our people may be permitted to trade with your people; but we shall not authorize them to break any law of your Empire. Our object is friendly commercial intercourse, and nothing more. You have many productions which we should be glad to buy; and we have productions which might suit your people.

Your Empire has a great abundance of coal. This is an article which our steamships, in going from

California to China, must use. They would be glad that a harbor in your Empire should be appointed to which coal might be brought, and where they might always be able to purchase it.

In many other respects, commerce between your Empire and our country would be useful to both. Let us consider well what new interests arise from the recent events which have brought our two countries so near together, and what purposes of friendship, amity and intercourse they ought to inspire into the breasts of those who govern both countries. Farewell.

Given under my hand and seal at the City of Washington, the 10th day of May, 1851, and of the Independence of the United States the seventy-fifth.

MILLARD FILLMORE.

By the President,
DANIEL WEBSTER, Secretary of State.

It was during the very month when the foregoing letters were written, that I became in reality Mr. Webster's Private Secretary, although my official position from that month to the following September, was that of Librarian of the War Department, after resigning which I was placed ostensibly in charge of the Copyright Bureau in the Department of State. I very well remember that on several occasions Mr. Webster and Commodore Perry had various consultations at the Department of State on the subject of the proposed expedition; but I cannot throw any light on the reasons which induced the Navy Department, at a subsequent period, to recall Commodore Aulick from the far East, and to turn over to Commodore Perry the entire control of the proposed expedition. That I should have been personally cognizant of Mr. Webster's action in regard to Japan in 1851, and that, just twenty years afterwards, I should, through Professor Joseph Henry, and without any action on my part, have become indentified with the Japanese Legation in Washington, is certainly to me a gratifying, if not important coincidence.

The commission to Commodore (then Captain) Aulick, was dated on the thirtieth of May, 1851, and the instructions which he soon afterwards received referred in hopeful terms to the time when the last link in the great chain of oceanic steam navigation should be formed, pointed out the manner in which the shipwrecked sailors should be delivered to the Japanese authorities, mentions various objects to be provided for in the proposed treaty, and also recommends the propriety of securing a period of three years for the exchange of ratifications.

The letter of instructions here mentioned was dated June 10, 1851, in all particulars characteristic of Mr. Webster, but nothing more so than the following sentence:

"It is considered important that you should avail yourself of every occasion to impress upon the Japanese officers, with whom you will be brought in contact, that the Government of the United States does not possess any power over the religion of its own citizens, and that there is, therefore, no cause to apprehend that it will interfere with the religion of other countries."

After Mr. Webster's death, as you know, his intimate friend Edward Everett became Secretary of State; his zeal and interest were no less conspicuous than those which had been manifested by Mr. Webster, and all the documents necessary to fit out Commodore Perry were duly prepared under the direction of Mr. Everett. It may be safely asserted, however, that had it not been for Mr. Webster's far-seeing statesmanship, the Empire of Japan would not at this time be universally acknowledged as one of the most patriotic, refined, sincere, and progressive of existing nations. Eight years have now elapsed since I began to study its beautiful scenery and the many interesting traits of its people, and to-day my enthusiasm is without a shadow of abatement.

I remain, dear General, sincerely yours,
CHARLES LANMAN.
GENERAL BENJAMIN ALVORD,
United States Army, Washington, D. C.

Since writing the foregoing letter I have procured some additional information bearing upon the earliest intercourse of the United States with Japan; and while it does not invalidate the claim I have made that Mr. Webster was the first whose efforts were really effectual, it is only just that I should send you the following interesting particulars:

From a manuscript in the Department of State, I learn that in 1832, Edmund Roberts, a sea captain of New Hampshire, was designated by President Andrew Jackson as an "agent for the purpose of examining in the Indian Ocean the means of extending the Commerce of the United States by commercial arrangements with the powers whose dominions border on those seas." He was directed to be very careful in obtaining information respecting Japan, the means of opening a communication with the Empire, and the value of its trade with the Dutch and Chinese. By the Secretary of State then in office, Edward

Livingston, he was instructed that the United States had it in contemplation to institute a separate mission to Japan. But nothing was accomplished.

In 1845, Alexander Everett, the Commissioner to China, under President Polk, was empowered to open negotiations with the Japanese Government, and Commodore James Biddle was instructed to take the utmost care to ascertain if the ports of Japan were accessible. He actually visited the Bay of Yedo in the ship *Columbus*, and remained several days, but the Japanese refused to open their ports, and the Commodore retired.

In 1849, Commander Glynn, U. S. N., was sent to Nagasaki to liberate some American sailors who had been imprisoned there, and was successful. On his return he expressed the opinion that then "was a favorable time to enter upon a negotiation with Japan." And again nothing was accomplished.

In 1851 the Dutch Government had the monopoly of foreign trade in Japan, and it was because the Dutch minister in Washington had reported to the United States Government that there would be no modification of her policy by Japan, that Daniel Webster took the step which led to success.

And now, by way of throwing still more light upon this interesting subject, I append the following communication sent from Boston, by a Japanese student, to the editor of the Tokio *Times*, on the sixth of November, 1879.

SIR:—I read with pleasure the correspondence of Mr. Charles Lanman, published in the Philadelphia *Progress*, and inserted in your issue of September 6th, 1879, giving the connection of Daniel Webster with the original movements for establishing intercourse between Japan and the United States of America. In bringing us over from secluded darkness into the light of the nineteenth century, we, the Japanese, owe a sea of gratitude to the Government and people of the United States, and any information which throws light upon the undertaking which has produced such a mighty result, will, without doubt, be welcomed by the world at large.

In the correspondence to which I refer, General Alvord claims the "inception" of Commodore Perry's expedition for Mr. Webster, while Mr. Lanman attributes it to Commodore Aulick. The following information which I have obtained from public and private sources seems to ship the authorship of the great idea upon another individual. It may be, however, that Daniel Webster, Com. Aulick and Mr. Pratt all conceived the idea independently from each other. History furnishes many instances of such cases.

During the winter of 1878-79, I received the following letter through a friend of mine:

Mt. Ida, Jan. 17th, 1879.

My dear Sir :— In reply to the note of your friend Shinichiro Saito, I beg to give the fact that Honorable Zadoc Pratt, Prattsville, Green County, N. Y., member of Congress, in February, 1845, laid before the House of Representatives a report in favor of taking preliminary measures for entering into commercial arrangements with the Empire of Japan, and the Kingdom of Corea. The report gave all the accessible statistics of these two great nations, and pointed out the advantages which would result from an intimate intercourse with them. The successful issue of the mission to China showed that an attempt to extend intercourse in that quarter of the globe might be safely undertaken.

Mr. Pratt was a tanner, and an uneducated man. John Quincy Adams — who was in Congress with him — said, "If he (Mr. Pratt) had our experience, with his practical knowledge, he would be a match for us all."

The proposition of Mr. Pratt was received with but little favor, and whether it was even alluded to when the expedition of Commodore Perry was authorized, I am unable to say. The *Congressional Record* would show. Our friend, doubtless, could obtain all the particulars by writing to Honorable C. M. Ingersoll, of New Haven, Connecticut, who is a son-in-law of the late Mr. Pratt, and has all his papers.

Believe me, etc., etc.,

NAHUM CAPEN.

Immediately upon the receipt of this letter, I wrote to Mr. Ingersoll, who sent me the following reply:

NEW HAVEN, Feb. 4th, 1879.

DEAR SIR: — .... I have no impression regarding the matter beyond that furnished to the public. My father-in-law told me that the importance of contracting relations with Japan occurred to him, and that he asked accordingly. I will look over the papers, and if I find any thing throwing light upon the subject I will communicate. . . . . .

Respectfully, etc.,

COLVIN M. INGERSOLL.

MR. SAITO, ETC.

The fourteenth volume of the *Congressional Globe*, page 294, shows the following:

Second Session, Twenty-Eighth Congress.
February 15th, 1845.
"Mr. Pratt, chairman of the select committee on statistics, remarking that, when the civil and diplomatic bill came up, he should move an amendment to defray the expenses of a mission to the Empire of Japan, laid on the table statistics and facts relative to that subject, which were ordered to be printed."

These "statistics and facts," ordered to be printed, form No. 138 of the Executive Documents, 2d session, 28th Congress;—which is as follows:

Extension of American Commerce — Proposed Mission to Japan and Corea.

February 15th, 1845: Read, and laid upon the table. Mr. Pratt submitted the following, in reference to proposed amendments, which he intends to submit in a bill now before the house.

*Proposed Mission to Japan and Corea.*—Whereas it is important to the general interests of the United States that steady and persevering efforts should be made for the extension of American commerce, connected as that commerce is with the agriculture and manufactures of our country; be it therefore —

*Resolved,* That in furtherance of this object, it is hereby recommended that immediate measures be taken for effecting commercial arrangements with the Empire of Japan and the Kingdom of Corea, for the following among other reasons :

*Memorandum concerning the proposed mission to Japan and Corea.* The importance of intercourse with the Japanese Empire has led to various attempts, by different nations, at sundry periods within the last three hundred years. Though all these attempts, excepting the Dutch, have proved abortive, that is not an adequate reason for our refraining from making a vigorous effort now.

The Chinese Empire, long barricaded against commercial intercourse or diplomatic relations with other countries, is now measurably thrown open for the enterprise of Americans, as among "the most favored nations;" and there is much reason for believing that a judicious embassy, characterized by justice, which should ever sway our Government, will succeed in establishing intercourse with Japan and Corea that may be largely beneficial to the American people.

Though Japan and Corea are much less extensive and populous than China (with which we have just concluded an advantageous treaty), both countries are well worthy of attention from the American people. Debarred from intercourse with Japan, the remainder of the world has paid less attention to that Empire than its character may justly demand. With a population exceeding fifty millions (about thrice as numerous as the whole population of the United States), the Japanese Empire combines a degree of civilization and power that may well render it respectable and formidable among the nations of the earth. That civilization, even judging from our imperfect knowledge concerning it, places Japan in advance of several countries with which our Government now maintained diplomatic and commercial relations. The industry of the Japanese is said to be comparable with that of the Chinese; and many of the leading arts of useful life are practised by them with a degree of success unsurpassed in some of the European nations with which we are on terms of political intercourse. Though nearly all foreign trade is forbidden, the internal commerce of Japan (the trade between its large cities and populous provinces) is very extensive; the intercourse between the great markets and all sections of the Empire being facilitated by numerous coasting vessels and well-conditioned roads.

The power of the Government may be estimated by the statement that the army ordinarily consists of about one hundred thousand infantry and twenty thousand cavalry, which force is increased in warfare to more than four hundred thousand men. And as for agriculture, where in the world is there a country more industriously cultivated? The few travellers who have ever "penetrated the interior," concur in stating that the soil of Japan, though not naturally fertile, has been so much improved as to be rendered extremely productive; and the face of the country, even on the mountain sides (which are formed into terraces, as in some parts of Italy and Persia) is so diligently cultivated that it would be difficult to find in the country a single nook of untilled land, even to the dry summits of the mountains. Jeddo, the chief town of the Empire, is reputed to be one of the largest cities of the world. Little as we know of Japan, in comparison with our knowledge of other countries, we know enough of it to render us desirous of a closer acquaintance.

Corea also possesses a large population, estimated at fifteen millions; and assimilates in character with the Chinese Empire, with which it is slightly connected in political relations. The Coreans and Chinese, it may be added, are now nearly the only foreigners with whom the Japanese allow any business intercourse, however limited. Though we cannot expect anything like equal advantages from intercourse with Corea, it seems desirable to include that country along with Japan in the projected mission, as negotiations may be despatched with little additional expense by the same ambassador.

With the successful issue of the late mission to the Chinese Empire, we may feel well encouraged to attempt an extension of our commercial intercourse with other nations nearly similarly situated; and where can we now find a better field for enterprise than is furnished by the countries included in the proposed mission — the Empire of Japan and the Kingdom of Corea, with their aggregate population of sixty or seventy millions.

The mission should be placed on a liberal basis. The day and the hour have now arrived for turning the enterprise of our merchants and seamen into the harbors and markets of those long secluded countries. Another year will not elapse before the American people will be able to rejoice in the knowledge that the Star Spangled Banner is recognized as an ample passport and protection for all who, of our enterprising countrymen, may be engaged in extending American commerce into the countries to which it is now proposed to despatch suitable diplomatic and commercial agents on behalf of Government.

Believing that the above communications and documents will prove of interest to all who are concerned in tracing the origin of relations between Japan and the American Republic, I submit them for publication in the *Tokio Times.*    Yours respectfully,
SHINICHIRO SAITO.

TREATY REVISION. — *Nichi Nichi Shimbun, Dec.* 20, '77.

Ever since the draft of the circular letter respecting Treaty revisions from our Government to the Japanese Ministers at the various Foreign Courts transpired in the *Herald* newspaper, this has been a question much discussed, but as the said draft is still a diplomatic secret, we are unable to inform our readers what progress the negotiations have made since then. According to public rumor, however, the proposals contained in it refer solely to the right of Customs Taxation, and it manifests an intention of allowing the stipulations of the original Treaties to stand so far as the question of extra territoriality is concerned. We are inclined to believe this rumor, but as we have never seen a complete copy of the draft, we cannot speak with certainty on this point. Without reference, however, to special secrets, the public, in discussing the question of the Revision of the Treaties, have assembled about it their sharpest spear-point of argument, and each writer has severally given expression to his own views. There are points of difference among them, it is true, but if we observe the substantial gist of their arguments, it is this: They all agree in being eager to devise means for the restoration of our rights as an independent nation, so that the prestige of this country may be maintained, and the preservation of peace and security may be ensured.

This is the position in which the question now stands, and now is the time for us newspaper editors who are the mediums of public opinion to devote our closest attention to it. We shall not fail to bring to our readers' notice any proposal or any opinion which has a bearing upon it.

In listening attentively to the arguments of both natives and foreigners, and noting the differences among them, we observe that for the most part those writers who argue chiefly from principles, contend that in this matter of the present revision it is necessary that we should recover at once both our great rights, viz.: of jurisdiction and taxation, while those whose reasonings are based on facts maintain that in the present revision the best plan is for us to endeavor to recover our right of Customs Taxation, and to wait until our civil and criminal law is reformed before claiming the restoration of our right of jurisdiction. This difference is not confined to the articles of native writers. We observe that the views of foreigners are distinguishable into two classes in the same way. Judging from present circumstances, however, we think with regret that we must after all confine ourselves to the results anticipated by the latter class of writers.

Now amongst those writers who are eager to cancel the stipulation of extra territorial rights at the earliest possible moment, some are in favor of adopting a modification of the new Egyptian Treaty and establishing mixed courts; others prefer to imitate an ancient known institution, and to establish Courts of Equity for the trial of all civil cases in which natives and foreigners are concerned. But we have heard that the gentlemen learned in law who were sent by the Government to Egypt for the express purpose of observing the working of the Egyptian courts, have reported that their advantages were equalled by their disadvantages, and that they were unsuitable for adoption in Japan. Again the proposal for the institution of new Courts of Equity has no doubt its advantages, but it is feared that if these courts were established concurrently with the ordinary courts there would be a clashing of jurisdictions. We believe that neither of these two proposals has yet been sufficiently discussed, and it is impossible at present to pronounce definitely in favor of either.

If both are rejected, what is then to be done?

Again, in regard to the revision of the tariff, there are some foreigners, who (though not even they think it unfair) would wish to establish a certain limit, and are averse to transferring entirely to this country the right of Customs Taxation. This idea, however, is contrary to natural principles, and as it proceeds from a selfish desire to encroach on the rights of another country, it can never be carried into execution, and if we consider that even among foreigners there are only a very small number who take this view, we see how little is the chance of its adoption. It is manifest that if we except these few, the united opinion of Japanese and foreigners is in favor of the right of Customs Taxation being restored to Japan in its entirety on the occasion of the present Revision, so that there is no reason for over anxiety as to the results of the negotiation. Now when this right has been restored to us, what is the next step? No doubt the Import Tariff will be revised, and additional duties imposed. But here the protectionist steps in, and urges that in order to encourage home production, duties of from fifty to one hundred per cent. should be imposed on imports until the good effects of protection are visible. Again the advocates of free trade will maintain that although for purpose of revenue an increase of duties is required, these duties should be as light as possible, that even granting that a protective duty might be levied on manufactures, the production of which there is some special reason for stimulating, protective duties in general are inadvisable. There is no sign of these two views becoming harmonized. Which is the more suitable for Japan under present circumstances?

Again in the collection of duties, there are two

systems, that of specific, and that of ad valorem duties. In the former case, the duty is levied at so much per catty, or foot, as for instance tobacco which is 3.75 momme per catty, cotton yarn which is seventy-five momme per picul. Ad valorem duties are levied at so much on the original value of the article, as glass and wines and spirits, which pay five per cent. on their original value. Both systems are combined in the present Tariff, specific or ad valorem duties being charged according to the kind of merchandize; but this combination is fruitful of much trouble to the Customs officials, and seems inadvisable. Again in the case of specified duties, no note is taken of the quality of the goods, so that articles of fine quality and high price are lucky in being charged a low duty, while coarse and cheap articles on the other hand are subjected to a burdensome tax. Nor is the ad valorem system free from objection. To prevent the Customs officials from being deceived by fraudulent invoices furnished them by importers, it is necessary to employ a staff of valuators. When the time comes therefore for the revision, will a system of specific or of ad valorem duties be adopted, or a combination of them retained as at present?

These are questions on which public opinion has not yet formed any definite conclusion, and they seem to be very important points. Another point is strongly urged by some, viz.: that foreigners should not be allowed to travel in the interior, and others suggest that in addition to the present entrance and clearance dues, harbor tonnage, and light dues should be imposed. These are questions on which our readers should form an opinion, and we therefore put them forward in order to elicit their views.

# ADDITIONAL NOTES.

IT was in 1868, the first year of the present Emperor's reign, that he issued a manifesto, to wit:

"Japanese learning has of late greatly declined, so that the honor of the country in its relations with foreign nations has been materially prejudiced. It is now the intention of the Government to take measures to revive Japanese learning, and it is earnestly desired that every one, by diligent study and by encouraging sound scholarship, should aid in this work."

It was in the second year of the Emperor's reign that he sanctioned the publication of newspapers. This is believed to have been the first public recognition of the modern newspaper, an institution which has received a remarkable development since that time in Japan. The bureau for their management was for a time connected with the Department of Education, but subsequently was transferred to the Department of Home Affairs. At the time of this first sanctioning of newspapers, there was also established a bureau for the compilation and correction of historical records.

It is now about eight years since the Government of Japan enacted a copyright law, and although it contains not less than twenty-eight articles, its leading provisions are that every manuscript shall be examined by the Librarian of the Interior Department, and when found to be free from disloyal opinions, or any matter calculated to injure the public morals, a certificate of protection is promptly issued.

When the authors reside in the provinces, remote from the capital, they are obliged to make their application for protection through the local authorities: the fees for certificates amount to the cost of six copies of the work protected, and three copies of the work have to be deposited in the Interior Department. This regulation holds good in regard to all the books published, whether they are original, or translations from foreign languages into the Japanese.

Under the direction of said Department there is a quarterly report issued, which gives a description of all the books published, and from the last of these reports, for the last quarter of 1879, which I have received, I find some particulars which give us an interesting idea of the manner in which the Oriental mind is developing itself under the influence of the Western nations. During the quarter alluded to, the total number of books published was three hundred and fifty-six, and the largest proportion of them are on the subjects of Education, Law, Medicine, and matters Parliamentary, with numerous dictionaries and other books of reference. Among them, moreover, there are not less than thirty-three works translated from the English, French and German languages. Most of the books from France are of a legal character, those from Germany chiefly on medicine, while the supply from the United States and England seems to be of a conglomerate character.

As straws show how the wind blows, so will the following list illustrate the bent of the Japanese mind, viz: *Paper Money Inflation*, by White; *Botany*, by Gray; *Conic Sections*, by Robinson; *Elections in*

## ADDITIONAL NOTES. 411

*America*, by Verbeck; *Seaman's Manual,* by Dana; *American Institutions,* by De Toqueville; *Lombard Street,* by Bagehot; *Gardening for Profit,* by Henderson; *Civilization,* by Buckle; *Essentials of Chemistry,* by Whitehouse; *British Commerce,* by May; *English Constitution,* by Creasy; several books by Herbert Spencer; *From the Earth to the Moon,* by Verne; with other works on Marriage, Education of Women, Science of Finance, Laws of Banking, Algebra, Bookkeeping, International Law, Penal Code, Microscope, Medicine, Topography, Anatomy, Civil Procedure, Pathology, Sociology, Physiology, and Martin's Year Book. All these books are handsomely printed, with illustrations when necessary, and while the paper and type may be purely Japanese, the binding is quite frequently in cloth or paper, after the American fashion.

But the facts connected with the newspaper press of Japan are even more wonderful than those of the book trade. The total number of newspapers and periodicals is not less than two hundred and fifty; in Tokio there are some ten daily papers (not including prices current), and among them is one named after its editor, and others entitled as translated, *Worldly News, Alphabet, Reading and Selling, Daylight,* as well as a *News* a *Post,* and an *Advertiser;* they also have several comic papers, after the manner of *Punch* and *Puck,* and various magazines devoted to the advancement of agriculture and other national interests. While there have been no material changes in the Press Laws of Japan within the last few years, the Government would appear to be much more lenient than it was fomerly, and editors may now speak their minds somewhat after the American fashion, which, according to the Constitution and Congress of the United States, may be considered the leading luxury of modern civilization, if not especially dignified nor truly patriotic.

With regard to the literary events of 1880, the two most important are the publication, in a series of volumes, of the Laws of Japan, which resemble in size and extent the Statutes at Large of the United States; and, secondly, the publication, in handsome style, of the New Testament in the Japanese language.

As an appropriate sequel to the foregoing, perhaps the following bit of Japanese Bibliography may interest the book-worm reader. When the Arctic discoverer, A. E. Nordenskiold, was in Japan, in 1879, he made a collection of books, written in the language of that country, which consisted of 1036 different works, but nearly six thousand volumes, and the subjects were as follows: History 176, Buddhism and Education 161, Shintoism 38, Christianity 1, Manners and Customs 33, Drama 13, Laws 5, Politics 24, Poetry and Fiction 137, Heraldry, Antiquities and Ceremonies 27, War, etc. 41, Chess 1, Coining 4, Dictionaries and Grammars 18, Geography 76, Natural History 68, Medicine 13, Arithmetic, Astronomy and Astrology 39, Agriculture and Handicrafts 43, Note Books 73, Horticulture 16, Bibliography 9, and Miscellaneous 20. Total 1036.

# ADDENDA.

# FOREIGN BIBLIOGRAPHY OF THE EMPIRE.

Account of Japan in 1631-38. By F. Caron. In Pinkerton's Voyages.

Across America and Asia. Notes of Five Years' Journey around the World, etc. By Raphael Pumpelly. New York, 1871.

Ambassades de la Compagnie, etc. vers le Japon. 2 vols. Paris, 1722.

Ambassades Mémorables de la Compagnie des Indes Orientales des Provinces — unies Verrs les Empereurs de Japon. Foleo. Amsterdam, 1680.

Agriculture and Husbandry of the Japanese Islands (The). By Quanno Keigokee. Tokio, 1879. Translated into English by William H. Doyle.

Caron F. Beschrijvinge van het Machtiyh Koninckrjke Japan. Amsterdam, 1649.

Castle of Yedo (The). By Thomas R. H. McClatchie. Tokio, 1877. Pamphlet.

China and Japan. A complete Guide to the open Ports of those Countries, together with Pekin, Yedo, Hong Kong and Macao, etc. etc. By W. F. Mayers, N. B. Dennys, and Charles King. London, 1876.

China and Japan; and a Voyage thither. By James B. Lawrence. Hartford, 1870.

China and Japan. A Record of Observations, etc. By I. W. Wiley. New York, 1878.

China and Japan. 2 vols., large folio calf, with Maps, and several full page and large folding Plates, Views, Cuts, etc., etc., illustrating the Cities, Temples, Religions, Laws, Wealth, Habits, Plants, Beasts, Rivers, etc., etc., of those Countries. By John Ogleby. London, 1670.

Chronicas de los Rel Descalzos de S. Francisco en las Isles Philipenas, etc. In three volumes, the last devoted to Japan. Minila, 1738.

Claims of Japan and Malaysia. By C. W. King and J. T. Lay. 2 vols. New York, 1839.

Cloisonné Enamels of Japan (The). By George Ashdown Audsley. Liverpool and Paris, 1880.

Coal Fields of Kiushiu, Japan (The). Paper read before the "Institut de France." By Prof. F. Fouque. Paris, 1882.

Colloquial Japanese, etc. By S. R. Brown. Shanghai, 1863.

Cornwallis K. Two Journeys to Japan. London, 1859.

Description of Formosa, etc. By G. Psalmanaazaar. London, 1704.

Descriptio Regni Japoni Auctore Bernardo Varenio. Tome II. Amstelodami, 1649. Same et Siam. Cantabrigiae, 1673.

Diary on the Coast of Japan in 1673. By John Pinkerton. London, 1808-14.

Dutch in Japan. By K. Matsukuri. Proceedings Asiatic Society of Tokio, 1880.

Education in Japan. A Series of Letters addressed by prominent Americans to Arinori Mori. New York, 1873.

English and Japanese Dictionary (An). Tokio, 1872.

English-Japanese Dictionary of Spoken Language (An). By Earnest Mason Satow. London, 1876.

Empire of Japan (The). Brief Sketch of the Geography, History and Constitution. Philadelphia, 1876. By Imperial Commission for the Philadelphia International Exhibition.

Ethnologische Studien über die Aino auf der Insel Yesso. Von Heinrich Von Siebold, Legations Seortar bei der K. and K. Mission in Japan. Berlin, 1881.

Faociculus e Japonicis Floribus suo adhuc Madentibus. Sanguine Compositus A. F. Cardim. Roma, 1646.

Fauna Japonica Crustacea elaborante. W. de Haan. P. F. Von Siebold, 1850.

Fidelle et Notable. Recit de la Conversion du Roy Ydata Macamune de Boin a Jappon; traduit des Copies imprimées en Espagnol. Tolose, 1618.

Financial Condition of Japan (The.) By Herr Liebscher. Leipsic and London, 1882.

Flora Japonica and Icones Plantarum Japonicarum. By Carl Peter Thunberg. Stockholm, 1784-1805.

Forbidden Land (A). By Ernest Oppert. London, 1880.

Fraissinet E. L'Expédition Americaine au Japan. Paris, 1855.

Fortune R. Yedo and Peking, etc. London, 1863.

Fugaku Hiyaku; or a Hundred Views of Fuji (Fusiyama). By Hokusai. Descriptions translated by F. V. Dickins. London, 1881.

Geographical and Ethnographical Elucidations to the Discoveries of Maerten Gerrits Vries 1643. In the East and North of Japan; to serve as a Mariner's Guide in the Navigation of the east Coast of Japan to Jezo, Krafto and the Kurils. From the Dutch by F. M. Cowan. Amstd... . 1 59.

Glimpse at the Art of Japan (A). By Jarvis. London and New York. 1880.

Grammar of the Japanese Written Language (A). By W. G. Aston. Tokio and London, 1877.

Grandmamma's Letters from Japan. By Mrs. Mary Pruyn. Boston, 1877.

Greater Britain. A Record of Travel in English-Speaking Countries during 1866–67. By Charles W. Dilke. London, 1868.

Halloran A. L. Visit to Japan. London, 1856.

Hand-Book of Northern and Central Japan. By Satow and Hawes. Yokohama, 1881.

Histoire et Description générale du Japon. By P. F. X. Charlevoix. 9 vols. Paris, 1785.

Histoire du Christianisme au Japan. By P. F. X. Charlevoix. 2 vols. Paris, 1828.

Historical Notes on Nagasaki. By W. A. Woolley. Yokohama, 1881.

History of Japan. Account of its Ancient and Present State of Government, etc. 2 vols. Written in High Dutch and translated by J. G. Scheuchzer. London, 1728. Same to be found in Pinkerton's Voyages.

History of Japan from the earliest Period to the present Time. By F. O. H. Adams. London, 1871.

Iancigny A. P. D. Histoire et Description du Japon. Paris, 1850.

Illustrations of Japan, consisting of private Memoirs and Anecdotes of the reigning Dynasty of the Djoyounsor Sovereign of Japan. By M. Titsingh. Translated from the French by F. Shoberl. London, 1822.

Introduction of Christianity into China and Japan. By John H. Gubbins. Tokio, 1877. Pamphlet.

Introduction of Tobacco into Japan (The). By Ernest M. Satow. Tokio, 1877. Pamphlet.

Invasion of Corea. By W. J. Aston. Proceedings Asiatic Society of Tokio. 1879.

Japan. By Bayard Taylor. New York, 1872.

Japan. By C. MacFarlan. London, 1852.

Japan and around the World. By J. W. Spalding. New York, 1855.

Japanese and English Dictionary. By J. C. Hepburn. Shanghai, 1876.

Japan and Her People. By A. Steinmetz. London, 1849.

Japan and the Japanese. Illustrated. By Aimé Humbert. Translated by Mrs. Cashel Hoey. London, 1874.

Japan and the Japanese, etc. 2 vols. By Captain Golowinin, of the Russian Navy. London, 1853.

Japan as It was and is. By Richard Hildreth. New York, 1855.

Japan. Encyclopædia Britannica. Edinburgh. 1881.

Japanese Episodes. By E. H. House. Boston, 1881.

Japan Expedition; a Voyage around the World. By J. W. Spalding. New York, 1859.

Japan, Historical and Descriptive. By Charles H. Eden. London, 1877.

Japan: Its History, Traditions, and Religions, etc. 2 vols. By Sir Edward J. Reed. London, 1880.

Japan nach Reisen und Studien. Von I. I. Rein. Leipzig, 1881.

Japanese Expedition to Formosa (The). By Edward H. House. Tokio, 1875.

Japanese Government and People. By M. Louis Bazangeou. Paris, 1881.

Japanese in America (The). By Charles Lanman. New York and London, 1872.

Japanese Islands. By M. Malte-Brun. Edinburgh, 1822.

Japanese Marks and Seals. By James L. Bowes. London, 1881.

Kæmpfer's History of Japan; translated from the Dutch by Scheuchzer, with Journal of a Voyage made to Japan by the English in 1673, and Appendix, numerous curious engravings and maps. 2 vols. in one, 1727.

Kagoshima. By E. H. House. Tokio, 1875.

Kak' Ké. By William Anderson. Tokio, 1878. Pamphlet.

Keramic Art of Japan. By Audsley. London, 1881.

Keramic Art of Japan. By G. A. Audsley and J. L. Bowes. Liverpool, 1879.

Kioto. By W. Gifford Palgrave. London (Fortnightly Review), 1881.

Lacquer Industry of Japan (The). By John J. Quinn. Pamphlet. Tokio, 1880.

Land of the Morning (The). By William Gray Dixon, M. A. Edinburgh, 1882.

La Relion des Japonais. Par Leon de Rosny. Paris, 1881.

Labor in Japan. By T. B. Van Buren. Washington, 1881.

Labor in Japan. [Official Report.] By Thomas B. Van Buren. Washington, 1880.

Leading Men of Japan; with an Historical Summary of the Empire. By Charles Lanman. Boston, 1882.

Le Gendre. Progressive Japan, etc. New York, 1879.

Le Japon de nos jours et les echelles de l'extrême Orient. Par Georges Bousquet. Paris, 1877.

L'Empire Japonais, Pays, Peuple, Histoire. Par Leon Metchnikoff. Genéve, 1881.

Leon de Rosny. La Civilization Japonaise, and other works. Paris, 1860.

Lieboèd Philip Franz. Fauna Japonica, Replilia elaborantibus. C. J. Temminck et H. Schlegel, 1838.

Lühdorf. Acht Montate in Japan, etc., etc. Bremen, 1860.

Lord Elgin's Mission to China and Japan. By L. Oliphant. London, 1859.

Loyal Ronins (The). By Tamenaga Shunsui. Translated by S. Saito and E. Greey. New York, 1880.

Manley R. English version of Caron. London, 1663.

Manners and Customs of the Japanese in the Nineteenth Century. New York, 1842.

Manners and Customs of the Japanese in the Nineteenth Century. From Recent Dutch Travels of Von Liebold and others. London, 1841 and 1852, and New York, 1841.

Meeting of the Sun : A Journey all around the World, etc. By William Simpson. London, 1874.

Memorials of the Empire of Japan in the Sixteenth and Seventeenth Centuries. By Randall. London, 1850.

Metchnikoff. L'Empire Japonais. Geneva, 1878.

Meylan G. F. Japan Voorgesteld in Schetsen. Amsterdam, 1830.

Mikado's Empire (The). By William E. Griffis. New York, 1877.

Montanus A. Denckwürdige gesand tschafften der ost indischen gesellschaft in den Vereinizten. Niederlanden an unterschi edliche Keyser Von Japan Amsterdam, 1669.

Narrative of the Expedition of an American Squadron to the Chinese Seas and Japan, etc. By Commodore M. C. Perry, U. S. N. Edited by Francis L. Hawks. 3 vols. Washington, 1856. Abridgement of the same, New York, 1856.

New Japan. By Samuel Mossman. London, 1873.

Notes and Sketches from the Wild Coast of Nipon. By Captain H. C. St. John. Edinburgh, 1880.

Notes on Loo-Choo. By E. Satow. Proceedings Asiatic Society of Tokio, 1879.

Notes on some of the Volcanic Mountains of Japan. By D. H. Marshall. Tokio 1878. Pamphlet.

Notes on the Early History of Printing in Japan. By Ernest Satow. Yokohama, 1881.

On the History of Japanese Keramics. By F. Brinkley. Japan Mail, 1881.

Our Life in Japan. By E. P. Elmhirst. London, 1869.

Outline History of Japanese Education (An). Prepared for the Philadelphia International Exhibition. New York, 1876. By the Japanese Department of Education. (Tanaka Fujimaro.)

Palmer, A. H. Documents and Facts, etc., about Japan. Washington, 1857.

Paupe Van Meerdewoort. Vijf jaren in Japan, 1857-63. Leyden, 1867.

Progressive Japan, a Study of the Political and Social Needs of the Empire. By General Le Gendre. Yokohama and New York, 1878.

Prussian Navara Expedition. Official Report. Berlin, 1864.

Reise um die Welt. 3 vols. By Von Adam Johann Krusenstern. 1812.

Rundall T. Memorials of the Empire of Japan. London, 1850.

Russian Descents in Sazhalin and Itorup in 1806-7. By W. J. Aston. Proceedings Asiatic Society of Tokio.

Satsuma Rebellion (The). An Episode in Modern Japanese History. By Augustus H. Mounsey. London, 1879.

Smith G. Ten Weeks in Japan. London, 1861.

Steinmetz A. Japan and her People. London, 1859.

Summary of the Japanese Penal Code (A). By Joseph H. Longford. From Proceedings of the Asiatic Society of Tokio. 1873.

Tales from Old Japan. By A. B. Mitford. London, 1871.

Thunberg. Voy. au Japon. Paris, 1795.

Titsingh. Memoires, etc. Paris, 1820.

Titsingh I. Illustrations of Japan from the French of F. Shoberl. London, 1859.

Tomes R. The Americans in Japan, etc. New York, 1857.

Travels around the World, etc. By William H. Seward. New York, 1873.

Tronson J. M. Personal Narrative of a Voyage to Japan. London, 1859.

Telley H. A. Japan, etc. London, 1861.

Unbeaten Track in Japan. 2 vols. By Isabella L. Bird. London, 1880.

Varenius or Varen B. Descriptio regni Japaniæ et Siam Cantabrigiae, 1673.

Voyages dans le nord du Japon par W . . . . Yokohama, 1880.

Voyage au Japon, exécuté pendant les années 1823-1830; Description de Iezo, des iles Kuriles méridionales, de Krafto, de le Corée des iles Liu Kiu, etc. By von Philipp Franz Siebold. Paris, 1830.

Voyage of La Perouse round the World in 1785-86-87-88, etc (The). 2 vols. By M. L. A. Milet Mureau. London, 1798.

Voyage of the *Vega* round Asia and Europe (The). By A. E. Nordenskiöld. Translated by Alexander Leslie. London. 2 vols. 1881. [Contains Information about Japan.]

Voyage to Corea and Loo-Choo. By B. Hall. Philadelphia, 1818.

Whittingham B. Notes of a Visit to Japan. London, 1856.

Young Japan, Yokohama and Yedo, etc. 2 vols By John R. Black. London, 1881.

Zwei Reisen nach dem Westen Japans in den Jahren 1369 and 1389. By Von Dr. August Pfizmaier. Wien 1881.

www.ingramcontent.com/pod-product-compliance
Lightning Source LLC
Chambersburg PA
CBHW051741300426
44115CB00007B/653